AFRICAN WRITERS SERIES

250

The Last of the Empire

AFRICAN WRITERS SERIES

FOUNDING EDITOR Chinua Achebe

PETER ABRAHAMS
* Mine Boy

CHINUA ACHEBE
* Things Fall Apart
* No Longer at Ease
* Arrow of God
* A Man of the People
* Anthills of the Savannah
100 Girls at War *
120 Beware Soul Brother †

THOMAS AKARE
241 The Slums

T. M. ALUKO
70 Chief, the Honourable
   Minister

ELECHI AMADI
* The Concubine
44 The Great Ponds
210 The Slave
* Estrangement

I. N. C. ANIEBO
206 The Journey Within

KOFI ANYIDOHO
261 A Harvest of Our Dreams †

AYI KWEI ARMAH
* The Beautyful Ones Are Not
   Yet Born
154 Fragments
155 Why Are We So Blest?
194 The Healers
218 Two Thousand Seasons

BEDIAKO ASARE
59 Rebel

KOFI AWOONOR
108 This Earth, My Brother

MARIAMA BÂ
* So Long a Letter

MONGO BETI
13 Mission to Kala
77 King Lazarus
88 The Poor Christ of Bomba
181 Perpetua and the Habit of
   Unhappiness
214 Remember Ruben

STEVE BIKO
* I Write What I Like §

OKOT P'BITEK
193 Hare and Hornbill *
266 Song of Lawino & Song of
   Ocol †

DENNIS BRUTUS
115 A Simple Lust †
208 Stubborn Hope †

SYL CHENEY-COKER
221 The Graveyard Also Has
   Teeth

DRISS CHRAIBI
79 Heirs to the Past

---

* Four colour trade editions
* Short Stories
† Poetry
‡ Plays
§ Biography/Politics

WILLIAM CONTON
12 The African

BERNARD B. DADIE
87 Climbié

MODIKWE DIKOBE
124 The Marabi Dance

MBELLA SONNE DIPOKO
57 Because of Women

AMU DJOLETO
41 The Strange Man
161 Money Galore

T. OBINKARAM ECHEWA
* The Crippled Dancer

CYPRIAN EKWENSI
2 Burning Grass
9 Lokotown *
84 Beautiful Feathers
185 Survive the Peace
* Jagua Nana

BUCHI EMECHETA
* The Joys of Motherhood

OLAUDAH EQUIANO
10 Equiano's Travels §

NURUDDIN FARAH
252 Sardines

NADINE GORDIMER
177 Some Monday for Sure *

BESSIE HEAD
* Maru
* A Question of Power
* When Rain Clouds Gather
182 The Collector of Treasures *
220 Serowe: Village of the Rain
   Wind §

LUIS BERNARDO HONWANA
60 We Killed Mangy-Dog *

OBOTUNDE IJIMÈRE
18 The Imprisonment of
   Obatala ‡

EDDIE IROH
189 Forty-Eight Guns for the
   General

KENJO JUMBAM
231 The White Man of God

CHEIKH HAMIDOU KANE
119 Ambiguous Adventure

FARIDA KARODIA
* Coming Home and Other
   Stories *

JOMO KENYATTA
219 Facing Mount Kenya §

ASARE KONADU
40 A Woman in her Prime
55 Ordained by the Oracle

AHMADOU KOUROUMA
239 The Suns of Independence

MAZISI KUNENE
211 Emperor Shaka the Great †

ALEX LA GUMA
* A Walk in the Night *
110 In the Fog of the Seasons
   End
* Time of the Butcherbird

DORIS LESSING
131 The Grass is Singing

HUGH LEWIN
251 Bandiet

HENRI LOPES
* Tribaliks

NELSON MANDELA
* No Easy Walk to Freedom §

JACK MAPANJE
236 Of Chameleons and Gods †

DAMBUDZO MARECHERA
207 The House of Hunger *
237 Black Sunlight

ALI A MAZRUI
97 The Trial of Christopher
   Okigbo

TOM MBOYA
81 The Challenge of Nationhood
   (Speeches) §

THOMAS MOFOLO
229 Chaka

DOMINIC MULAISHO
204 The Smoke that Thunders

JOHN MUNONYE
21 The Only Son
45 Obi
94 Oil Man of Obange
153 A Dancer of Fortune
195 Bridge to a Wedding

MEJA MWANGI
143 Kill Me Quick
176 Going Down River Road

JOHN NAGENDA
* The Seasons of Thomas Tebo

NGUGI WA THIONG O
  ✳ Weep Not, Child
  ✳ The River Between
  ✳ A Grain of Wheat
  51 The Black Hermit‡
150 Secret Lives*
  ✳ Petals of Blood
  ✳ Devil on the Cross
240 Detained§
  ✳ Matigari

NGUGI & MICERE MUGO
191 The Trial of Dedan Kimathi‡

NGUGI & NGUGI WA MIRII
246 I Will Marry When I Want‡

REBEKA NJAU
203 Ripples in the Pool

NKEM NWANKWO
67 Danda

FLORA NWAPA
26 Efuru
56 Idu

GABRIEL OKARA
68 The Voice

CHRISTOPHER OKIGBO
62 Labyrinths†

KOLE OMOTOSO
122 The Combat

SEMBENE OUSMANE
  ✳ God's Bits of Wood
  ✳ The Money-Order with White
     Genesis
175 Xala
250 The Last of the Empire
  ✳ Black Docker

YAMBO OUOLOGUEM
99 Bound to Violence

FERDINANDO OYONO
29 Houseboy
39 The Old Man and the Medal

PEPETELA
269 Mayombe

R. L. PETENI
178 Hill of Fools

LENRIE PETERS
22 The Second Round
238 Selected Poetry†

MOLEFE PHETO
258 And Night Fell§

SOL T. PLAATJE
201 Mhudi

ALIFA RIFAAT
  ✳ Distant View of a Minaret*

RICHARD RIVE
  ✳ Buckingham Palace: District
     Six

STANLAKE SAMKANGE
33 On Trial for my Country
169 The Mourned One
190 Year of the Uprising

KOBINA SEKYI
136 The Blinkards‡

FRANCIS SELORMEY
27 The Narrow Path

SIPHO SEPAMLA
268 A Ride on the Whirlwind

MONGANE SEROTE
263 To Every Birth Its Blood

WOLE SOYINKA
76 The Interpreters

OLIVER TAMBO
  ✳ Oliver Tambo Speaks

TIMOTHY WANGUSA
  ✳ Upon This Mountain

DANIACHEW WORKU
125 The Thirteenth Sun

ASIEDU YIRENKYI
216 Kivuli and Other Plays†

D. M. ZWELONKE
128 Robben Island

COLLECTIONS OF PROSE
23 The Origin of Life and Death
48 Not Even God is Ripe Enough
61 The Way We Lived*
118 Amadu's Bundle
132 Two Centuries of African
     English
254 Stories from Central and
     Southern Africa
256 Unwinding Threads
  ✳ African Short Stories

ANTHOLOGIES OF POETRY
164 Black Poets in South Africa
171 Poems of Black Africa
192 Anthology of Swahili Poetry
230 Poets to the People
257 Summer Fires: New Poetry
     from Africa
308 A New Book of African Verse

COLLECTIONS OF PLAYS
34 Ten One-Act Plays
179 African Plays for Playing 2

The Last of the Empire

A Senegalese novel

SEMBENE OUSMANE

Translated from the French by Adrian Adams

HEINEMANN

Heinemann International
a division of Heinemann Educational Books Ltd
Halley Court, Jordan Hill, Oxford OX2 8EJ

Heinemann Educational Books Inc
361 Hanover Street, Portsmouth, New Hampshire, 03801, USA

Heinemann Educational Books (Nigeria) Ltd
PMB 5205, Ibadan
Heinemann Kenya Ltd
PO Box 45314, Nairobi, Kenya
Heinemann Educational Boleswa
PO Box 10103, Village Post Office, Gaborone, Botswana
Heinemann Publishers (Caribbean) Ltd
175 Mountain View Avenue, Kingston 6, Jamaica

LONDON EDINBURGH MELBOURNE SYDNEY
AUCKLAND SINGAPORE MADRID
HARARE ATHENS BOLOGNA

British Library Cataloguing in Publication Data
Ousmane, Sembene
The Last of the Empire.—(African writers series)
I. Title   II. Le Dernier de l'Empire. *English*
III. Series
843[F]   PQ3989.0/
ISBN 0-435-90250-4

Set in 10pt Times New Roman, by Performance Typesetting,
Milton Keynes
Printed in Great Britain by
Cox & Wyman Ltd, Reading, Berkshire

90 91 92 93 94 95 10 9 8 7 6 5

To my wife from far away
Carrie D. 'Malawi'
To the children
Alioune Alain
Mame Moussa
I dedicate this book that
deprived them for so long
of the all-pervading odour
of my pipe.

Sembene

Author's Foreword

This book is not to be taken for anything other than a work of imagination.

Our dear and beautiful country has borne and bred only men and women worthy of our esteem and entire trust, worthy of the position they occupy even fleetingly.

These men and women of our dear SUNUGAL – Senegal – are far superior to the mediocre types portrayed in this book. I will (never) forgive any reader who makes any comparison, any connection even covert between these 'fictional characters' and our valiant fellow citizens, devoted unto death (however it may strike) to building our future. I will not hesitate to have recourse to our laws (which are fair and just).

Sembene
Galle Ceddo
August 1976 – January 1981

GLOSSARY

Bambara geec Slave from the West Indies.

BCEAO Banque Centrale des Etats d'Afrique de l'Ouest.

Boy-bi Term used to address a junior. (Wolof)

Caaf da Xëm The roasted groundnuts have burnt.

Cëbu Jën Rice with fish.

Couz Short for the French 'cousin'.

Debbo Woman (Pulaar)

Diola A people of the Casamance region in southern Senegal.

Doyen Honorific term denoting the senior member of a group.

Fadjar Early-morning prayers.

FEANF Fédération des Etudians d'Afrique Noire en France.

Geew A circle. Hence *gueewel*, to form a circle about someone; and by association *guewel*, the caste of praise-singers and musicians.

Gran-bi Term used to address an elder. (Wolof)

Guelewar A prince.

Jam u geec Slave from overseas.

Joom Galle The master of the house (Pulaar).

Mawdo Term of address showing respect. (Pulaar)

Ndey San Denotes sorrowful compassion. (Wolof)

OAU Organization of African Unity.

Safara A kind of holy water.

SDEC Service de Documentation Extérieure et de Contre-Espionnage.

Tirailleurs Sénégalais A corps that included men from all France's colonies in Black Africa.

Tonton A synonym of 'uncle', used to show filial respect for a mentor.

Tubabs bu nuls Black Europeans.

UMOA Union Monétaire Ouest Africaine.

Yenekat Town criers.

CHAPTER 1

Friday, 6.30 a.m.

Gun at hip, his face expressionless, the guard raised his right hand and motioned him to wait, and then moved off on bandy legs down the corridor, silent at this very early hour. A door, which was padded with imitation leather, swallowed him up.

For years now Mam Lat Soukabé, Minister of Finance and the Economy, had walked down this corridor once a week. He knew every door on the way to the chamber where Cabinet meetings were held. Puzzled by the guard's stern demeanour, he wondered why the President of the Republic, Léon Mignane, had summoned him so early. It must be somewhere between 6.15 and 6.25. Less than four hours from now, he was due to sign the official agreement with the International Aid Fund. The text of the agreement had been drawn up under his personal supervision.

Mam Lat Soukabé gazed down the corridor. At the opposite end he glimpsed the shadow of another guard, with a rifle. He began to be obsessed with a possible reversal of fortune. He had a growing sense of unease and insecurity. Why all these armed men? 'If the Venerable One hadn't called for me, I'd get the hell out of here!' No sooner had he thought that, than he started, switched the Samsonite from one hand to the other, and looked the other way. Another guard, with a military bearing, was drawing near.

'Good morning, Minister,' said the man in uniform as he came up to him. The greeting soothed Mam Lat Soukabé. He acknowledged it with a grunt, and breathed more heavily. Following the man's gaze, he saw the first guard returning, accompanied by Corréa, the Minister of the Interior. Relief at the sight of a colleague renewed his self-confidence. He moved quickly towards Corréa.

'Hullo,' he said with alacrity, and added inquiringly: 'What's going on here?'

'Come along,' was Corréa's only reply.

Mam Lat Soukabé was wearing a silky tropical-weight suit purchased on Fifth Avenue in New York, a shirt of India silk, a striped yellow tie, and platform shoes to add to his height. He dyed his hair, coquettishly leaving a few white hairs in his crescent-shaped moustache. No one knew whether he owed his innumerable female conquests to the care he took with his appearance, or to his control of the country's finances.

Five people were already seated in the room. Mam Lat Soukabé let his gaze rest on each in turn: Wade, Minister of Defence; Haïdara, Minister of Foreign Affairs; Doyen Cheikh Tidiane Sall, Minister of Justice; Mapathé, Minister of Information and Parliamentary Affairs; and last, Daouda (David to his friends), the Prime Minister. Their eyes betrayed weariness. They had fallen silent as he came in. On the long table, the ashtrays set in front of the smokers were full to overflowing.

'We looked for you everywhere last night, and couldn't find you. It seems you were at a meeting,' said Daouda, seated in his usual place to the right of the President's empty chair.

'Why are you questioning me?' asked Mam Lat Soukabé aggressively, glaring at the Prime Minister.

'We want to know,' replied the Prime Minister, meaning, 'I want to know.' Raising his voice, he asked again: 'Where did you spend the night?' He added at once, to make the question sound less indiscreet: 'It's very important.'

The rivalry between the two men had split the government, the administration and the ruling party. At every level, each had his followers.

'I was told over the telephone that the President wanted to see me.'

Mam Lat Soukabé was reasserting himself. Prime Minister Daouda had spoken with authority, but it hadn't quite come off.

'Where did I spend the night? Frankly, I'm not going to tell you.'

Still standing, Mam Lat Soukabé eyed the only European present, seated behind Corréa.

'Adolphe, it was you who rang to say the Venerable One wanted to see me; where is he?'

Adolphe remained silent.

The presence of the Minister of Finance and the Economy at this emergency meeting had been felt to be undesirable. Doyen Cheikh Tidiane Sall had been opposed to such ostracism. He had argued: 'Mam Lat is of equal rank to all of us here. To leave him out, to pretend he doesn't exist, would be a mistake even more serious than the object of this meeting.' He was trying to make peace but the trio of Corréa, Wade and the Prime Minister reacted angrily to his words. Usually, the President's presence alone could make the two clans hold their peace. In his absence, the rift between the groups would widen. The battle to succeed him had started well before this particular Friday morning.

'Doyen, can you guarantee that Mam Lat will listen to reason?'

'Since when am I responsible for the behaviour of the Finance Minister?' exclaimed the old man.

Haïdara hesitated to answer. The Minister of Foreign Affairs wanted the transfer of power to take place smoothly. The prospect of a struggle between the two contenders hung like a storm on the horizon.

'No one knows where he is, anyway. They've tried all his women,' said Corréa, a hint of denigration in his voice.

'I object to this sectarian spirit. As a minister, he enjoys the same prerogatives we do. He always starts work early. We can contact him at his ministry before we leave here.'

Cheikh Tidiane pulled out his pocket-watch, attached to his waistcoat by a chain. To end the argument, he suggested:

'Let us ask Monsieur Adolphe to ring him.'

That is how Monsieur Adolphe – personal adviser to the President of the Republic – came to take the liberty of summoning the minister in the President's name.

'I'm listening, Monsieur Adolphe,' Mam Lat Soukabé said evenly, addressing the European.

'Sit down, Mam,' said Cheikh Tidiane with all the authority he could muster, pulling out a chair.

Mam Lat sat down, his hands on his attaché case.

'Might I know where you spent the night? I don't mean right now; but later.'

The Minister of Foreign Affairs spoke in a comradely tone of voice. He had weak eyes, and wore very dark glasses with thin gold rims. In profile, his flat face and the heavy lenses shielding his eyes gave him the look of a chameleon.

'To you especially, Haïdara, I will say nothing,' stated Mam Lat Soukabé. 'May I, in turn, ask what is going on? Where is the Venerable One?'

No one answered. He turned to his right and asked:

'Doyen, what's happening?'

'Tell me where you spent the night,' urged the old man.

'With a woman, not my wife. I won't say anything more. What's going on?'

Cheikh Tidiane glanced sideways at Daouda.

(It needs to be said that the two men never addressed each other directly, but always through a third person.)

'Mam Lat, we found out last night that Léon has disappeared.'

Being the President's elder, Cheikh Tidiane called him by his first name.

'Doyen . . . you . . .'

He could scarcely finish his sentence. The earth was giving way beneath his feet. He seemed to be floating in space, as if in a nightmare.

3

'Is he . . .?' he brought out with difficulty.

'No! No! Not dead. At least we hope not. Léon has simply disappeared,' answered the Doyen.

Mam Lat Soukabé's gaze shifted from the Doyen's face to the 'empty throne'. He said:

'It's not the first of April. But it must be a joke!'

Without knowing it, he was repeating what the others had said hours before.

'All the same, it's true; as true as it is that you and I are sitting here now.'

'Doyen, it's not possible! A president can't disappear just like that. The palace is guarded night and day.'

'Who said it happened at the palace?' asked Corréa quickly, policeman-style.

'Where did it happen, then? Let's stop the joking . . . I'm meant to be signing the IAF agreement this morning.'

'Nobody's joking, Mam Lat. The Venerable One really did disappear last night. We are the only people to have heard the sad news.'

Mam Lat Soukabé remained silent, as if stunned.

The wake-like gloom deepened.

The five of them, and the Prime Minister, were Léon Mignane's right-hand men. Each, within his field, was the President's confidant. His absence hung over them like a damp, numbing pall. Their eyelids were swollen with lack of sleep. They sat with drawn faces and loosened ties, each listening to his beating heart.

'The Venerable One can't have vanished just like that. Ask his adviser . . . Monsieur Adolphe?'

Adolphe, an expatriate, was startled by Mam Lat's remark. Since the start of their conclave, no one had thought, or ventured, to address Monsieur Adolphe. The European felt awkward. Mam Lat's sudden query, and the way everyone looked at him, made him ill at ease. He felt his former authority slipping from his grasp, like an actor who doesn't know his lines well, and is disconcerted by every change of scenery. For the first time in all his decades in the country, he felt like an alien.

In 1950, having successfully completed secondary school, Adolphe joined his country's army. After a few months' initiation at Corniche-Kléber in Strasbourg, he spent some time in occupied Germany – the French zone. He then went to Indo-China. He was noticed, earned honours and was mentioned in dispatches. He was one of the thousands defeated with the French expeditionary force at

Dien Bien Phu. He was deeply wounded by this humiliating major defeat, a blot on the renown of the nation's army. Ruminating thoughts of revenge, he studied at Saint-Maixent and became an officer. His head full of stories of the 'empire-builders', he showed boundless hatred for the politicians who were selling out their colonial inheritance. He soon had his revenge when Charles de Gaulle made the politicos toe the line.

He next turned up in Algeria, as a lieutenant. He roamed the Sahara with the Camel Corps, defending France. He knocked off plenty of *fellagha*. For a soldier defeated in the rice-fields of Indo-China, to fail once more in the Algerian *bled* would be a disaster. He was wont to say, echoing the words of a very famous figure, that 'The Mediterranean flows through France, just as the Seine flows through Paris.'

He threw himself into the action, no holds barred, in the best gunboat tradition, and won his third row of gold braid. Algeria too was lost. After this traumatic blow to his pride, he returned home an embittered man.

With the help of some *esprit de corps*, he was sent to Senegal. No longer in uniform, with no troops to command, he was now special adviser for politico-military affairs to the President of the Republic. With Corréa he formed a group in charge of secret files and covert operations. He was answerable to the President alone, and had private access to the French Embassy. In fact, he had precedence over all current ministers.

'Monsieur Adolphe, you still haven't answered my question,' repeated Mam Lat Soukabé.

In a flash, Adolphe realized that he was no match for the technocrat. Mam Lat's insistence flustered him. He took out a filtertip Gauloise and lit it, before saying:

'I can't answer your question, minister. Let us hope it may turn out to be a practical joke.'

'The Venerable One's doddering now, is he? We have all kinds of police, secret, official, subsecret and God knows what else, and you say . . . perhaps it's a practical joke! What about you, Corréa; where were your police all this time? You owe us an explanation,' thundered Mam Lat Soukabé.

'You turned up last, don't make us repeat everything.'

Annoyed, Corréa had raised his voice. He gazed accusingly at Doyen Cheikh Tidiane: 'What did we tell you? Mam's Lat's being here is making for trouble.'

'I want to know,' snapped back Mam Lat. 'I have the same responsibilities as everyone else here. The President of the Republic disappears, and you want me just to shut up. What were your men doing?'

5

'Ever since his driver, old Siin, was found dead, we've been checking out the entire Cap-Vert area.'

'So there's a dead body as well,' said Mam Lat, taking over Daouda's role in chairing the discussion.

'Yes.'

'And I thought it happened at the palace!'

'It happened in town, on the Western Corniche,' explained Corréa.

'What the hell was he doing there?'

The question remained unanswered.

Each man had devised his own explanation, but refrained from airing it.

'Let's say it's the Black Squadron gang that did it,' quipped Mam Lat, pleased with his sally. One corner of his mouth lengthened into a wry half-smile, stretching his thick salt-and-pepper moustache.

'What connection can there be between our country and terrorists?' enquired Cheikh Tidiane.

'I don't know,' answered Mam Lat.' 'Maybe the Minister of the Interior can answer that question.'

'What? Every leader of an opposition party, legal or not, is under surveillance. I myself have checked all nationals and foreigners entering and leaving the country. All calls are being tapped. Wires from journalists and press agencies are being discreetly checked, to avoid leaks.'

'Let's say it's the Israelis who've staged a second Entebbe in Dakar.'

'Idi Amin's no longer in office. He's fled . . .'

'And where's our man right now?' challenged Mam Lat sharply, a mocking gleam in his eye.

'What about the Palestinians, then?'

'Might I inquire, Haïdara, what motive the Palestinians might have, in your view, for such action?'

Doyen Cheikh Tidiane Sall had spoken slowly and deliberately, looking Haïdara in the face. Léon Mignane's elder, he was his oldest companion and had witnessed his rise to power. He had often disagreed with the younger man, now also in his seventies. That had several times earned him a reprimand from one or the other of the ministers of the second post-Independence generation. During one session where all the twenty-two ministers and the Venerable One were present, Daouda had exclaimed: 'Doyen, there's no age limit for foolishness. There's no head nor tail to what you're saying.' Africa has lost her respect for elders. It's a mere survival now.

As one meeting followed another, Cheikh Tidiane noted that he had become a target for repeated verbal attacks. Léon Mignane had realized that his age-mate was not immune to well-aimed sarcasm.

As if he himself were neutral, above the fray, he would console him:

'In a democracy, everyone must express his opinions. We must acknowledge, without false shame, that it was the *Tubabs* who taught us modern democracy. Under the palaver tree of the Africa of yore, truth was the monopoly of the elders.'

Cheikh Tidiane had stoically accepted the situation. Since then he had refrained from talking or thinking too much. Week after week his relationship with Léon Mignane had deteriorated. During the weekly meetings they exchanged only a few words, for appearances' sake. He was startled when after a Cabinet meeting Léon came up to him and said with apparent modesty: 'Cheikh, I'd like to consult you about something.' He quickly added: 'If you're free of course. I'll be at the palace on Sunday afternoon.'

That Sunday, after a refreshing nap, Cheikh Tidiane had gone to the palace. Like an elderly couple the two men strolled down to the garden, on the seaward side. On the horizon the smooth liquid azure blended with a cloudless sky. Vultures wheeled overhead. Their shoes crunched on gravel as they walked along the path. The conversation languished. Cheikh Tidiane Sall listened warily, punctuating pauses with a 'Hm! Hm!', while nodding his freshly shaven gleaming black head.

Suddenly, Léon blurted out:

'What if we resumed diplomatic relations with Israel? Sadat is a great African, and he showed courage in signing a peace treaty with the Jews.'

Cheikh Tidiane stopped in his tracks. Three paces ahead, Léon Mignane stood waiting for him. For a short time they stared at each other; then Cheikh Tidiane joined him without speaking, his jacket unbuttoned, his hands clasped behind his back.

'In that part of the world, the political context has changed. The Middle East must know peace at last. The sleep of the just,' added Léon Mignane. From a distance, his gaze was following the armed sentry pacing the low red stone wall reinforced with electric wire.

Cheikh Tidiane eyed the President, struggling to repress the thoughts crowding to his lips, then said:

'Explain yourself, Léon! What context? The Arab countries have broken with Sadat.'

'That's their attitude at the moment. But it's temporary. One has to consider how things will evolve. Some Arab countries will re-establish diplomatic relations with Sadat. We ought to be thinking along those lines . . .'

'All the Arab countries condemned Sadat at the Baghdad con-

7

ference. Furthermore, the headquarters of the Arab League have been transferred to Tunis. Why do you want to swim against the tide of history?'

From his full height Cheikh Tidiane gazed down upon the other man's dyed hair.

'It's not a question of swimming against the tide, Cheikh. One must face facts. Sadat had the courage to do what he's done. He deserves his Nobel Peace Prize,' said Léon Mignane, scratching his cheek.

'What about the PLO? Explain yourself, Léon! I don't follow you. Who are you trying to whitewash? Sadat? The Hebrew state? Or who else?'

'No! No! It's not a question of whitewashing,' Léon Mignane protested.

He drew in his lower lip, changing the shape of his mouth.

'In that case, Léon, wait for the OAU's decision. And don't forget the aid you've requested from certain Gulf States.'

'What are you getting at, Cheikh?'

'I want to refresh your memory a bit, Léon.'

Despite his self-control, Léon Mignane had been wounded by this remark. He didn't like people to point out his lapses. His grimace deepened into a sneer of contempt.

'If the petro-dollars stop flowing, we'll call on our partners for help.'

'What partners?'

'The Europeans! Have the Arabs broken with the European countries, who have maintained relations with Israel throughout? Why should I be more particular than they are?'

Léon Mignane emphasized the end of his sentence by drawing himself up on tiptoe. He lost his balance, exclaiming 'Oops!', then regained his footing.

A smile lit up Cheikh Tidiane's face. He recalled an article he had read in the European Press: 'Secret meetings are taking place in Black Africa as well as in Europe, in order to convince certain countries to recognize the Jewish State.' Further on, he had read: 'The United States, Great Britain, Canada, France and Federal Germany, along with Israel, would be prepared to compensate for losses caused by the withdrawal of Arab donor nations. By this operation, the "Great Powers" would consolidate the position of Egypt, faced with the hostility of the Muslim world, while helping the Jewish State to break out of isolation.' Cheikh Tidiane no longer doubted the truth of these allegations.

'You're prepared to sacrifice the PLO then, Léon? For what price?'

'Who, me? You know me, Cheikh; I never yield an inch. *Muug!*'

he exclaimed, lifting his head. He thought it wise to add: 'Israel has never demanded that PLO representatives leave Paris, London, Bonn or Rome . . .'

'For the simple reason that Israel has no way of applying pressure to those governments. Furthermore, those countries need petrol . . .'

'I repeat, Cheikh, that no one can apply pressure to me. Neither today nor tomorrow.'

A look of malice appeared on Cheikh Tidiane Sall's elderly countenance. The smile spread as far as his eyes. Léon Mignane detested his companion's superior expression.

'Léon, you won't resist pressure from the West. I know you too well. The West has more influence over you than over any other present-day Head of State on its periphery.'

Léon Mignane was disappointed. He regretted having asked Cheikh to come. He recalled the times Cheikh had directly opposed him: he had been against buying a Boeing, against his seventieth birthday celebrations; he had refused to come to the airport to welcome him home; he had been against sending a contingent of troops to Shaba (Zaïre). Like an elderly couple accustomed to living with each other, they hesitated to part. Léon Mignane was afraid of being forsaken. But he was vexed, and struck back:

'We were having a friendly chat, and now you've offended me. You seem more and more lacking in self-control. In Africa, old age usually brings wisdom.'

'Léon, age and experience afford me the privilege of not beating round the bush when I want to tell a friend the truth. All the more so when I've been asked for my opinion. At the moment, I'm not addressing the Head of State. Forget your act and be frank with me. Why are you in such a hurry to renew diplomatic relations with Israel?'

'No one's manipulating me. Do you think I'm keeping something from you?'

'Yes, Léon! Yes.'

It was a direct hit.

They walked on in silence, side by side. A pair of cranes stalked down the grassy slope, moving from the shadow of the building into the sunshine.

Léon Mignane's face crumpled with disappointment. Twisting his fingers, he finally said:

'We'll continue this conversation some other time, Cheikh.'

'I don't think there's any point in it, Léon,' said Cheikh Tidiane. He felt sorry for his old friend.

The Doyen stared at Daouda, then at Corréa. Did they know that

Léon intended to re-establish relations with Israel? Turning to Haïdara, he asked:

'Did Léon ever ask you to consider a plan for re-establishing diplomatic relations with Israel?

'During our weekly work sessions, the Venerable One and I looked closely at the situation in that part of the world, in the light of recent events involving Jerusalem and Cairo. But no decision has been taken. We are awaiting reports from our accredited diplomatic representatives in the Egyptian capital.'

Haïdara never made a decision without specific instructions from the Venerable One. The country's foreign policy was the sole responsibility of the President. Léon Mignane occasionally summoned home a diplomat stationed abroad in order to reprimand him, without advising the head of the Diplomatic Service. Ambassadors would send their reports direct to the Head of State, then send a copy to their superiors.

'We're saying that it's a second Aldo Moro affair,' Mam Lat resumed, a cigar between his teeth.

'Legally speaking, if there's no corpse, you can't say a person's been murdered.'

'The Venerable One isn't a person,' proclaimed the Prime Minister with deliberate brutality, addressing Cheikh Tidiane ... He was trying to recover the authority he had lost since Mam Lat's arrival. He added: 'Even though you belong to the same age group, you ought to bear in mind that you're speaking of our country's Chief Executive.'

Cheikh Tidiane stared at him, amazed. What was the meaning of Daouda's attack? According to the Constitution, he was the President's direct successor.

'How could a thing like this happen? You'd think our oh-so-expensive army, or the Interior, could bloody well protect us from ... a thing like this.'

'You're accusing us of negligence; what would our motive be?'

'It's up to you, Corréa, to tell us where the Venerable One is.'

'The army is guarding our borders,' opined Wade (Defence).

Mam Lat turned towards Wade, waving away his cigar smoke. Everything about him at that moment showed how little respect he had for that particular colleague.

'Then let's send the *yenekat* to find the Venerable One.'

'Show a bit of respect, Mam Lat,' snapped Corréa.

'How long will we be able to keep this secret and how will we govern the country? What if it's the run-up to a coup?'

Mam Lat's gaze rested on each of them in turn, the Prime Minister last. Daouda's head was bowed on this long stork's neck. The very mention of a possible *putsch* was enough to chill his blood.

The Venerable One's absence distressed them all. Not one of them had stood for election. Few of them could rely on any degree of electoral support. Léon Mignane had recruited them, and entrusted each of them with a portfolio under his supervision. With the exception of Cheikh Tidiane Sall, not one of them had yet reached the age of fifty. When ousting his former associates of the 1940s, 1950s and 1960s, Léon Mignane had told Cheikh Tidiane: 'I'm going to call on the young. The second generation of Independence.' He alone had raised Daouda (whom he called David) to the Prime Minister's pedestal. By tapping this second generation and channelling it into his government, Léon Mignane had broadened and strengthened his power base.

Daouda had not striven to be Number Two. Was he not the Venerable One's spiritual heir, then? No. He just did as he was told. Now he was anxious at the prospect of having to make decisions. He knew just how vulnerable his position was. Deep within himself, Daouda suffered from the handicap of his origins.

'What solution shall we adopt, gentlemen?' he asked.

'First of all we must observe the rules, and enforce them. If the supreme power should fall vacant, once the fact is duly acknowledged by the judiciary, the PM becomes President for the duration of the then current assembly.'

'*Muug!* Never! Never! I never agreed to that clause. I was always against it; and now more than ever. The country isn't a piece of private property, to be willed as the owner wishes . . .'

'What about respect for the law, Mam Lat?'

'What law, doyen? Right here, I told the Venerable One to his face that that clause was an abuse of power, even a piece of despotism. Each of us here knows that. The country isn't an empire. I maintain my position.'

Corréa and Haïdara eyed each other. They both found intolerable such a lack of respect for the Prime Minister. Indeed, they had suggested to the President that he get rid of Mam Lat Soukabé . . .

Cheikh Tidiane was polishing his spectacles. With lowered gaze, he said to himself: 'Here we go! The struggle is on.' He could guess what would follow. This very morning, he was resigning from the government. The decision had been made a long time ago.

'So you're setting yourself against the government, Mam Lat?'

'I've never been responsible to the PM. I take my orders from the Venerable One. Maintaining the clause that has the Prime Minister succeed the Venerable One will give rise to violence in the country.'

Ever since the Venerable One had confided in him that he planned to retire soon, Mam Lat Soukabé had been hoping to provoke a crisis that would sweep Daouda from office. The occasion was to hand. Here was his chance; he wasn't going to miss it. He had flung down his challenge straight away.

'We can cope with all eventualities, Mister Mam Lat,' snapped Corréa, losing patience.

'Once you start using violence, Corréa, you'll have to tighten the screws every day . . .'

'Furthermore, doyen,' interrupted Mam Lat, depositing his cigar stump in an ashtray and leaning forward to look Corréa full in the face, 'once you begin to use violence, there's no turning back; every day you have to step it up. The economy wouldn't survive. In order to pay government employees, I have to . . . borrow, or scrape the bottom of the barrel of public funds. The country is living beyond its means and potential. It's bankrupt. I know what I'm talking about.'

They all acknowledged this. The next few days would be tense.

'What do you suggest, Mam Lat?' asked Mapathé.

'What I suggest,' repeated Mam Lat in a superior tone, 'is that we dissolve the assembly and government, and call an election.'

'You've lost all sense of proportion. You're all like lost souls. What if Léon Mignane were having us on?' said the doyen, breaking the silence.

'Doyen!' exclaimed Corréa. He was infuriated by this suggestion, which seemed to him monstrous. 'Doyen, why would the Venerable One play hide-and-seek with us? And what about the dead driver?'

Cheikh Tidiane gazed at the clear-cut shape of the Bambara antelope carving. Ever since he had heard of Léon Mignane's disappearance, he had been having doubts. He knew that in his quest for power, which intoxicated him, Léon was unhindered by ethical considerations of any kind. He had surrounded himself with younger men simply in order to consolidate his autocratic hold.

'Explain yourself, doyen!' requested Mapathé.

'That was just my own personal conclusion,' he stated calmly. 'I suggest a few days' patience. Today is Friday, tomorrow Saturday, then Sunday. There's a long weekend ahead. On Saturdays and Sundays Léon has few commitments. On Monday . . . you'll make whatever decision needs to be made.'

Haïdara glanced at Daouda. Encouraged by a blink from him, he agreed:

'Those are words of wisdom . . . We will keep this heavy secret until Monday.'

'I won't be able to keep the whole city under surveillance without arousing suspicions.'

Mam Lat glanced at his electronic watch. It was ten past eight; they were all aware of it. He asked Mapathé: 'Will Information be present for the signing of the IAF agreement later on?' The other man confirmed that people from both radio and television would be present.

12

'One more thing; I'm leaving, as of today,' said the doyen. 'The PM has accepted my resignation, which I had already tendered to Léon. It's an unfortunate coincidence . . . but I must go. Thank you all.'

Daouda improvised a farewell speech, ending with:

'We must not leave our homes. We must keep all our engagements, even in the absence of the Venerable One. That's all.'

Mam Lat was the first to leave . . .

The bureaucrats who worked in the President's office, both men and women, had arrived on time. Model employees, discreetly dressed, they conversed in low voices, with friendly smiles rather than laughter. Working so near the Venerable One, do they not each possess a few crumbs of state secrets? They did not hang about the corridors. Behind the numbered padded doors rose the gentle clatter of typewriters. The few guards or policemen glimpsed here and there aroused no suspicions. Everyone was planning his weekend leisure.

CHAPTER 2

Friday, 8.42 a.m.

'Did Doyen Cheikh Tidiane really mean what he said about the Venerable One?' asked Haïdara, breaking into a silence that seemed to have lasted forever.

The four ministers (Information, Defence, Foreign Affairs, Interior) were ruminating the same thoughts. 'A put-up job by the Venerable One? Why? What about the murder of his personal driver?' Each refused to supply an answer to this series of questions. The President of the Republic doesn't take to his heels like a common criminal.

Adolphe, huddled in a corner, was reserving judgement. His task was to maintain his country's influence at all costs. Daouda was still a mystery to him. Would he be able to handle his new responsibilities? Adolphe knew that all the ministers, except Corréa, harboured resentment towards him. He watched Mapathé stand up and offer a reply to Haïdara's question.

13

'I don't know . . .'

From the window, through the curtains, he could see the garden. The gardener was squatting, pulling weeds.

'I can't believe it's a trick by the Venerable One. He's above such things.'

'There's the dead driver, though,' repeated Mapathé, taking his seat.

'Yes! It's an unaccountable situation . . . We must be prepared for all eventualities, once the news is out. I haven't much confidence in Mam Lat Soukabé. He's keeping himself to himself.'

'Why not bring about a meeting with opposition leaders? Take the initiative . . . and isolate Mam Lat Soukabé,' suggested Haïdara.

'Apart from the clandestine communists, the whole legal opposition was set up by the Venerable One,' declared Corréa, his weary gaze scanning Daouda's face.

He lit what must have been at least his twentieth cigarette. He never voiced more than a third of what he was thinking.

'We're no worse off with that semblance of democracy, even if it was created by the Venerable One. It's a victory for him abroad, enhancing his reputation. It's good to hear new ideas from time to time. We'll have to wait till Monday before deciding anything . . .'

With a gesture of his hand, Mapathé stopped Corréa from interrupting him. He continued in a calculating tone:

'The law is on our side. The PM is Assistant Secretary-General of the party. That clause of the Constitution automatically makes him President and Commander-in-Chief of the Armed Forces.'

'True,' remarked Corréa. 'But many things can happen from now until Monday. We mustn't let ourselves be taken by surprise. A vancancy at the top is a temptation . . . I'll keep the constabulary on the job, confine the Legion of Intervention to barracks, and put the police on call. The thing that bothers me most is the match the police and civil service teams are due to play on Sunday.'

'So you see, we mustn't rush things. I'll give the match treble time on the air . . . That's a good idea.'

'The Armed Forces are confined to barracks,' added Wade, pleased with the turn of the conversation.

A sustained buzz sounded. They all looked at the telephone.

Adolphe lifted the receiver and said:

'The President's palace! Yes . . . yes . . . Good morning, Madame. Yes, the Prime Minister's here . . . '

He turned towards Daouda.

'It's your wife.'

'I'll stay right here,' said Daouda to the others, taking the receiver.

The three men filed out, followed by Adolphe, who closed the door behind them.

14

'Yes, darling, it's me,' said Daouda, his voice tinged with disappointment. He had hoped it might be the Venerable One, ringing even from the ends of the earth. He grunted hoarsely, scratching his narrow forehead. Little by little, his anxiety lifted: 'After all, darling, they're only children. Yes! they're spoiled brats, I agree ... No! nothing special. Really not. He's only meant to be going somewhere ... You know the Venerable One. He's never tired! Yes, I have the pills [he felt his pockets]. Right! Till this evening, then, darling.'

Daouda replaced the receiver. His doe-like gaze slid over the green table. The ashtrays were full to overflowing; all twenty-two chairs were empty; statues, masks, all was still. Leaning back in his chair, he raised his right hand to his eyes and rubbed his eyelids.

That second seemed to last forever ...

To bestir himself, Daouda stood on his long legs and walked over to the middle window, swinging his large feet forward at each stride. He wore only custom-made shoes. He was taller than average, with a coconut-shaped head joined to his body by a long cylindrical neck as slender as the rest of him: skinny, in fact. No muscles could be discerned beneath his copper-coloured skin. From the window he could see the Peugeot 604s leaving the grounds. A guard had stopped the traffic to let the ministers out.

Daouda had never wanted to be the cynosure of all eyes, nor even to be well known. His present position had not been reached by a long and tedious climb up the party ladder. Docile and studious, he did not have a brilliant or profound mind. He was, however, endowed with an uncommon memory, a quality he had inherited. The atmosphere in which he grew up, his initial education, had made an introvert of him. His fellow students knew little about him. While they, in Dakar and in Paris, were courting girls, exchanging them, sharing them, he took refuge in books like a timid recluse. This recourse to study, which his acquaintances took for a sign of devotion to hard work, was in fact a complex. His father, Gorgui Massamba, praise-singer of the Ayane dynasty (Mam Lat Soukabé's family), had told him time and again: 'Whatever the future may hold for you, Daouda, you must keep to your station in life.' These words of his father's clung to him like a second skin, like a shadow that preceded or followed him as the sun moved along its course.

He was to feel the truth of his father's words. Daouda fell in love with Madeleine, a Senegalese student, a Christian. After they had known each other for two years, he asked her to marry him. Two weeks before the wedding, Madeleine suddenly told him:

'Neither my father nor my mother will consent to our marriage.'

This painful disappointment in love heightened his sensitivity. It left a gaping wound. He withdrew into himself, and once more

15

dedicated himself to study. Although his fellow students trusted him, he refused to accept any position of responsibility within the African students' association, the FEANF. He married Guylène, a West Indian who had a son from a former marriage. He gave this woman from distant isles two more children: a girl and a boy. First of his class, equipped with all his diplomas and two degrees, he returned to Senegal.

Daouda hoped to be a humble cog in the new administration.

Léon Mignane called him to his side, and made him his new personal assistant. Daouda did his best, and proved a good organizer: young, disciplined, discreet. Without making a confidant of him, the President sometimes asked his advice. His remarks, the notes he pencilled in margins, his succinct reports won him an ever-higher place in the esteem of the Head of State. At Léon Mignane's side, Daouda became familiar with a leader's role. Under his paternal wing he learned to fence and parry. A faithful servant, a clever assistant, he carried out orders without asking questions. Turmoil and internal upheavals had never shaken his filial loyalty.

After the ousting of Ahmet Ndour (the Cabinet head) Léon Mignane appointed Daouda Prime Minister. Unknown both to the public and to his party, he was imposed on them. Thanks to skilfully-fed information, his profile began to emerge. Had he not been for years the trusted right-hand man of the Father of the Nation? That which grows at the foot of the baobab tree must have absorbed its sap.

When the keepers of knowledge disappear, there will be no choice but to consult those who were formerly their servants.

With one finger, Daouda pushed back the cuff of his white shirt to check the time: 9.25 a.m. He had summoned the French Ambassador, a friend. For the moment, he was very much alone. Propelled to the forefront of current events in a tormented Africa, faced with vast and weighty responsibilities, he tried to control his feeling of confusion.

He was pacing up and down the conference room that he had not left since two o'clock in the morning. Before, whenever he had to stand in for the Venerable One, the latter told him what to do. He fought back the questions that rose within him, and tried not to give way to doubt. 'What if the Venerable One has fled? The failure of his economic policy? Financial bankruptcy?' The solutions proffered are no more than palliatives. But Daouda dispelled this cruel and evident truth by a surge of blind faith in the Venerable One. 'There are poorer countries in Africa,' he argued to himself, to preserve the image of his paternal protector. 'What if he's been killed? But why?'

16

Brooding over this string of questions, Daouda kept turning towards the President's chair, the 'throne' as everyone called it. He examined it from all angles, followed every line of carving. He had never sat there, not even when he was replacing the President.

This throne was carved of *ekume* wood, with decorative motifs and legendary symbols belonging to the various peoples of the continent. Its mass rested upon four legs each bearing the dignified mask of a bearded Ibibio; the arms were reinforced by two ebony *tyi-warra;* on the back a couched leopard, fangs bared, lay ready to leap upon its prey.

Daouda was discovering the throne for the first time. He was fascinated, as if attracted by a supernatural power. Timidly he drew near. The hand-embroidered cushion of Kashmir silk charmed him. He held out his hand to touch the fabric. His heart beat twice as fast. A tide of warm blood flooded up his arm from his fingers. When his middle finger touched the cushion's seam, his blood flowed more quickly, piercingly chill. It seized his whole body. He withdrew his hand as if scorched, breathing heavily. He glanced fearfully at the walls, the folds of the curtains, the masks and statues. He was certain someone was spying on him. He turned around quickly. No one! But the feeling remained.

This sudden fright reminded him that the Venerable One practised fetishist rites. Before every trip, he would summon masters of the art for consultation. He himself, Daouda, had several times carried messages to these sages. He had more than once seen Léon Mignane anointing himself with *safara*. And he would not soon forget the story of the infant stolen from a maternity ward to be offered up as a sacrifice.

One day the Venerable One, in an expansive mood, had whispered to him:

'Africa is irrational! Or else its rationality is such as to startle the modern world ... One has to make use of such practices ... to protect oneself against enemies within.'

Remembering those words, Daouda felt certain that there was a spell upon the throne. 'The Venerable One isn't dead,' he said to himself, moving away.

Soutapha knocked and entered. He came to announce that 'the Minister of Foreign Affairs and the French Ambassador were waiting ..'

CHAPTER 3

Daouda composed his features into a smile of welcome. Now in his sixties, the senior member of the diplomatic corps accredited to Senegal, the French Ambassador had been the last European vice-chancellor of the university, before the post was taken over by a Senegalese. Most of the present ministers were former students of his. He had established a personal relationship with some of them.

Jean de Savognard had been informed by Adolphe of Léon Mignane's disappearance before Daouda's initiative. Daouda did not know this. While the five ministers of state were conferring this Friday night, Jean de Savognard had summoned his advisers to his residence to examine the situation and decide what steps needed to be taken in the first instance. He had also immediately alerted the (French) Minister of Defence and the Secretary for African Affairs. That very night an emergency meeting had taken place at the Elysée, in the presence of the (French) President . . .

Daouda led Jean de Savognard towards the low table surrounded by armchairs upholstered in greenish plush. Once comfortably seated, the latter enquired about the Prime Minister's family. They exchanged the usual polite remarks. The ambassador said that he would take advantage of this interview to clear up a few routine matters. He raised the case of some imprisoned French citizens. This deliberate diversion allowed him to study Daouda, and try to fathom his thoughts and intentions. He had kept track of the Prime Minister's career. However sudden and unexpected the disappearance of Léon Mignane, one of the best products of colonial schooling, Daouda was a chip off the old block.

Like a good father concerned for the future, Léon Mignane had himself introduced his heir to the European political and financial world. As Prime Minister, Daouda had paid official visits to his peers and future partners. A suitor must call on his parents-in-law.

The interview was beginning to seem a mere formality, when Daouda announced in a hoarse voice, with deliberate slowness:

'This room is not unworthy of what I am about to tell you in confidence . . .'

He paused, and his gaze rested on the throne. The emblematic leopard was gazing at him. Jean de Savognard looked about, and said in a flattering tone:

'A really beautiful room!'

'The Venerable One himself supervised the interior decoration, as they call it these days.'

18

'What admirable taste! A true artist,' added the ambassador.

The three men admired their surroundings.

'I asked to see you,' began Daouda once more, as if recalling a momentarily forgotten train of thought, 'to inform you of a sad piece of news. I myself hope it is only temporary. Last night, the Venerable One disappeared.'

Frowning, Jean de Savognard asked:

'When was his absence noticed?'

Daouda told him what he knew.

'And his personal bodyguards?'

'This morning, they were all questioned discreetly. The Venerable One had given them the evening off. I was briefed by the Minister of the Interior, who had it from Adolphe. We found the Peugeot 403 and the bullet-riddled body of the driver. There are bullet holes where the Venerable One would have been sitting, but no traces of blood.'

'Has the blood found in the car been analyzed?'

'It doesn't belong to his blood group.'

'Oh?' said Jean de Savognard, puzzled.

'Yes,' insisted Haïdara. 'The Venerable One belongs to a blood group that exists only in northern Europe. So we can't say if he's been wounded or killed.'

After this statement by the Minister of Foreign Affairs, the ambassador remained silent, while thinking: 'Since when is there such a thing as an Aryan Negro?'

'Have you informed any other embassies?'

'No, not even his family. They're in France at the moment.'

'What if it's a coup?'

'A coup?' repeated Haïdara, removing his cigarette from his mouth. 'The radio station's not been taken over, and there's been no movement of troops anywhere in the country.'

'Could he have been taken hostage?'

'It's difficult to say.'

'What were his relations with the PLO?'

The two Africans eyed each other. Was that question meant to inform them, or to focus their investigation?

'Nothing out of the ordinary has been reported concerning travellers entering or leaving the country,' replied Daouda.

He realized that the ambassador knew about the meetings being held between Europeans and Africans to negotiate diplomatic recognition for Israel.

'Might one not try a different approach . . .'

'Yes? I'm listening,' said Daouda, breaking the silence that followed the diplomat's pause.

He raised his arms, stretched them then let them fall.

Jean de Savognard mistakenly interpreted this gesture as a sign of arrogance. In fact it betokened only fatigue. He mistrusted this second generation, capable of switching from the extremes of xenophobic nationalism to those of dogmatic communism.

'What if the President . . . had . . .'

He fell silent. He felt he was going a bit too far, and regretted having spoken. He pressed the tip of his tongue against his plastic false teeth.

'Suppose the President . . . this is just speculation, mind you,' he added, 'suppose the President was having an extra-marital affair. It might all have happened there.'

He had said this all at one go, while observing Daouda closely. The sudden change in Daouda's expression, the slump in his posture did not escape him. His sources had informed him of the President's habits. His predecessor had left him a list of 'lady friends'. He was not interested in Léon Mignane as a person, but in what he represented as a pawn in the West's global strategy.

Daouda's Adam's apple suddenly blocked his throat. No one was entitled to talk about his Father's private life . . . His gaze became infinitely sad. He glanced at Haïdara. The latter, reticent and respectful of the precepts of old Africa, was indignant at the European's lack of respect. He asserted in a toneless voice:

'The Venerable One is above all that. Furthermore, we Africans have a different point of view where women are concerned.'

Jean de Savognard had touched a sensitive spot. As one greatly interested in African sociology, he murmured to himself: 'A pair of orphans.' He tactfully resumed the conversation:

'I believe you should investigate all possibilities. However, I have great respect for the President.'

Haïdara was relieved.

'A great man,' exclaimed Daouda with sincerity.

That awkward moment past, Jean de Savognard once more took up the subject under discussion.

'How far have you got with your investigation?'

'Things are under way. I would like your police to help us, discreetly. This request will not be put in writing.'

In spite of the gravity of the occasion, Jean de Savognard smiled. He felt Daouda was proving to be a tactful partner. He admired the concise clarity of his remarks.

'Our services have always collaborated closely. My country is not likely to let yours down at a time like this. With your permission, even verbal, I can alert my Government.'

Daouda looked at Haïdara. No answer. He stated firmly:

'Please wait. I'll advise you in good time.'

The confident tone of Daouda's reply, the way in which he took it upon himself to decide things in his own name, startled the ambassador. He thought of Adolphe: 'Will he be able to influence this young man?'

'You are optimistic,' he said.

He added to himself: 'You'll have to assert yourself . . .'

'You must think me a fool! What would I do with a foreign army, however friendly, on my hands in the circumstances. I have no proof of the Venerable One's death.'

'The driver was killed . . .'

'True, there has been a death . . .'

(Both men, in their conversation, had avoided the word murder.)

'The presence of an army doesn't guarantee security. And I've the opposition to deal with as well. I must avoid a Chad-type situation.'

The ambassador acknowledged that this was so. He subtly broadened the topic of conversation:

'What does Cheikh Tidiane Sall think about all this?'

Daouda frowned. He analyzed everything he heard, to discover its hidden meaning. Did they intend to try and foist the old man on him?

'He's handed in his resignation. It's been accepted,' said Daouda, looking the European full in the face without seeking to avoid his reptilian gaze.

'Why don't you ask him to reconsider?'

Daouda stiffened, and placed his clasped hands between his knees.

'He left of his own accord. The Venerable One knew he was resigning.'

'Aren't you afraid he may join one of the opposition groups?'

'No,' asserted Daouda with youthful certainty. 'If it hadn't been for the Venerable One, the doyen would have been dead and buried long ago, in political terms.'

'It's a strange coincidence!'

'It won't stop the world from turning.'

'You have faith in the future . . .'

'The Venerable One taught me that nothing is as it seems,' answered Daouda, clinging to shreds of Léon Mignane's ideas, which bolstered his confidence . . .

He felt under no obligation to justify himself to the white man.

'According to the Constitution, you're his successor.'

Daouda became meditative. He shifted in his seat. His eyes darted from one man to the other with unexpected swiftness. He said in a modest tone:

'I'm only carrying on until the President returns.'

Jean de Savognard wondered if the son would be of the same stamp as the father. For him to be of *the same stamp* meant to honour western values and the western way of life. He would have to use all available means to channel his country's values and priorities through these men's veins.

The conversation flowed on, broaching other topics. Jean de Savognard was testing the Prime Minister, to determine the scope and depth of his competence. Tomorrow, perhaps even today! this youth would be a Head of State. Was it wise to stake one's country's reputation on him, as well as the remainder of one's career? Where would they find another man, easier to manage? The name of Mam Lat Soukabé occurred to him. He too was a contender . . .

Daouda backed up his incisive judgements with flawless reasoning. He analyzed the political situation with subtle insight, without falling into any of the traps laid for him by the ambassador.

'Quite so! Quite so! I hadn't seen it that way,' said the European, impressed by the range of Daouda's knowledge.

Won over, Jean de Savognard muttered to himself, 'Daouda's the man we need. His youth is no handicap . . . On the contrary.'

Daouda did not feature in the files kept in the Rue Monsieur; unlike many students at the time, he had not had relations with the French Communist Party, nor had he been active in the FEANF. The decisive factor in his support for Daouda was his grooming as heir apparent. He had grown and taken root in the shadow of Léon Mignane. There had been talk of replacing the President, now too old. However well kept, the secret of the Venerable One's senility was beginning to leak out.

'What if relations between our two countries were to take a turn for the worse?'

'We will never change our options, nor go back on the reciprocal agreements signed by the Venerable One,' Daouda stated openly without avoiding the white man's gaze.

'We'll manage! Trust us,' asserted Haïdara.

Upon leaving, Jean de Savognard promised his support as before. Daouda escorted him to the door.

'Goodbye, Mr President,' said the Ambassador.

Daouda started. He was annoyed at being thus addressed. He stood tall as a palm tree, head and shoulders above the others. Jean de Savognard raised his eyes to his face; but there was no sign there of his inner torment.

'Goodbye, Your Excellency.'

Haïdara ushered the ambassador out.

Alone once more, Daouda looked the throne up and down. His fear of a moment ago had vanished. His fascination with the throne was dispelled by the pangs of hunger. He rang up his office and asked his secretary to bring him 'a good breakfast'. He summoned his personal assistant and principal private secretary.

22

The two men had only to cross the street. Ten minutes later, they were in the conference room. Daouda conferred with them, and corrected three or four memos. He delegated one of them to represent him at a routine meeting.

The two men, both younger than he was, left just as Victorine, his secretary, entered carrying a carefully wrapped carton. In the corridor, the private secretary, who was wearing a kaftan, remarked to his colleague:

'The PM looks determined.'

'He's rehearsing his role as Head of State,' replied the other.

Victorine, fragrant with perfume, set the carton down on the long table and opened it: coffee, milk, croissants, hard-boiled eggs, sugar, orange juice . . . She served him.

Victorine had been working for him for the past five years. She always had a ready smile, and never complained about the work.

Seated unawares where the French Ambassador had been, she checked through the letters to be signed. She admired the room . . . and its mild temperature. She was shocked to see that it hadn't been cleaned.

When he had finished his meal, Daouda dictated a letter to be sent to the governors of the country's eight regions, and signed a few letters and memos. He cancelled all his appointments.

Victorine left with the rough drafts, trailing a cloud of perfume. She was disappointed: Daouda had not complimented her . . .

Daouda summoned Soutapha, the President's personal assistant. Thirty-two years old, he too was an unconditional supporter of the theory of Authenegraficanitus, and the lynch-pin of the party's youth movement. He was an important figure, occupying the position Daouda had held ten years ago . . .

They sat down at one end of the table, and Soutapha brought him up to date on the President's commitments. Daouda made a note: 'Find a Minister of Justice.'

CHAPTER 4

Doyen Cheikh Tidiane Sall had returned to his office on the fourth floor of the *Building Administratif*, with a heavy heart. As recently as the day before yesterday, Wednesday, he had reminded Léon Mignane that he intended to resign on Friday. Léon Mignane had tightened his lips, avoiding his gaze. 'Please, Cheikh, in the name of our old friendship, don't reveal anything . . . to the Press. I ask it as a favour,' he pleaded.

Cheikh Tidiane Sall had hesitated to give his word. Various things, one after the other, had damaged their friendship of more than fifty years. Out of altruistic feeling, he promised not to reveal anything about his resignation. Léon Mignane patted him on the back, adding: 'That's more like you! That's truly African. I'll come and see you once you've retired.' This morning he regretted having yielded and given his word. What use had his silence been? . . .

Cheikh Tidiane Sall, born with the century (ours), was the son of a sergeant in the corps of *tirailleurs*. His father, Abdoulaye Sall, a model auxiliary, had won his stripes by taking an active part in the 'pacification' and colonial penetration of the Upper Senegal. He knew how to enforce respect for 'civilization', with stick or gun. A tall man with a loud voice, he would pin trouble-makers to the ground and beat them.

The traditional chief — or king — of the village of Tch. . . had rebelled against the new authority of the *Tubabs* and their auxiliaries. The captain commanding the fort of Tch. . . meted out justice: his justice. In the space of a night, the authentic chief, his wives and children were deported, and Abdoulaye Sall was made village chief. Sometime in the 1930s, before his death, old Abdoulaye Sall pinned to his breast the Legion of Honour 'for services rendered to France'.

A fervent Muslim, Abdoulaye Sall attracted scholars to the royal compound to teach all his children the Koran. His son Cheikh Tidiane Sall (one of thirty) attended this straw-roofed *medersa* until the age of ten, when he was enrolled in a French school: the *Ecole des Otages* or Hostages' School, later renamed the School for Chiefs' Sons. The school was built of mud bricks, with a thatched roof. It was run by an old soldier from Brittany. After four years of schooling, it was decided that the chief's son would continue his secondary education at Saint-Louis (Senegal).

Saint-Louis — or Ndar, to give it its Wolof name — was a melting-pot of the Arabic and French-speaking intelligentsia, seething with new ideas. A crossroads, a trading and administrative centre, since 1848 the town had been run by the Creole or mulatto families, related to Frenchmen from the *métropole,* who controlled trade and municipal affairs. They alone had the right to elect a deputy to the National Assembly in Paris. Their offspring alone received scholarships enabling them to study in Europe.

Black youths educated in French schools, who could not progress beyond secondary education, rebelled against this segregation. Steeped in the ideals of the French Revolution of 1789, they fought with their pens, with all the tenacity of a grain of millet sown on rocky ground. Their struggle for assimilation reached a high point in 1914, when Pascal Wellé, a black man, stood for election to the National Assembly. The deputy's mandate had always been Creole property.

Cheikh Tidiane had arrived in the town at the beginning of the 1909–10 school year. He was intimidated at first by his unruly classmates, but soon adapted himself. His future was clear: he would either become a schoolteacher, or succeed his father.

On Thursdays, their day off, young Cheikh Tidiane Sall would go to court, not for the pleasure of seeing justice rendered, but to admire the robes and be charmed by the lawyers' seductive speeches. He dreamed of becoming one of them ... But to become a lawyer he would have to pass both baccalaureate examinations at the end of secondary school, then go to university overseas, in France.

Pascal Wellé's appearance on the scene was to trouble the city's surface calm.

Among French-speakers the electoral campaign was in full swing. The black élite seized this opportunity to divert people's minds from this electoral excitement towards their basic grievances. The native officials, schoolteachers, clerks, interpreters, customs officers, whose access to education was restricted by local laws, launched an attack. Their campaign, tinged with rancour, took a frightening turn ... and people were frightened.

During an electoral meeting at the Dakar Chamber of Commerce, attended by merchants, trading-post managers, major tradesmen, administrators and heads of oil refineries, Pascal Wellé was harassed with questions about the colony's future. He was asked if, once elected, he planned to kill the Europeans and Creoles. The smile of a man-about-town (he was that) playing on his lips, his gaze swept the audience, composed entirely of whites. He proclaimed in the voice of a man who has faith in destiny:

'I am black, a Christian and educated. I have a white wife and Creole children. I ask you therefore, what part of myself am I to kill?'

The audience, startled, gaped at him.

Pascal, well used to such republican subtleties, ended his speech by saying:

'I represent a synthesis.'

That witty reply calmed the fears of merchants and administrators.

In Saint-Louis Cheikh Tidiane, one of the best and most effective publicists of his generation, dashed off an article entitled 'The Defence of the Mother Country'. The substance of what he wrote was as follows:

25

France is at war. Our duty as beloved sons of martyred France is to go and defend her. We demand to enlist in the army of the valiant defenders of our mother country, attacked by cowardly foes.

With courage, self-sacrifice and honour our fathers took part in the noble civilizing mission of France. The France of Victor Hugo, Lamartine, Musset, Jean-Jacques Rousseau, Robespierre, Danton etc. is in danger. We, black sons of that France, are prepared to die for this eternal France . . . in the name of freedom.

The article aroused tremendous interest. It was distributed in the streets of Saint-Louis, Dakar, Gorée and Rufisque. Its patriotic content stirred heroic impulses in the young people of the day. Black youths paraded through the streets, beneath the wooden balconies, singing the 'Marseillaise'.

The war coincided with Pascal Wellé's electoral campaign. He seized the opportunity, and the defence of the mother country became his campaign theme.

Once elected, Pascal Wellé did the rounds to thank his supporters. In Saint-Louis (Ndar) he was hailed as a liberator by the determined young people. The 'Young Senegalese' group tore him away from a crowd of revanchist admirers. They had grievances to air. Cheikh Tidiane, as their spokesman, formulated their demands.

'We want to enlist in the army. We don't want to be second-rate Frenchmen any more. If we take part in this war, you'll be able to demand scholarships for everyone.'

'You'll have to pass the baccalaureate examinations before embarking on further studies.'

'Just give us a chance! White or Creole children are no more intelligent that we are. You know that, Monsieur le Député.'

Pascal Wellé bit his lower lip. He felt ill at ease. He himself had not progressed beyond secondary school, yet he had made his way in the administration.

'I'll do my best in Paris.'

'Make that the topic of your first speech in the National Assembly. Where there are rights, there are also duties.'

There was something about that young man he didn't like.

In Europe war was raging between the two peoples, German and French. The armed conflict between the two colonialist states extended as far as their tropical possessions.

In 1917 a law was voted (in Paris) which stated that France's Africans were to take part in the defence of the mother country. Pascal Wellé was given the task of 'recruiting *Tirailleurs Sénégalais'*.

Cheikh Tidiane, now a schoolteacher, pursued his studies alone:

he began to learn Latin and Greek. But he had not given up his plan to become a lawyer.

Among the thousands of soldiers sent off to the chill horizons, only one enjoyed an exceptional situation: Cheikh Tidiane Sall. As a protégé of the deputy's, and also because of the renown of his father, six of whose sons had been recruited straight away, he never came under fire.

In 1918 he passed his baccaulaureate and at last enrolled in the Paris Law School. Three of his brothers had died in the war. Victorious France joyfully welcomed back her defenders.

On that day of victory, Cheikh Tidiane wept for sadness. Pascal Wellé, celebrating with champagne, asked him: 'Why are you crying on a day like this, my boy?'

Cheikh Tidiane Sall, whose opthalmologist had just prescribed spectacles, removed them, laid them on the table and answered:

'How many Africans had to die before I was allowed access to higher studies?'

The guests (all metropolitan French) remained silent.

'If you keep on thinking along those lines, my boy, you may turn into an unconscious racist.'

Cheikh Tidiane looked at Mme Wellé, who was seated at the table with them. He put his spectacles back on, and replied:

'We must recognize that if it had not been for this war, the doors of the university would still be closed to black Africans. That's not denigration, it's just a statement of fact.'

Two months earlier, the two had come to words. During an exchange of opinions, Pascal Wellé had asserted that 'blacks are incapable of scientific thought'. Cheikh Tidiane had indignantly denied this:

'You know nothing about Africa. How can you say that?'

'A future lawyer needs to keep his mind in fighting trim,' Mme Wellé interjected to soothe the two men.

As time passed, Cheikh Tidiane was more and more on his own. He hung about the organizers of the 'Communist League'; then he quietly withdrew, as discreetly as he had come. He often went to the café 'Le Croissant'. Jean Jaurés had been assassinated there in 1914. He had read all of his work, and admired him in silence.

His visits to Pascal Wellé had become less and less frequent. It was there that he met the young Léon Mignane, just arrived from home. At that time Léon Mignane was skinny, with an aggressive forehead jutting over a shifty-eyed face. They often met elsewhere than at the Wellés'; their relationship was like that of elder and younger brother.

At the end of the 1930s, having won all his certificates and diplomas, Cheikh Tidiane returned to Senegal. He settled in Dakar. A prominent figure, with an intellectual sphere of influence greater than that of any other black man south of the Sahara, and a partisan of assimilation, he practised his profession in a liberal manner. He remained aloof from the intrigues of politicians, as from the Freemasons, then gaining a foothold in Senegal. He married a distant cousin.

When the second European war (between the same tribes as in 1914–18) broke out in 1939, he was at the peak of his career. A patriot in word and spirit, he supported Pétain for a time, then joined the small group of pro-Gaullist Africans.

As soon as the war was over, he used his position as an influential man to send groups of students to Paris. He convinced his peers by saying: 'We can benefit from the *Tubabs'* war ... We must train cadres.'

He wrote to Léon Mignane, who had remained in Paris, to urge him to return home and 'take part in the struggle for a free and democratic *Union Française'*. Léon Mignane then usurped his place at the head of the campaign he himself had initiated. Demoted to second place, for more than half a century he was to serve as a mere figure-head. He soon began to have second thoughts.

Thinking back over his life, this Friday morning, made clear to him the flaws of his character ... These memories were deeply painful. Regret welled up in him like a bitter underground stream.

From 1914 to the present he had been nothing more than a floating tree-trunk, helping others to cross the river.

From his office he had a fine view over the tiled roofs of the colonial-style houses of this part of the city: the Plateau. He could see evidence of Dakar's growth as a modern city, the emergence of tall buildings. As he stared at the dome of the cathedral, his memories clashed and blended into a seething mass.

Gazing at the Pasteur building, he watched the vultures in flight. He often wondered about vultures: 'What makes them fly over the city, from one place to another?'

That day, he had other things in mind. Narcissus-like, he kept returning to his own difficulties.

He had been intending to resign for about a year; since before the official celebration of Léon Mignane's seventieth birthday. He knew that Léon was older than was stated on his birth certificate.

There had been a Cabinet meeting, chaired by the Prime Minister to plan the celebrations. Badara, Minister of Culture, was in charge of organizing the festivities. Delighted with this chance to be in the news, he read out the programme of activities: 'Holiday throughout the country; conferences and African-style evening gatherings to study the works of the Venerable One; colloquium on the theory of Authenegraficanitus, with prominent European, African and Arab scholars, as well as scholars of the Black Diaspora; inaugural meeting to be addressed by Doyen Sall.' As he finished, his sharp eyes glanced from one side of the table to the other, seeking a smile or gesture of approval.

'You forgot to mention radio, television and the *National Daily*,' remarked Mapathé, who did not want to be left out.

'Yes . . . I was coming to that.'

'Very good,' interrupted Mam Lat Soukabé . . . 'For my part, I suggest that we purchase a Boeing . . . as a gift for the Venerable One.'

Three glossy flight magazines were passed from hand to hand. Each man displayed his knowledge of aeronautics: 'Automatic pilot, safety measures, wing-span, turbine.'

'There's a bathroom,' exclaimed the Minister of Public Works, marvelling. 'So what!' grumbled his neighbour, the Minister of Hydraulics. 'That's a commonplace model in the States. All the big bosses own at least one.' He had spent five years in New York as a member of the permanent delegation to the UN.

'Does everyone agree?'

'Might I ask how much this plaything is going to cost us?' asked the doyen. 'The first crate we bought has proved expensive enough, according to the Ministry of Finance.'

'Doyen, stop right there,' called out Mam Lat. 'I don't remember saying the first aeroplane was expensive. I said, right here, that the frequent need for repairs was creating a great risk for the nation. It was at that very same Cabinet meeting that I suggested buying a Boeing. I was the one who first thought of it.'

'Very well!' pronounced the doyen.

A half-smile flattened Mam Lat Soukabé's bushy tinted moustache; he was pleased to have dealt with that obstacle. Of all the twenty-two ministers Cheikh Tidiane Sall was the only one for whom he left off his arrogant domineering manner.

'I haven't finished! How much will this aeroplane cost?'

'Three thousand million and some.'

'CFA Francs?'

'Yes.'

'How can our people pay such a sum? With groundnut husks or with oilcake? You seem to have forgotten about the drought.'

'We're negotiating with the manufacturers.'

'Through a bank. Bankers aren't choirboys.'

'Are we choirboys, then?' demanded Mam Lat, pounding on the table to impress him, his anthracite-black face taut with rage.

According to legend, an angry lion licks his chops. He did the same, furious. His breathing was audible.

For a moment they all thought he was going to punch the doyen.

Whatever the circumstances, the old man always insisted on being honest, to the point of naïvety. 'A politician must never tell the whole truth,' Pascal Wellé had told him. That phrase was meant as a warning; he refused to heed it. He replied calmly:

'In view of the awesome nature of the charge entrusted to us, Mam Lat, I would say: Yes.'

They were all astonished; because of his forcefulness, his self-control, or the harsh truth? The Minister of Public Works launched the furious counter-attack. They vied with one another in releasing floods of invective. He had become their scapegoat. They hoped, by abusing him, to win the favour of the Prime Minister and the Minister of Finance. The two rival factions had at last found common ground.

Reassured by their unanimous response, Daouda let his opponent Mam Lat Soukabé conduct the attack. He refrained from intervening, to stay clear of his fury. He exchanged glances with Corréa and Haïdara.

Talla, Minister of Higher Education, seated at the end of the table opposite the empty throne, was shocked by this verbal onslaught; he flinched as if stung at each unpleasant phrase directed at the doyen. The tip of his pink tongue resting on his lower lip, he observed the old man. The doyen, his arms crossed, looked each assailant full in the face. He remained serene, almost unperturbed by this lack of respect for his years. That was why Talla did not intervene on the doyen's behalf, as his conscience prompted him to do. He himself was not in favour of purchasing a Boeing at a time of natural disasters. 'Three thousand and some million, plus interest, would be better used by our peasant farmers, or the university, than in pandering to an old man's megalomania.' He kept his thoughts to himself. He was distressed at not having the courage to support the doyen.

Nafissatou, Minister for Women's Affairs, stared at Talla. Her eyes flashed a clear message: 'Say something! You are a *man*.'

Just then Badara leaned towards Talla and muttered: 'Bugger the old fool. What does the money aspect matter?' Talla did not answer.

'Gentlemen, gentlemen, the doyen isn't against buying the aeroplane. Let him state his case,' said Nafissatou, unable to stand being a silent onlooker.

'The doyen can speak for himself, Nafissatou,' Mam Lat Soukabé angrily replied, intent on carrying his point.

'Doyen, why are you against this aeroplane?' intervened Wade.

30

Cheikh Tidiane took a deep breath, then replied:

'A period of drought is not the time to indulge in such an expensive toy. Not only is the price high, there is interest to pay as well. Who will endorse this loan? The state, on behalf of our impoverished people? Such a gift, at a time like this, is a misappropriation of public funds.'

'Doyen, you must remember the cultural aspect of this celebration. The Venerable One is the founder of modern Senegal,' asserted Badara.

'Waste and culture are not the same thing. And I'm not likely to change my opinion on this topic, at a time when we're asking for aid all over the world.'

At that meeting Cheikh Tidiane Sall had openly clashed with the ministers, clearly intent on eliminating him. He himself suddenly felt his age . . . over seventy-five.

A week later, during a private conversation, Léon Mignane had teased him:

'What's this? What's this? You've upset the boys [he called the ministers this because of their age]. You must realize that this aeroplane is not my private property.'

Cheikh Tidiane scanned the President's face, and said:

'This aeroplane is not indispensable, nor is it a priority for our country. A superfluous gadget, that will cost us very dear, Léon.'

'I must travel! I must have personal contacts with my counterparts, the bosses' bosses, in order to attract investment here . . .'

Cheikh Tidiane shook his shaven head and said:

'Léon, be assured that one can't relive childhood in old age.'

Stung by these harsh words, Léon Mignane concealed his feelings behind a wry smile.

For days afterwards, Cheikh said to himself: 'Léon is a monarch.'

It was one afternoon towards the end of the dry season. The elderly Sall couple had settled in a corner of their pillared veranda, to enjoy what little breeze there was. A fine-meshed green nylon screen protected them from insects. A few bold sunbeams pierced the foliage of the flame-tree, near which stood a baobab. Shadows danced in the wind, and the sea roared not far away. Along the wall lay a varied flower-bed . . .

'Would you like me to call a doctor?' asked the woman, her eyes fixed on Cheikh Tidiane.

'It's nothing physical,' replied the old man, brushing away a small spider dangling from the wooden roof by an invisible thread. 'I'm thinking of resigning from the government.'

Djia Umrel Ba sighed, and looked away. A beam of light struck

31

her eyes, and she turned her head aside.

Betrothed to this man since birth in accordance with tradition, at the age of seven she had been enrolled in the French school to be a suitable wife for Cheikh Tidiane. She was given in marriage at the age of twelve; the marriage was consummated when she was sixteen and Cheikh Tidiane almost thirty-three. After marrying she attended the Ecole Normale for girls, then left to fulfil her duties as a wife.

Now aged over fifty, she dressed in the old-fashioned style of the Signaras of Saint-Louis. Her white hair was covered with a mauve scarf; her spectacles were on a gold chain hung round her neck. In 1938 she was the only black woman to drive a four-wheel-drive Citroën. She had entertained governors, lawyers, schoolteachers, writers and intellectuals at her table. She also entertained film stars: Georges Milton, come to film *Bouboul, premier roi nègre*; Josephine Baker at the peak of her fame; Annie Ducaux, Habib Benglia, Henri Baur, here to work on another film *L'homme du Niger*. She was very quick-witted, and this quality was heightened as she grew older.

'So that's what's troubling you!' she said.

She had noticed her husband's moodiness and insomnia.

'Yes.'

'What will Léon say?' (She too called him Léon.)

'I don't know.'

She picked up her glass, and gazed compassionately at her husband. She did not want to harass him with questions. After so many years of life together, she knew what he was like.

'Do you think he'll be resentful, or angry?'

She answered herself, thinking: 'Léon will be furious. Spiteful as he is, he'll try to humiliate you.'

'I'm very old! It's time for me to retire.'

She knew he wasn't telling the truth, but she didn't want to show him that she knew him better than he knew himself. He and Léon Mignane had a few things in common. She put down the glass of home-made lemonade.

'That's true! We're old now. I congratulate you on your decision. On the day, we should have the children here to celebrate your exit, don't you think?'

'Yes,' he agreed.

Perched in a tree, a grey dove cooed over and over.

Djia Umrel had never liked Léon Mignane. The first time she saw him, in 1945, she said to her husband: 'That man is of the hyena breed,' meaning deceitful.

Badou, his younger son, a teacher of modern literature, came to see them one evening. His father and mother had just finished their evening meal.

'Come in, come in! We're listening to music.'

She clasped both her son's hands in hers. He was a head taller than she was.

'How's your family? The children?'

'We're all well.'

'*Joom Galle* is here.'

Father and son embraced each other warmly.

'How are you doing, son?'

'Senegalese-style . . . What about you, *Joom Galle?*'

'As you see me.'

Saying that, the old man flung his arms out, nearly hitting his wife with his right arm. The old man was wearing a dressing-gown, and smelled of lavender.

'Sit here . . .' invited his mother. 'I went by your house this week, to borrow a book.'

'Yes, I know.'

'Still active?'

'I do what I can, *Joom Galle.*'

'It's good to have faith. You should do away with that . . . [he pointed at his son's beard.] It doesn't suit you. Hasn't your wife told you?'

'Yes.'

'Maybe his wife likes him like that,' said Djia Umrel.

'Have a port, a real Sandeman; now that there aren't any more Portuguese colonies.'

'Yes,' replied Badou.

'I'll get it,' said his father, leaving the room.

Djia Umrel drew nearer her son, and whispered anxiously:

'Nothing wrong at home, I hope?'

'Nothing at all, mother. The whole family's well,' answered Badou, gazing into the old woman's eyes.

'*Alhamdulillahi!* I'm glad to hear that.'

'Just imagine, son; your mother is in much better shape than I am,' remarked Cheikh Tidiane, returning with the bottle under his arm and glasses in his hand.

'That's only to be expected, I'm younger. But I'm ill much more often.'

'That's true.'

The conversation took up the topic of men and women's life span and the life-expectancy of Africans.

The Daphnis and Chloë Symphony filled in the moments of silence. From time to time, the two men sipped at their drinks.

'Shall I leave you alone?'

They looked at each other.

'Yes, mother.'

'My son, are you still an anti-feminist, after Women's Year?'

'I didn't say the woman should go. I asked my mother ... to excuse me ...'

'That's very subtle ... But I understand ...'

'*Debbo*, I would gladly come with you ... but I'm being detained here by force.'

'And the bottle of Sandeman is your gaoler ...'

'One can keep nothing from you, *Debbo.*'

She shrugged, then kissed Badou and wished him goodnight.

'*Joom Galle,* don't take advantage of my absence to make free with the port.'

'I promise ...'

She left, and they had another drink. Badou looked at the room's furnishings, strewn with nineteenth-century European ornamental knick-knacks.

'*Joom Galle,* the drought is playing havoc with people and livestock in the countryside. And we're about to squander our savings and go into debt for the sake of a masquerade! And it's you who are going to preside over this ritual pledge of allegiance, this deification.'

'Is that what you came to tell me?'

'Yes, *Joom Galle.*'

Cheikh Tidiane had had many quarrels with his younger son. Badou had joined the PCF (the French Communist Party) during the colonial period, and had been very well known among students. Because of his extreme opinions, his relations with his father were very tense.

When General Charles de Gaulle stopped in Dakar in 1958, to offer France's overseas colonies a form of community association, he had been confronted with these youths of the 1940s. A big meeting had been held in the Place Protet (now Place de l'Indépendance). The general had made his key speech. The stands were full of prominent people, traditional chiefs, administrators, elected representatives. Armed soldiers stood guard ...

Badou had slipped past the guards and appeared in front of the general, who was making his speech. He unfurled a banner which read: 'WE WANT INDEPENDENCE NOW.' Annoyed by this lout, De Gaulle stopped speaking, and announced: 'If the banner-wavers want independence, let them take it.' With these haughty words the general brought the meeting to a close.

Cheikh Tidiane, seated in the middle of the stand, like everyone else had recognized his son. Looks of disapproval were aimed at him from all sides. At that moment, if he had had a gun he would gladly have shot Badou. Cheikh was suspected of links with the communists; General de Gaulle refused to receive him, as did the Governor-General of French West Africa. Cheikh cut off Badou's allowance, and Badou also lost his scholarship.

Badou continued his studies unassisted, except for what his mother could secretly give him. He lived in poverty, but did not budge an inch. In 1960 Djia Umrel brought about a reconciliation between father and son.

'What do you expect me to do, son?' asked the father.

'Just refrain from presiding over this farce.'

'I can't lie to you, nor to myself. I've agreed to do it . . .'

'Joom Galle, Léon Mignane is just using you. And I've heard those high-and-mighty ministers are treating you disrespectfully.'

Without showing annoyance, the father acknowledged that this was so. He had not expected such frankness.

'Badou, if I were to refuse to preside over this ceremony, do you think Léon Mignane would fall from office? Or that the country would rise up in arms? Or that the drought would end?'

'No! Frankly, no! Whether you take part or not will have no immediate effect on the sufferings of the people. However, as a son who is aware of what is at stake, I would say to myself proudly: "My father has behaved as a man should." Léon Mignane with his Authenegraficanitus has nothing African but his black skin. If he could turn white he would. I haven't come to talk to you as a communist . . . Just as a son whom you owe some respect, just as he owes it to you.'

Cheikh Tidiane's gaze wandered about the room. The light of the standard lamp defined his features sharply. A grave expression stole over his face. This private conversation had suddenly reminded him of something he had thought a long time ago: 'When a man is told his father was a Don Juan, the son is proud. But if this same son is told his father was a coward, he becomes angry.'

He began, in the tone of one making a confession:

'I belong to two epochs. For over half of this century I convinced myself that I was French. I had done everything necessary to be acknowledged as such. And in the end, I myself was convinced. You know, that period was the most important of my life. As I grew, like a sunflower I was irresistibly drawn towards France. There was my sun, the light I needed for my spiritual life. Look around you. Nothing here comes from our country. Nothing was handed down by my father or my grandfather. On these bookshelves, books on Africa occupy a very small place; furthermore, they're written by Europeans. On the other hand, if you want books in Greek, Latin, German, English, Italian, French — here they are.'

They turned their gaze towards the shelves, with their tastefully bound books. The father was revealing his most secret thoughts. Each sentence had required a long search of his innermost being, both day and night. He continued:

'My Frenchness affects me here. [He passed his hand over his shaven head.] It's choking me. I refused to opt for dual nationality, so did your mother. I didn't believe in Independence. I voted in favour of the *Communauté Franco-Africaine,* and I was responsible for evicting from administrative posts all those who did not share this option at the time. I'm not pretending to be more guilty than I am.'

Badou was saddened by his father's confidences. His father was not as he had imagined him. He had been prepared for a confrontation; but his father's amiable mood left him feeling sheepish. He listened.

'I was never a coward. Timid? Yes. I was a publicist for Pascal Wellé. I was Léon Mignane's footstool. My life was spent between those two men. What do you expect, son?' he asked.

His son kept quiet, as if yielding him out of courtesy the right to speak again . . .

'I saw aeroplanes evolve from Jean Mermoz' crate to the rocket taking the first man to the moon. In Paris, I heard about the Bolshevik Revolution; I lived through the end of the First World War. I witnessed the Rif war, the Italian invasion of Ethiopia . . . and its liberation, the Spanish Civil War, the Russian attack on Finland, the Second World War, the end of colonial dominion, African independence. I have one wish left: to see our whole continent free . . .'

'It's a matter of years, *Joom Galle,'* ventured Badou.

The father smiled, to conceal the gravity of what he was thinking: death would deprive him of that last chance. He automatically smoothed his eyebrows, and repeated:

'Everything's just a matter of time.' Then he asked him, in a firm tone: 'Do you believe in the inevitable victory of communism?'

'Yes, *Joom Galle*. It may take a long time, but I'm convinced of it.'

'As the poet says, "You are like rocks."'

'Sembène's right.'

'Where did you get what flows through your veins? You've rejected all of me, my social milieu, my environment. How did you manage, with all your education, to elude the spell of Europe? I, Léon Mignane, the old soldiers of both wars, although our relations with Europe have somewhat cooled, remain attached to her. If you can't have your mother's breast, you'll suckle your stepmother's.'

He paused once more, like a good housewife who lets water settle and deposit its impurities at the bottom of the water jar. He then recited this verse: 'My existence has been but a fraction of a second on the face of time.'

'Sembène again,' said Badou. '*Joom Galle*, Europe no longer has the power to attract us. Nor does any other country.'

The father lifted his spectacles towards his son and asked: 'Not even the Soviet Union?'

'No, *Joom Galle*.'

'I hope all your comrades are as determined as you are.'

'They are.'

'In that case, son, you are carrying on a struggle our forefathers started over five centuries ago. But you must realize that the African continent is at stake in the world's future. The quality of life in the coming century will depend on Africans. As for me, I will make the inaugural speech on Léon's so-called seventieth birthday. Thank you for spending the evening with me, and for teaching me something. Don't forget, either, that Léon recruits his sycophants among those of your generation.'

Cheikh Tidiane moved towards the front door. Badou stood looking at him for a moment, then understood and followed him.

'All the best to your family,' said the father, looking him full in the face.

He was remembering the banner waved at de Gaulle.

Once his son had gone, he locked the door.

Days folded into weeks. The media's full batteries were trained on the celebrations, to prepare the ground psychologically. The Venerable One's birthday took precedence over current events. Terms of praise vied with one another: supreme, enlightened . . .

A foundation was created, bearing his name.

Djia Umrel was alarmed at her husband's taciturn manner. He would toss and turn in bed, his eyes open, then get up to drink some water. Before his wife could ask him anything, he would explain: 'I'm thinking over my speech.'

'Don't please other people,' she advised.

Meaning: if you can't say publicly what you yourself think, don't speak.

'Thank you,' he answered.

The Place de l'Etoile was throbbing to the rhythm of drums, xylophones, lutes and songs in praise of the Venerable One. It was too small to hold the crowd. People were waving pictures of the Father of the Nation. Policemen were directing the heavy traffic with shrill whistles. Official vehicles displaying rosettes moved along in a solid stream. Buses were bringing in members of Léon Mignane's party from the crowded outlying districts of the city. Boys in the uniform of the party youth movement, the 'Pioneers', lined the pavement behind the blue-clad policemen.

The gentle morning sun heightened the warm, glowing, shimmering colours.

In his luxury Citroen DS, an official car, Cheikh Tidiane and his wife sat in silence, each contemplating the crowd streaming along in the same direction.

At the foot of a man-made waterfall, two uniformed porters ran to open their car doors. The officer of the guard, in a red dolman, called out: 'Preseeent . . . sabres.' The stainless-steel sabres flashed through the air. A little girl came forward to present a bouquet to Djia Umrel. The old lady kissed her as photographers and cameramen went into action.

Djia was dressed in an old-fashioned style, with a cloche hat; her spectacles hung on a chain round her neck. She clung to her husband's elbow as they entered the hall. The old man was wearing a dress-suit, but no medals, national or international. As they were dressing, his wife had remarked on this. 'I don't see any need for them,' he had replied.

In the hall of the National Assembly, party officials and religious leaders, Catholic, Muslim and Protestant, rubbed shoulders with the judiciary in full regalia, caps and ermine cloaks; the civil service in full dress; high-ranking officers of all three forces; deputies in dinner-jackets; and all their ladies in evening dress. Above their varied headgear floated the indistinct hum of voices, the fragrance of scent. People were meeting, embracing, gossiping about each other. Television cameras swept this high-society gathering, while a volley of photographers' flash bulbs captured images for posterity.

The clear light streaming through tinted plate glass bathed the scene in an atmosphere of cordiality.

Doyen Cheikh Tidiane was affably greeting people here and there, deputies, ambassadors, magistrates, dignitaries . . .

His elder son Diouldé, a deputy, wearing a midnight-blue dinner-jacket and black bow-tie, came to meet them. He relieved his mother of her bouquet. A playboy, Diouldé was strutting with manifest pride, a pair of sunglasses perched on his nose.

The day after his younger brother's visit, Diouldé had been to call on his father. During their conversation, he had claimed that the celebration had positive aspects. The ceremony, he announced, was a symbol of unity in support of the Venerable One.

'Do you want to write my speech, Diouldé?'

'No, *Joom Galle,* no!' he had answered, ill at ease.

As he was leaving, he whispered to his mother: 'Is *Joom Galle* feeling all right?'

'Yes, he's quite well . . .'

'I see . . . Fine.'

The sirens of the Prime Minister's escort rent the air.

Daouda entered with his wife Guylène and their children. Guylène duly received her bouquet. The Speaker of the National Assembly, Maguette Kane, in full dress, along with his Chief of Protocol, came forward to greet the Prime Minister. In their wake bobbed Badara, stouter than ever in his burgundy dinner-jacket.

The bell tinkled several times.

People slowly drifted into the hemicycle. Each group of guests had their allotted seats.

Maguette Kane, as host, opened with a few words of welcome before yielding the microphone to Badara. The Minister of Culture introduced the theme of the ceremony. He recalled the Venerable One's exemplary life, then announced the next speaker, 'the man who, still alive today, was his comrade in arms'. The audience applauded as Doyen Cheikh Tidiane Sall moved to stand behind the rostrum. He directed his gaze, first at the row where the entire government was seated, then towards the deputies, the diplomatic corps, the judiciary and the public. He had written nothing down. In a calm, precise voice, he began to evoke the long winding path the country had taken. He recalled those who had passed away, from 1914 to the present . . . the illustrious unknown names of our history. As he spoke, he gradually raised his voice.

'. . . In my youth, the system then prevailing, commonly known by the name of colonialism, assimilated the first cadres it trained; its aim was two-fold, to make us into "Frenchmen" and to take possession of our land. That method has now had its day. However, we must have the honesty to perceive and acknowledge, we the leaders of today, that that very same system, hide and hair, has reappeared in a new guise. Let us further acknowledge that colonialism no longer consists in occupying land, but in demeaning the minds, crushing the culture and distorting the growth of a society, and imposing an armada of obtuse advisers whose role within our new administration is not to help us, but to curb every daring reform, every enterprising spirit.

'Our one chance lies in the youth of our people. We must educate our young, train them to develop our country. Instead, we lie . . . We lie to them when we say "We are preparing your future." A dark, deadly future it is. Our educational system, our schools in particular, are not places for imparting culture. They serve only to manufacture mandarins. The young of today, born far away from the sacred

39

woods of old, circumcised in dispensaries and hospitals, grow up in families whose world is in collapse: lost, torn apart, without any faith to live by. We the elders, the enlightened guides, are compelled to recognize that the old morality has to relevance to today. How then can it be assimilated? Who sets an example for the young? A set of individuals engaged in legalized plunder of the national economy, who constitute a privileged élite. These same individuals are making fortunes out of the drought; in search of authenticity, they deck their homilies in the rags and tatters of the old culture now in its death-throes.'

Doyen Cheikh Tidiane Sall paused, and poured himself a glass of mineral water.

Dismay reigned. The audience was transfixed with astonishment. Murmurs of disapproval rose from where government members, legislators and dignitaries were seated. On all sides fluttered sounds of 'hush! hush!'

Daouda, indignant, bent his head to avoid searching glances. Corréa leaned over towards Mapathé. The latter rose, as did Badara. Mapathé ordered the technicians of his department to cut the live broadcast of the speech. When they returned, the doyen was continuing:

'When the sun sets each day as it did the day before, these young people become aware that the best part of themselves has been murdered. They sense that their dreams of tomorrow are dead; they sense that they are failing in their cruelly atrophied roles as fathers and mothers. Every sunset is but one more mournful step towards the old age that awaits them. Take a closer look at our traffic lights! One often sees there an old man and a crowd of children, begging. The former is drawing near the end of a life of farming toil. The latter are just starting out in life. What future do they have? Look at them, listen to them, these children, these girls, these men and women, these fugitives from our countryside. At every sunset their voices rise in accusation. Today anger vented in words; but tomorrow, a justified rebellion ... that those in power will seek to crush. Decrees, orders and laws are fashioned into a muzzle, to protect a tiny minority; this muzzle dangles over the people's heads, they flout them. The space allowed the free exercise of democratic freedoms grows smaller every day. Freedom is not something which can be handed out to any individual or group. It – freedom – is the way in which individuals, or the people as a whole, can remedy abuses. Depriving a group or an individual of freedom, sooner or later leads to revolt. We must do everything in our power to ensure that our children master this technological age. For they are, they will be, the creators of a new kind of life, of culture, of civilization. They must embrace and weld together all the races to fashion the new Africa,

40

not imitate a dying civilization. To conclude, I will say this: the blindness of certain rulers is clouding our country's future. May our country forever be twenty years old.'

He had finished. His old eyes scanned the audience. Everyone was turning round to confer with his neighbour. In the rows reserved for the public, someone clapped, shattering the silence. The ovation spread to fill the house. Everyone rose. There were shouts of 'Bravo!', 'That's the truth!', 'Long live Doyen Sall!' Indescribable turmoil broke out. All the government members had hastily withdrawn, to escape the journalists, especially those from Europe.

Representatives of the European Press had rushed up to the doyen and were firing questions at him.

'Minister, have you thought of how the President will react?'

'Minister, may I have a copy of your speech?'

'After making this speech, do you intend to resign from the government?'

The doyen declined to answer any questions.

A ten minute pause in the proceedings was announced.

Djia Umrel had trouble joining her husband, advancing with difficulty through the throng. They finally met. He took her by the arm. People stood aside to let them pass. While remaining silent, the old man nodded in response to congratulations.

In the hall, on the balcony, people were commenting on the speech, interpreting particular words and phrases. Some boldly came forward to shake the couple's hands.

'Is that what you meant to say, *Joom Galle?*' asked the old lady, looking up . . .

'Yes!' the doyen replied, seeking to measure his worth in his wife's gaze. 'Did I say it well?' he asked.

'I could have wished for nothing better.'

'Thank you,' he said, squeezing his wife's elbow, happy to be admired. In spite of his advanced age, he felt the need to be acknowledged as a true man.

O! Women, give us the courage, the strength of mind never to drape ourselves in falsehood . . .

O! Men, take your wives as the measure of your daring.

An elderly dignitary in sumptuous attire, his chest covered with medals, separated him from his wife and declared:

'Cheikh, everything you said was the honest truth.'

The Minister of Justice looked him up and down. Deep down, he knew that this man had understood nothing, not even the meaning of the French words he had used.

The assembly's Chief of Protocol came over to fetch him. The other man clung to his wrist and muttered:

'Cheikh, tell Mignane I must see him. I have important things to tell him. Please . . . Don't forget me.'

Cheikh Tidiane sadly eyed the man's coal-black countenance. That very man would be prepared to disown him, no later than this evening, if Léon Mignane told him to. He went over to Djia Umrel and spoke to her, before following the Chief of Protocol.

Her heart heavy, Djia Umrel kept her eyes on her husband's back. Someone inadvertently blocked her field of vision. It was a journalist.

'Good morning, Madame! What do you think of your husband's speech?'

Taken by surprise, the woman started; her mouth trembled, but the quivering soon ceased. Just then, her elder son Dioulde rushed towards her. He knew which Paris newspaper the European worked for. The journalist took advantage of his presence . . .

'Monsieur le Député, I ask you the question I've just asked Madame your mother: what do you think of the speech made by the Minister of Justice?'

Despite his sunglasses, Dioulde's face was grey. He remained silent. Djia Umrel saw that her son was in an awkward position, and helped him.

'Please excuse us, Monsieur.'

Having said that, she drew her son towards the staircase. They sat on a sofa yielded to them by two men.

'Dioulde, why didn't you answer that journalist?' she asked, watching the European approach someone else in the distance.

'What did he want to know?'

'What you think of *Joom Galle's* speech.'

The old lady fixed her gaze upon her son's profile. Between lens and eyelid darted his gleaming eye.

A guest came over to greet her, bowing respectfully.

'*Joom Galle* should not have said such things in public. Especially on the occasion of the President's seventieth birthday. He made a personal attack on him . . . The European Press will once more denigrate the country . . . and black people in general,' Dioulde declared when the man had gone.

'Did *Joom Galle* speak the truth, or not?'

'Mother, it's not a question of basic truth. *Joom Galle* should have known this was not the time or place. He should have refrained from speaking. *Joom Galle* isn't just anyone! He's a member of the government and a political leader.'

They fell silent.

Highly displeased, Dioulde gazed at the people moving to and fro. In the crowd he caught sight of a young woman who'd once made a date with him, then failed to turn up.

'Where is *Joom Galle?*' asked Djia Umrel, suddenly worried.

'With the PM. Really, mother, I don't know how to make you see what a political mistake *Joom Galle's* made.'

'Go and see where he is now.'

Diouldé repressed a grumble. His mother's demand annoyed and vexed him. He knew he wouldn't be allowed access to the VIPs' lounge. He strolled towards the lift, without hurrying. On the way, he caught up with the woman who'd once let him down. He turned, and saw that his mother was watching him. She signalled to him not to stop.

The ambassador of an African country came to kiss her hand, and sat down beside her.

'For technical reasons, this morning's session is postponed until two o'clock this afternoon,' announced an usher, his gaze sweeping the hall.

The crowd withdrew.

That afternoon Doyen Cheikh Tidiane did not go to the National Assembly, where the colloquium on Authenegraficanitus was being held.

Two days later, Léon Mignane sent him two volumes of Lenin and Mao. The gesture reduced the old couple to tears of laughter. Responding in the same vein, Cheikh Tidiane sent him two volumes of Nkrumah, *Class Struggle in Africa* and *Consciencism,* as well as the works of Franz Fanon and two records by the Bembeya Jazz Ensemble, called *A Look at the Past.*

Léon Mignane ordered the ministers and party organizers who wanted to get rid of Cheikh Tidiane to do nothing ... 'I don't want that old man to become a martyr. By keeping him on, we show how democratic we are.'

The telephone rang insistently, tearing him away from his personal preoccupations. He searched the overcast sky for vultures. 'We're in for bad weather,' he said to himself. His scattered thoughts were now collected, focused on today's business. 'A President who disappears into thin air! A trick? Why? To what end?'

Cheikh Tidiane lifted the receiver and a woman's voice announced:

'Attorney Ndaw is here.'

'Please show him in, Madame.'

Cheikh Tidiane was courteous with his subordinates. He used his influence on their behalf. He had forgotten that he'd asked to see Ndaw.

Ndaw, in his fifties, with ash-grey hair, was wearing a white kaftan, the neck embroidered in cream-coloured silk, and held in his hand a small black leather case.

'*Tonton,*' he said, while warmly shaking hands with the Minister of Justice.

Cheikh Tidiane led him over to the armchairs. They both sat

down. Cheikh Tidiane had dreamed of Ndaw succeeding him. But things had happened otherwise. He knew Ndaw to be honest, clear-sighted and perspicacious. Both men appreciated each other. Like anonymous heroes they opposed the abuses of the executive branch. They talked shop, discussed the careerists and upstarts of the Judiciary, the increased incidence of assaults, bad cheques and embezzlements. Each remark darkened an already gloomy picture.

'I'm leaving,' said Cheikh Tidiane. 'I wanted you to be the last person I received in this office. I would have been very glad to see you become Minister of Justice.'

Ndaw shifted in his chair. His energetic face tightened, and the cleft in his chin deepened.

'I'd heard of a Cabinet reshuffle, through Radio Street-Corner, but not that you were leaving, *Tonton,*' he said, gazing at the old man's drawn face.

The pouches under his eyes had sagged still further below the rim of his spectacles. Cheikh Tidiane's jowls and scalp were bristling with white hairs.

'My decision has nothing to do with the Cabinet reshuffle,' he stated solemnly, as if he were being asked to reconsider his decision. 'I'm retiring, once and for all.'

Ndaw perceived the note of frustration in his voice.

'What's going on, *Tonton?*'

The need to confide in someone led Cheikh Tidiane to reveal 'Léon's escapade' and the death — not from natural causes — of the driver.

'That means that the highest position in the country is in abeyance.'

'And Daouda will be invested with that office, according to our Constitution.'

'The Judiciary must first ascertain the facts,' replied Ndaw sharply, lifting his head. Then he leaned back slowly. Passionately attached to justice, he could brook no irregularities. 'So Daouda will ascend the throne,' he thought, before asking: 'What does the Minister of the Interior have to say?'

'Corréa is going to exert his influence over Daouda. I won't pass judgement in advance! But their group is capable of anything ... And Mam Lat Soukabé isn't going to sit about with his arms crossed.'

'The President's disappearance creates an exceptional situation — and there's no proof.'

'The Constitution isn't a sacred truth. It functions as a law without being one. We should know that, you and I. You and I modified the former Constitution to introduce the clause that makes the Prime Minister the President's official successor should the

44

position fall vacant. And the PM will inherit unlimited power. We hadn't foreseen this trick of Léon's . . . You and I dug the grave of our freedom. We're responsible for what may happen any minute. Morally responsible, I mean.'

The attorney sat up to reach for the standing ashtray. He lit a cigar, and gazed over the smoke at the photograph of Léon Mignane. In his own office, on the wall above his head, was the same framed photograph of the President.

'But, *Tonton* . . .'

He didn't finish his sentence. His mouth was frozen in a mirthless grin.

'The way Léon Mignane had himself re-elected, with a made-to-order Constitution! . . . It's pure Machiavelli! I can't believe in this latest prank, *Tonton*.' He shook his head, dispelling the cloud of smoke.

'Unfortunately, it's true. Pure Jesuitry. Léon can't be found anywhere.'

The two men looked at each other.

'What will the people do?'

The attorney's question diverted the attention of the Minister of Justice. Lost in private speculation and suppositions, he raised his hand to his mouth. His beard prickled. He slid his fingers over his cheeks; they were rough.

They discussed future prospects.

Bringing the conversation to a close, Cheikh Tidiane said:

'We look like two conspirators.'

Ndaw smiled, shook the old man's hand, and said:

'It's Friday, I'm off to the mosque . . . to pray for everyone.'

'I should have more time to devote to Allah now. But I'm very stiff . . .'

'You should come and play tennis with me every morning. It's very good for your health and mental equilibrium.'

'At my age?'

'Why not? We Africans don't exercise much past a certain age, but it's highly recommended.'

'I'll see.'

This conversation somewhat cheered Cheikh Tidiane. Ndaw promised to visit him.

After saying goodbye to his staff, Cheikh Tidiane left the building by the main exit. He had declined their suggestion of a farewell gathering over drinks. He wanted to leave quietly, he said.

He walked along the pavement in front of the palace. Above the building, just under the country's flag, fluttered the flag of the Commander-in-Chief of the Armed Forces: the sign that the Head of State was at home. Groups of tourists were aiming Japanese

45

cameras at the guard on sentry duty by the great closed gates. Two armed policemen were pacing up and down.

The bus braked at the traffic-light with a sound of creaking metal. Cheikh Tidiane raised his head. The driver waved, inviting him to cross. Passengers were pointing him out to each other through the open windows. Someone shouted: 'Hullo, Doyen Sall.' He responded in kind once he had reached the far pavement.

The bus continued on its way, towards the harbour.

It was a very long time since he had been, and felt, so free. He examined buildings and shop windows. Pedestrians turned to look as he passed, or stopped to stare. Their whispers pursued him.

A watchman sitting on a bench, listening to the Friday religious programme on the radio, stood up and greeted him as he drew near. Cheikh greeted him in reply. A young bootblack walking in the same direction insistently proffered his services. He smiled at him.

A taxi-driver attracted his attention by hooting his horn. He declined the offer. At the corner by the Ecole Jeanne d'Arc, he waited for the light to turn red. He was surprised at the number of cars speeding past.

'Doyen, may I drop you anywhere?'

Cheikh Tidiane leaned towards the young driver, who repeated his offer.

'No, thank you, son,' he replied, pleased with this token of attention.

How ideas can suddenly strike you! He was startled to notice that no one – European or African – was wearing a solar topi. 'In what year did people stop wearing them?' he wondered. He looked about for one. He himself hadn't worn one for a long time. 'Is the climate milder now? Or have people changed somehow?' He told himself that he'd ask Djia Umrel. At this point in his monologue he strolled past the cathedral. A bizarre sight caught his eye: a leper, with folded arms and old socks drawn over his stumps, was scraping his hunched back against the wall. His ragged body swung from left to right. His disfigured face was contorted with pleasure.

Doyen Cheikh Tidiane was shocked . . .

'Say! *Couz* Nam Salla!'

Hearing the name Salla, he thought he was being addressed, and turned around, startled. Who? . . . Two individuals were pressing each other's hands and forearms while exchanging the customary greetings.

'Samb! How is your family?'

'Accept my condolences, *Couz*. I heard the sad news,' declared the member of the Samb family.

He was wearing a silky midnight-blue kaftan, embroidered in thread of the same colour. His reddish bonnet, the peak crushed to

46

one side out of masculine coquetry, was aslant on his head.

'We share the same sorrow! I too offer condolences, Samb,' replied *Couz* Salla, thus returning the courtesy. He was plump, with a round face and gold canine teeth. Dressed all in white, with a cap on his shaven head and a silk scarf carelessly tossed over his shoulders, he gave off a heady scent of musk. He added fervently: 'Let us implore the mercy of God upon her and ourselves! We live only to die. She had cancer,' he added, as if seeking the other man's sympathy.

'Ndey San!'

'A dreadful illness! She was butchered ... simply butchered ... her breasts ...'

'Ndey San!'

'She left me with three children. To die at twenty-five! *Allahou akbar!* Luckily my first wife has been very good about it. She's agreed to care for the dead woman's children as well as our own seven.'

'Ndey San! Sometimes our wives surprise us,' said Samb prosaically. He caught the eye of Doyen Cheikh Tidiane Sall, nodded his chin at him in greeting, and asked: *'Couz,* you're all dressed up; where are you going?'

'I'm going to the Friday mosque. I always try to pray inside the mosque. Outside, the heat from the asphalt is unbearable.'

'Every Friday after prayers, I have a headache.'

'It's because of the heat outdoors. I'll keep you a place in our row. I'll be in the third row behind the Imam, by the windows ... The first window.'

'Thank you, *Inch Allah*. Once more, accept my condolences ... Salla.'

'We share the same sorrow, Samb.'

In spite of himself, Cheikh Tidiane had heard everything. A banal conversation, in fact. His gaze followed *Couz* Salla, as he thought of Attorney Ndaw. He himself didn't worry about not practising his religion, attending only christenings, weddings and funerals. He had just learned why the faithful rushed inside the mosque on Fridays: for fear of sunstroke.

He turned. The leper was crossing to the opposite pavement. He quickened his pace towards home, feeling tired.

His villa was in the old part of the Plateau. He had bought this colonial-style house, built of freestone, at a preferential price, at the time of Independence. A bougainvillea hedge surrounded the house; a horseshoe-shaped path led up to it.

Djia Umrel Ba saw him push open the little gate. Startled, she put down the book she was reading and removed her spectacles, frowning.

'What's happened, *Joom Galle?*'

'I was stretching my legs,' he answered, lowering himself into the rocking-chair.

He loosened his tie, and began to unbutton his waistcoat.

'Wait a bit! You'll catch cold,' she said, and called out: 'Mamadou?'

The servant arrived, a blue apron round his waist.

'Bring a glass of water and *Joom Galle's* slippers.'

Birds were twittering among the leaves.

Mamadou returned with a tray; he handed over the glass, and put the slippers on the floor. 'Thank you, Mamadou,' said the old man, slowly sipping the water.

'Can you tell me in what year we stopped wearing solar topis?'

'Topis?'

'The headgear we used to wear to keep off the sun.'

'That was a very long time ago.'

'I know, *Debbo*. But what year did people stop wearing them . . . '

The old woman gazed at him, her thoughts elsewhere. She counted on her fingers while speaking, beginning with the thumb.

'At Independence, people weren't wearing them. I'm certain of that. Well now! Before then! in 1958, at the meeting with de Gaulle? no . . . Badou wasn't wearing a topi that day. In 1955, Diouldé didn't wear one . . . In 1950? No . . . In 1945–6, soldiers back from the war weren't wearing them either. I think it must have been the 1939–45 war that ruined the manufacturers. And solar topis lost their prestige . . . '

'Yes, that's right! So in the late 1940s, solar topis had already lost their elegance and their protective function. The world, our world, changes.'

'Is that a useful thing to know?'

'Quite useless! I was looking at people in the street, and it struck me. Just an idea to toy with . . . Invite the children over. Both of them, with their wives.'

He put down the empty glass, and put on the slippers.

Djia Umrel was watching her husband. She was impatient to know what had happened last night.

'Diouldé's marriage is near breaking-point.'

'Your son is a skirt-chaser, *Debbo*.'

'Can't you tell me what's happened?'

'Yes. But let me rest a bit first.'

Having said that, he stretched, rocking to and fro.

'You'll have a bath before your nap.'

Although they had three servants, Djia Umrel Ba always cared for her husband herself. Once he was in the bath, she would summon her sons . . .

CHAPTER 5

The building that housed the Ministry of the Interior was known as the 'Coffin House'. When Corréa had taken over the premises (formerly the headquarters of the colonial airforce) he had added on two storeys and covered the building's outside walls with cement slabs. This lugubrious decoration, resembling rows of coffins, had earned the building its name. Corréa had set up a projection room in the basement for film censoring.

Files, phone-tapping, all the departments in charge of surveillance of people and political parties were gathered here.

Corréa was the master here having succeeded Doyen Cheikh Tidiane Sall, who had refused to allow demonstrators to be assaulted.

Corréa was a mulatto from Saint-Louis-du-Sénégal. His family was a branch of an aristocratic lineage of the city, whose origins dated back to the time when the first trading-posts were established there.

It was since Independence that the Corréas and allied families had begun contracting matrimonial links with blacks. Previously, young mulattos returning home from studies in Europe would bring back a wife. But once Independence had come, with fewer soldiers (of the colonial army), settlers and administrators, mulatto girls had to make do with dark-skinned educated Christians. Some of them, in order not to remain spinsters, were converted to the Muslim faith and became second or third wives.

Corréa had always supported Léon Mignane's party. After a spell as Minister of Finance, he yielded that post to Mam Lat Soukabé and was entrusted with the country's internal security.

After the secret meeting of the ministers of state, he hurried back to the 'Coffin House'. This unforeseen absence of the Venerable One struck him as a personal insult. From the start, he had placed the city under close surveillance, reinforcing the guard by the harbour and airport police. He had a list drawn up of all foreigners who had entered or left the country during the past week, and another list of nationals currently abroad. The police had discreetly checked all hotels. None of this had yielded anything.

A map of the city covered the entire wall opposite his desk. He scanned the streets with a piercing gaze.

A musical peal drew his attention. He swung round in his swivel armchair, mounted on wheels. He loved it ... With one finger he extinguished the white light . . . and lifted the receiver.

'Oh, yes . . . Thank you! Show him in.'

A stocky man with bloodshot eyes came in.

'Hullo, Diatta. Sit down.'

Diatta was holding a sand-coloured folder.

'Well?'

'I've got something.'

Diatta leaned forward to hand Corréa a sheet of paper. He was an expert in manipulating public opinion by rumour and innuendo, in charge of mass psychology. Whenever the Minister of the Interior had a special problem, Diatta was called upon to solve it. Today's problem was how to find some way of returning the body of Léon Mignane's driver to his family.

'That's a bit much,' said Corréa, looking up.

'Well, you wanted something quickly. Give me until tomorrow, maybe this evening. It's not easy to slip something past on its own, without a counter-weight to attract people's attention . . . I'll think about it . . .'

'Find something! Believe me, it's urgent.'

'I'll see you this evening, then . . . What about our match against the civil service team?'

'The police team ought to win! They're in good shape . . .'

'The public don't support you . . .'

'True! But if we play a good game, we'll win their support in the first ten minutes. I've seen my team at work.'

'I know the way out . . . Bye . . . Till this evening.'

'Right . . .'

Corréa felt guilty. Wasn't it his job to keep watch over the Venerable One? To protect him? To ensure his security when he travelled anywhere? Hadn't one of the Venerable One's lady friends received him . . . these past five nights?

Someone knocked repeatedly at the door. He called out:

'Come in.'

It was his secretary.

'Good morning, Aïda.'

She laid a thick pile of letters on the table. At a glance, she noted the bristles sprouting from his ears and chin, and the dark circles under his eyes.

'Are you ill?' she asked in an affectionate tone of voice.

'Just tired.'

'You work too hard . . . day and night . . . you ought to go on holiday.'

Aïda had moved round the table, and began tenderly to stroke the nape of his neck. He yielded to her, his face pressed against her belly. He put his arms round her waist. One arm slid down her leg, then

50

moved up between her thighs. A flood of warmth pervaded him.

'Someone's waiting outside,' she whispered, still holding his head in her hands.

'Local colour?'

'Your cousin Alfred . . .'

'Damn . . .'

Aïda straightened her clothing before leaving.

Alfred entered hurriedly. The cut of his suit, his shirt, his tie, his polished boots and attaché case all suggested a frivolous person, more inclined to shady deals than serious work. He embraced his cousin . . .

'You'll excuse me, Alfred; I'm very busy. Wait for me at home.'

'I came down from Saint-Louis overnight. It's urgent business! My brother Jean-Louis, the hotel manager, has been arrested. A man died after a fight. There's presumptive evidence against Jean-Louis. He's still in custody.'

'Troubles never come one at a time,' Corréa remarked to himself, out loud.

'I can't do anything for Jean-Louis. You'll have to see the police superintendent up there. Without the police report, it's hard to see what I could do.'

'Here's a copy of the statements made by witnesses. As you can see, Jean-Louis has been accused unjustly. The guy was a thug . . . He was already known to the police.'

Corréa read the witnesses' statements carefully. He admired the style of the thing. The inspector who drew it up knew his job all right. Corréa could tell that the conclusions were one-sided. With a report like that, no magistrate would detain an accused person. He would have liked to know how much it had cost Alfred. He was a wheeler-dealer in real estate, using his whole family as straw men.

'What about the victim? Any relatives?'

'No . . . He was from out of town.'

'What does the superintendent say?'

Alfred leaned towards him:

'You're the only one who can do something about it.'

'How?'

Still leaning towards him, Alfred suggested:

'Have the hotel shut down. I admit it's seedy, even dirty! As for Jean-Louis, I'll send him to France for training in the tourism business until things blow over. I've already mentioned it to your wife.'

Corréa felt bitter. Alfred had spoken to Jeanne to get her to intercede in his favour.

'Very well!' he said at last, with a long, weary sigh.

He rang for his secretary.

Alfred turned slightly. He looked closely at the woman. Her tight-fitting indigo outfit concealed nothing of her well-rounded figure. He winked at Corréa with a crudely salacious look, then shifted his gaze back to the woman's body: 'A dish fit for a king,' he said in a low voice.

Corréa dictated an unofficial letter to the police superintendent, suggesting 'closing the hotel as a public health measure, and conveying Jean-Louis to Dakar, if there were nothing to detain him, in the care of his brother Alfred', he concluded, addressing Alfred.

'Wait outside . . .'

Careful and methodical, Alfred gathered up his papers and followed Aïda . . .

Bounama came in to report, having been delayed by Alfred's sudden arrival. Plump and pleasant, he knew his 'boss' well and didn't indulge in superfluous comments. He had worked with Corréa for ten years. As principal private secretary, he enjoyed all the prerogatives of a sub-minister. He began:

'I've read through the projects on penal reform. You'll find my comments on the last page. Our gaols are full to overflowing . . . A majority of young people.'

'I'll go through all that this evening. Sit down,' Corréa invited, looking closely at Bounama's clothes.

He was wearing the traditional three-piece outfit, a robe worn over matching shirt and trousers, in white damask. Corréa remembered that it was Friday, the day when people all gathered for midday prayers. 'Well, what's new?'

'People are getting excited about our match with the civil service. But our team is better trained.'

Corréa, amazed at such innocence at a time like the present, bit his lower lip then released it to ask:

'What about Radio Street-Corner?'

'Only unfounded rumours.'

'What kind of rumours?'

'The next Cabinet reshuffle; nothing much apart from that,' explained Bounama.

'Good,' remarked Corréa, with a forced smile.

The telephone rang. Corréa pushed his chair back with his foot, and leaned over the table.

'Hullo! Yes. One minute . . . Bounama, could you come back later?'

The door shut. Corréa spoke once more:

'. . . Yes! I'm listening. (It was Adolphe on the line.) Wait a minute, I'll look at my diary . . . I'm supposed to go and see our team; but I can send someone else. Right! I won't budge . . . See you later . . . OK!'

Corréa hung up. Aïda came in, followed by Alfred. Corréa never signed anything without having read it, corrected grammatical errors and added punctuation. Delighted, Alfred hugged his cousin. He invited Aïda to come and spend a weekend at his expense. 'Why don't you come with the minister?'

He left rapidly.

'Cancel all my appointments . . . and tomorrow's as well. I'm not available to anyone except the President's office. Tell Bounama to come in.'

Corréa rose from his chair. He stretched to his full height, then opened the sliding door that led to a terrace overlooking the roundabout. A blast of scorching heat struck him in the face. 'Dreadful weather,' he said to himself.

At his feet, the leafy branches of trees formed a shadowy dome. There was a group of people from the radio station. Policemen came and went. A file of cars slipped one by one round the dried-up fountain.

The racket of a heavy motorcycle shattered his eardrums. It wove in and out of the traffic, ridden by a pair of teenagers. The girl, her rear moulded in tight jeans, was clinging to the driver and saying something in his ear. They rounded the corner, leaning far over, and sped off towards the *lycée* . . .

Corréa's head nodded.

'Yes.'

He turned round, and collected himself; once more, he became the chief.

'Bounama, you'll replace me for the talk to the football team.'

'Is there anything special to tell them?'

'Just encourage them, and promise a bigger bonus than usual if they win.'

'Fine . . .'

The telephone rang again.

'What a day!' he exclaimed.

'They're here, Monsieur.'

'All right, Aïda . . . Bounama, show Monsieur Adolphe into the workroom.'

Once alone, he opened a safe behind his desk and took out a red folder; then departed by another door, on his left . . .

CHAPTER 6

That Friday, signing the agreement with the IAF, Mam Lat Soukabé threw himself wholly into the part. He signed the document like a lord, beneath the newsreel cameras' spotlights. Those who had worked with him longest could not recall his ever having been more eloquent than this morning. A convinced and convincing adept, he imitated the Venerable One's way of speaking so well that those who listened to him thought for a moment that he was Léon Mignane reincarnated. The ceremony was crowned by champagne, courtesy of the Minister of State in charge of Finance.

He was the heir to a famous name, enriched and renewed by local history from generation to generation; a name with which he identified himself. The praise-singers who chronicled their deeds could name more than thirty-seven of his ancestors who had died weapon in hand, defending their own, on numerous battlefields, and this added lustre to the history of the clan. These same praise-singers also named those who did not return from the cold lands of the men with red ears.

Mam Lat Soukabé was raised amidst tales of his ancestors' heroic deeds. He dreamed of continuing this lineage of bygone heroes. Accustomed to praise, like a graven image hanging in the Louvre, he would tell his age-mates: 'Don't forget that I'm a Lat Soukabé!'

His father, the Bourba Ayane, a *chef de canton* and second in command over its villages under the watchful gaze of the colonial administrator, knew how to appear submissive.

The Bourba Ayane had as an adviser Gorgui Massamba, a praise-singer by birth, Daouda's father. The two fathers lived in harmony, even though within their society they were separated by a tangible social frontier. They were circumcised by the same *Ngaman*. The dawn wind had not yet dried the blood of the one on the purifying blade, when the other straddled the mortar stained with red droplets. The drop of blood fell on his tied foreskin, before the impure skin was severed forever. The two men were more than brothers.

But one was the Bourba, and the other the keeper of the village chronicles. Their children were raised differently, from early childhood.

The French school was to disrupt that order; but the consequences would remain.

The two youths followed the same course of study and received the same diplomas from the same faculty.

Léon Mignane, then a deputy in Paris, representing the rural pop-

54

ulation, acted *in loco parentis* to the Bourba's son. When he became President, in order to use the clan's influence, he made Mam Lat Soukabé a governor.

(Governors of regions are responsible directly to the President. The governor is the chief administrator of his region, and *préfets* are under his orders.)

In his region, Mam Lat Soukabé behaved like a head of state, riding in an open car preceded by two motorcycle policemen and a pennant. He had his subordinates punished and whipped as he liked. He took undue advantage of his position ... He would arrest peasants or have them kept by force in humiliating postures. He had acquired a taste for firearms, and would shoot at people belonging to the opposition. He once fired almost an entire barrel at a supporter of Ahmet Ndour, the *Président du Conseil* or Cabinet head.

Ahmet Ndour took offence. His authority and prestige were threatened. Furious, he decided to punish the governor. Carried away by anger, he harassed Léon Mignane immoderately.

'How can that young so-and-so get away with such behaviour, as if he were above the law?'

'Ahmet, you must be mistaken ...'

'Tell me then, why does this so-called prince get away with gunning down citizens? I'm the head of the government. The people rely on me ...'

'Quite! Quite! All day long I hear *"Monsieur le Président"*, *"Monsieur le Président"* on the radio. It creates confusion, Ahmet!'

'In any case, I take note of the fact that governors are now superior to the Cabinet head. We'll have to do something about that ... As for this Mam Lat, I'm going to give him the sack.'

'Just a minute, Ahmet! After all, I'm the Head of State. You shouldn't shout at me like that ...'

'We're alone.'

'All the more reason for you to speak softly, without raising your voice. The President's residence isn't a palaver tree.'

Ahmet Ndour was furious. He was certain the two men were in league. His left eye, striated with reddish fibres, was fixed upon Léon Mignane. The latter, subjugated, could feel his gaze, like pins piercing his flesh.

'The law applies to everyone,' said Léon Mignane, ill at ease, seeking to avoid that defiant stare.

'I repeat that you're favouring those governors. As Head of Cabinet, I have no hold over them. They're untouchable. We'll have to reconsider their status.'

'What is it you're after, Ahmet?' asked Léon Mignane condescendingly. He intertwined his fingers and cracked his knuckles, one after the other. This series of incongruous sounds annoyed Ahmet Ndour.

Léon continued:

'Ahmet, you're trying to create divisions within the party.

'I'm very well informed . . .'

'By the governors?'

'What difference does it make . . . Why are you doing it? What are you after?' inquired Léon Mignane, scratching his nose.

At bottom, he was not displeased with Mam Lat Soukabé's behaviour. This affront to the pride of his second-in-command revealed the latter's weak points. He resented the renown of the Head of Cabinet. Ahmet Ndour was more widely known that he was himself. He decided to multiply such pinpricks, to incite him to rebellion. With the skill of an experienced poker player, he smiled affably, and added:

'You're the head of government . . . I don't know much about what actually goes on. I'm just a referee . . . I apologize; do as you like,' he said, with perverse pleasure.

He devised a strategy.

Ahmet Ndour, in all sincerity, took pleasure in his victory . . .

During the next few weeks, there was a massive reshuffle of governors and *préfets*. It swept Mam Lat Soukabé back to the capital city. The president granted him an audience.

'Mam Lat, a *Guelewar* like you mustn't take potshots at the citizenry. We're living in a republic,' said Léon Mignane, flattering him.

He often fanned, then appeased conflict between his subordinates, taking advantage of their differences.

Months passed . . .

One morning, a distant hollow voice, issuing from within the batteries and wires of the 'talking box' astonished the country.

'There has been an attempted coup. The Head of Cabinet, Ahmet Ndour, has had the National Assembly evacuated by troops. Rejecting a motion of censure against his economic policy, deposited by the deputies of his own party, he has challenged the Republic. The President of the Republic has decreed a state of emergency . . .'

From one house to another, from one village to another, night and day, the transistors poured out the same broadcasts. (My aunt, who had the sharpest and most venomous tongue in the neighbourhood, declared: 'It's the talking box that links us with Independence . . . The talking box chatters away, and never answers our questions. The people who own the thing can make it say what they like . . .')

Ahmet Ndour, Léon Mignane's companion for over fifteen years, was sent to prison . . .

The second Constitution was revised. The post of Head of Cabinet was eliminated. Léon Mignane alone held sway, an uncrowned monarch. 'A poor country cannot afford to have two heads,' he said in concluding the speech announcing his programme.

Mam Lat Soukabé was given a portfolio: the Ministry of Finance and the Economy, where he replaced Corréa, transferred to the Interior. Entering the government as controller of the exchequer, he was courted and flattered by industrialists, merchants and businessmen. His promising career took another step forward: he stood in for the President during the latter's absence. He was gaining weight in both senses of the term. His belly grew round, his cheeks swelled. He was fond of display and dressed accordingly, in custom-made suits from master tailors. His prematurely white hair was dyed black.

Years of solitary, undivided presidential power had taken their toll. Exhausted by overwork, Léon Mignane was growing weaker. His health and strength were waning. He experienced long, very long spells of dizziness and fainting. His personal physician, Fall, the doyen of the medical corps, diagnosed a state of deficiency and a long-standing case of pernicious anemia. He advised him to work less hard: 'You're no longer young.' To spare him, the doctor did not tell him the whole truth.

Léon Mignane confided in Cheikh Tidiane Sall.

'I'm having problems with my health. It might be an idea to create a Prime Minister's post . . . You never know.'

'It would mean a new version of the Constitution.'

'Of course! Of course! I'll go even further: democratize politics, recognize the three or four currents of opinion present in our society. The Prime Minister should be directly answerable to the President, and replace him until the end of his term in office should the Presidency fall vacant.'

Doyen Cheikh Tidiane, Attorney Ndaw and other jurists set to work drafting a third Constitution.

By a referendum followed by legislative and presidential elections, the voters approved everything. Léon Mignane, sole candidate to the presidency, was elected. His (single) party swept up all the votes. Léon then began cutting out the dead wood. He got rid of a number of veterans, keeping only three time-hallowed baobabs: Cheikh Tidiane Sall, Corréa and Mam Lat Soukabé. He kept them on in their former posts (those they now occupied).

Overruling all objections, Léon Mignane made Daouda Prime Minister.

Mam Lat Soukabé openly displayed his opposition. He expressed it to the President.

Léon Mignane summoned his two protégés, and said: 'I trained both of you. I shaped your future! I'm convinced that one of you will succeed me. You must work together. You complement each other.'

Mam Lat never came to terms with being placed in a subordinate

57

position. He was discourteous to the Prime Minister, and taunted him with hurtful allusions. For his part, the head of government had no control over the Minister of State in charge of Finance and the Economy.

Léon Mignane fostered this climate of rivalry between his two ministers. He promised each that he would succeed him, the better to retain his power over them.

This Friday, Mignane having vanished, Mam Lat decided to make his bid for power. After the reception, he summoned his brain trust. His ministry was an extension of his clan. As chief political organizer of his region, he could count on a block of voters. He decided to work from within, to unseat Daouda. He had a large following of hangers-on, and summoned them to his residence after midday prayers. Before noon, his messengers had been dispatched to round up his 'friends'.

CHAPTER 7

Friday is a holy day. A day of prayer. From *Fadjar* on, people visit the graves of their dead. Prayer-beads in hand, kneeling near the head of the deceased, they commune with him and beg Allah to have mercy upon him. All along the rows of graves, people invoke the dead and mutter prayers.

On Friday, cadres, bureaucrats, civil servants cast off their European clothes and donned traditional attire: robes, kaftans, tunics, djellabahs. The myriad bright colours gladdened the eye.

On Friday too, as if sprung from the bowels of the earth, legions of the blind and crippled, old and young, men and women, took up position at dawn at the cemetery gates; they then turned to stores, workshops, bars, restaurants, public transport, markets, banks, chemists' shops and post offices, begging alms here and there. On this holy day they clustered about traffic-lights ... to grasp hold of the privileged ones who drove cars.

They thronged the steps of the Friday mosques, chanting verses of the Koran. Some of the faithful would drop coins into their begging bowls, or onto a worn sheepskin.

On all four sides of the green-domed minarets, loudspeakers poured forth recitations of the Koran.

On Friday, whether in the public, para-public or private sectors, work started again at three o'clock in the afternoon.

After midday prayers, the weather changed. The fine young

morning sun, clad in old-gold gauze, began to lose its shining lustre. The sky was slowly clouding over with a film of dust. The air became dry, burning hot, laden with the scent of the desert. It penetrated everywhere, every bodily cranny, every fibre of cloth.

Fetid vapours from sewers, waste-water pipes, open-air urinals, ill-kept markets and heaps of garbage blended together to offend the delicate nostrils of people living in the Plateau area – the commercial centre of the capital.

The wind was blowing from the north.

CHAPTER 8

Luxury cars drew up one after the other in front of the residence of the Minister of State in charge of Finance: members of the Political Bureau, deputies, important merchants and ministers. Mam Lat Soukabé, who could make or break them, was organizing his supporters. Without mincing matters, he described the present situation. Without any mention of Daouda's genealogy, he warned them about the economic situation . . . for which the PM was responsible. In concluding, he evoked the prospect of a state of economic depression that could lead to rioting. Alarmed, his hearers asked why the Venerable One remained silent. He replied that he was too old. His strategy was to put his troops on the alert, before launching an attack . . .

Mam Lat Soukabé privately wished that the Venerable One would come back . . .

CHAPTER 9

At 3.37 p.m. that same day, Mapathé, Minister of State in charge of Information and government spokesman, was deeply shaken. His state of tension focused on the telex. As he read, he was seized with fright. He could no longer hear the machine's clatter. Censorship had been imposed, discreetly. No agency could send dispatches without their being subject to scrutiny. Coded texts had to be deciphered.

Mapathé swiftly tore out the sheet of paper and reread the text:

Since this morning the President of the Republic, Léon Mignane, has performed none of his duties. All his appointments have been postponed to a later date. Contradictory rumours are to be heard in well-informed circles.

The Minister of State in charge of Justice handed in his resignation last night, at a top-secret meeting. As of today, local banks are refusing to transfer French funds to the EEC countries and the US.

The forces of order are checking vehicles, the borders and airfields. Their presence, although discreet, is highly noticeable in town.

The resignation of Cheikh Tidiane Sall, in his eighties like Léon Mignane, has clearly shown that ever since a contingent of troops was sent to Shaba — in Zaïre — relations between the generations have not been what they were . . .

The Director of Information burst into the office. He was holding a copy of the wire.

'Who sent this?'

Furious, Mapathé greeted him thus.

'It was sent from Banjul, by the European Press Agency,' said the director, who was wearing a light-coloured suit.

His left shoulder sagged.

The jaws of the telex began to grind once more.

Mapathé darted forward, his gaze devouring each word. The director read over his shoulder:

'Fidel Castro has now arrived in Ethiopia . . .'

Mapathé returned to his chair, and asked:

'Does the European Press Agency have an accredited representative here?'

'Yes. One of their people, Kad, rang up three times.'

'Did you receive him?'

'No, Sir.'

Mapathé angrily grabbed the telephone, and barked: 'Yes! Tell the journalists I'm at a meeting. But the director will see them now.'

The director stared at him, nonplussed. He had nothing to tell the journalists.

'Tell them it's not true! We must issue an official denial,' instructed the minister, who then made his escape through a side door.

He went to the palace.

Young Soutapha took him in to Daouda, who had taken over the President's office.

'Have you read this?' asked Mapathé once they were alone, showing him the text.

'It came through here, too. I've summoned Corréa and Adolphe.'

When Daouda had read the newsflash, he had been disconcerted. This leak upset his plans. Daouda had not sought popularity for himself; he had never envisaged having to compete for the position he held today. The Venerable One had often reproached him for his timidity and lack of drive.

He had just been reviewing current problems in a meeting with Soutapha, the Venerable One's personal assistant. There were any number of plausible candidates for the post of Minister of Justice. The judiciary must be considered. Attorney Ndaw would do very well. 'Best hold someone else in reserve! The Professor of Law, Djibril Saar, is a loyal party worker,' suggested Soutapha.

'All right! All right!' agreed Daouda. He couldn't fit a face to the name Djibril Saar. 'Ask Djibril Saar to be here tomorrow at eleven ... But first make an appointment with Attorney Ndaw ... for ten tomorrow.'

Corréa and Adolphe arrived together. The former had changed his suit, and shaved. He laid a pair of dark glasses in front of Daouda. Since the departure of Cheikh Tidiane Sall, Corréa was the oldest among them, and the oldest still active companion of the Venerable One.

'Do you have the cable?' he asked Mapathé.

'Yes. We should expel that agency ... Kad works for them, you see.'

'Kad's Senegalese.'

'I don't like the young so-and-so.'

'You're not the only one, if it makes you feel any better. The dispatch was sent from a foreign country,' said Corréa, who had his suspicions about the leak concerning last night's meeting. He and Adolphe had thought of a way out: 'Hold a press conference to deny the news. Professor Fall, the Venerable One's personal physician, will provide a medical certificate.' In an elder-brother tone, he continued: 'Professor Fall will attend the press conference. Mapathé, you'll sign the press release to be given to the *National Daily* for tomorrow's issue, Saturday's.'

'What about the vehicle checks?'

'That's for the Ministry of Transport to answer. A routine check on behalf of the Ministry of the Interior. Same thing for the banks: ask the Minister of State in charge of Finance.'

Mapathé was afraid of the Press, especially the European Press. The Venerable One had no mercy for clumsy replies and ill-worded statements. 'If Corréa knows all the answers, why doesn't he handle it instead of me?' thought Mapathé. Press conferences were usually prepared in advance, with a list of selected questions returned to those who were to ask them.

'We'll hold a press conference, then,' decided Daouda,

instinctively clutching the dark glasses. 'Another thing: the ministers of state will meet this evening at ten. A statement will be drawn up, eh, Adolphe?'

The white man understood what was required of him. He nodded in agreement.

'Corréa, wait a minute,' said Daouda.

The two others moved towards the door.

'Try them! Yes . . .' ordered Corréa.

Daouda put on the glasses. Objects became dark and two-dimensional.

'They change your face. They're a bit wide . . . but keep them . . .'

Daouda unburdened himself by telling him of his intention to appoint Attorney Ndaw as Minister of Justice.

'I have reservations about him. He's too friendly with Doyen Cheikh Tidiane Sall. And it won't be easy to get him to share our views. He called on the doyen this morning, and stayed a long time. What about Djibril Saar? He's reliable, and young.'

A discreet buzz sounded. The two men started nervously.

Daouda hastily removed the dark glasses. This number was strictly private. His heart beat faster with hope; the Venerable One was back! In a boyish tone of voice, he said:

'Hullo! . . . Hullo! . . .'

Two fraught seconds of silence increased his hopes.

'Hullo! . . . Hullo! . . .'

Still no answer.

The two men looked at each other. Hope sparkled in their eyes. Corréa, an expert at telephone-tapping, had a feeling the call was long-distance.

'Hullo! Good afternoon, Madame. Yes! The President?' repeated Daouda. Dark despondency and distress clouded his narrow forehead. The pleasure that had swelled his heart a few seconds earlier, melted away like a lump of shea-butter in the midday sun. Boundless disappointment paralyzed his mental processes. He was unable to react: 'No! . . . No! . . . I haven't hung up, Madame. Yes . . . Yes . . . The President . . .'

He quickly murmured to Corréa: 'It's Madame.' Corréa frowned inquiringly. *'Madame la Présidente?'* The old animosity surfaced strongly.

Once, while he was still the President's personal assistant, the Venerable One, then travelling abroad, had sent a parcel to be given to Madame. Late in the afternoon, he had gone over to the palace. He had only to cross the garden. The steward, who knew him, was occupied elsewhere, and left him on his own. After a long wait, he set out to look for Madame. He knocked at each door, once, twice, thrice, before looking in. He eventually reached the bedroom. He knocked, but there was no answer; so he surreptitiously risked a glance.

Horror! Sprawled across the double bed in an unequivocal posture, Mam Lat Soukabé, naked, was embracing Madame.

He closed the door and fled, pursued by the woman's moans. His stomach rejected what his eyes had seen. Deeply depressed, he left the parcel with the steward. Himself an honest man, he could not forgive Madame for betraying his 'spiritual father'. His hatred for Madame increased threefold when he thought of Mam Lat Soukabé. 'Screwing the wife of the President! Your protector! Morally, it's like incest!' he thought to himself. And when he saw them dancing or chatting in public, always observing protocol, his bitterness grew and the picture of them copulating grew vivid in his mind. He did not know whether to denounce the unfaithful wife, or keep silent. He decided in the end that the Venerable One, the wise and dignified Father of the Nation, was above such filth.

'Yes, Madame, I'm here! I'm listening . . .'

With his free hand, Daouda signalled Corréa for help. The latter leaned forward and scribbled: 'He's in good health! And so on and so forth . . .' Daouda narrowed his eyes to read the message, and said:

'The Venerable One! He's well. Quite! Quite! A bit of a chill. We're having rotten weather here these days. No! . . . Yes . . . He's much better. In fact, he's gone to the National Assembly. That's right! The newsflash? No truth in it . . . except that Doyen Cheikh *has* left the government. Don't talk to journalists, or even answer written questions. I understand. He'll ring you back. I'm not in his office. I'm in mine . . . Yes! Yes! Very well! Mam Lat Soukabé! I'll pass on the message . . . Good day!'

While talking, Daouda had passed his hand over his face as if to sweep away cobwebs. His opponent's name revived his anger. He gazed at Corréa without seeing him, his mind elsewhere. He could not remember what he had said.

'I wouldn't wish this situation on anyone. I had completely forgotten about the Venerable One's family,' he said, talking to himself rather than the other man. Then, sharply: 'Why must we keep the truth from that woman? From the nation? Tell me, Corréa?'

'What can I tell you?'

'The truth!'

'I don't know the truth.'

'Till this evening, then,' said Daouda.

Thus dismissed, the Minister of the Interior rose.

Had there ever been anything like this before in history? A President vanishes without a trace. He violently rejected the idea that the Venerable One might have instigated the whole thing himself . . . Why? And what about the dead driver?

CHAPTER 10

Djia Umrel Ba, the wife of old Cheikh Tidiane Sall, wondered what she should serve for dinner. She had a long talk with Ly, the cook-steward, who promised to perform wonders.

Her two sons had accepted their father's sudden invitation. They wanted to know the reason for it. 'An old man's whim,' she had replied. She was worried about the two brothers being together this evening. Whenever they met, it ended in a political argument. Sprung from the same root, each now drew his sap from a different source. It was Badou, the younger one, who had the hardest time of it. It's not easy, these days, to claim to be a communist. Dioulde, the elder brother, was a pleasure-loving deputy, and his social life was a success. As for her daughters-in-law, each took her man's side.

Elderly and eager for culture, Djia Umrel Ba had joined a reading circle. The women members met once a month at the house of one of their number, to discuss a book. She enjoyed it, and it enriched her life. This month's book was *Femme de'Afrique**. Swinging to and fro in the rocking-chair, she could not keep her mind on the page. She was remembering how *Joom Galle* had confided in her: 'I've left the government, and given up politics . . . For good! . . . I swear it . . .'

'You needn't swear, *Joom Galle.*'

The electric shaver moved over his head, sweeping away the bristles of white hair. She smoothed the shaven surface with her hand. Seated on a foot-stool in the bathroom, Cheikh Tidiane continued in a mocking tone of voice:

'Your "friend" Léon has done a bunk . . .'

With her thumb, she switched off the shaver. She leaned to one side to look at her husband. Flaps of skin hung beneath his chin.

'The President of the Republic, Léon Mignane, can't be found anywhere . . .'

They looked at each other, without speaking.

'A coup?' she asked.

'Come now! Would you and I be sitting here quietly, if that were the case? . . .'

She did not know what to answer.

**Aoua Keita, Présence Africaine.

'Your "friend" has just vanished.'

He told her everything he knew.

The shaving finished, Cheikh Tidiane stood up, his belly flaccid, his muscles limp. He had a bath before going to lie down.

The old woman was momentarily unable to formulate her thoughts. She tried to revive her mind by reading ... But it didn't work ...

Twilight lasted only three blinks of an eye. Night fell, and the watchman lit up the garden.

She supervised the setting of the table, showing Ly how to lay out the silver tableware from Christofle, bought before the Second World War. 'Could't *Joom Galle* manage not to mention Léon?' One word out of place could set off a chain reaction. This intimate family gathering mustn't be turned into a platform for the two brothers. 'What if it were a plot? Were their lives threatened?' This monologue sent a chill through her veins. She was prepared to speak out, if need be.

'Ly ... don't forget the screens. The wind blows in through here ...' she called out.

'I'll take care of it.'

'Are you up already?'

'Do you think I've no legs any more? What about the alarm clock!' replied *Joom Galle*, appearing from the back of the room ...

'Do you think you could refrain from talking to them about your "friend"?' she asked.

'Yes, I won't say anything on the subject.'

'Thank you ...'

Cheikh Tidiane was surprised by this 'thank you'. Even when she's old, a woman is still a woman, he said to himself, while adjusting the blinds for proper ventilation of the sitting-room.

Badou and Fatimata turned up first. Badou was got up in a traditional three-piece outfit of white damask. He had trimmed his beard and cut his mop of hair, accentuating his thin, sharp-featured face. His wife Fatimata was wearing an ankle-length tunic that made her look even slimmer. Her eyelids had a touch of kohl. Her hair had black wool plaited into it, to make it longer.

Her mother-in-law put on her spectacles, the better to see the new arrivals ...

'It's the Badous,' she said, kissing Fatimata. 'Oh! you smell good, Fatimata! Where did you find that *gongo*?'

'I made it myself! I'll send some over.'

Djia Umrel Ba sniffed her a second time. The young woman gave off an aromatic scent. Turning towards her son:

'And you, my lad, how are you? Let me look at you ... You've lost weight ...'

'No, mother, I've trimmed my beard . . .'

'Fatimata, you should take advantage of your man's sleep to shave all that off. He looks like a Greek Orthodox pope without a church.'

Both women were passionately fond of reading. They both belonged to a reading club. They began to discuss this month's book, the author's life, the problems she had encountered as a wife, a midwife and an active member of the *Rassemblement Démocratique Africain*.

'I don't see *Joom Galle,'* remarked Badou.

'He's dressing up . . .'

Badou left the room, saying: 'I'm going to see the working class,' meaning the servants.

Hearing the sudden hoot of a horn, Mamadou ran to open the gate. A Peugeot 604, glittering under the garden lights, drove up to the front steps.

Diouldé, a man of the world, sported an ash-grey alpaca suit of Dormeuil cut, with a shirt and tie from Yves Saint-Laurent. He had the delicate features and alert stance of his Pulaar ancestry. A pair of dark glasses was perched on his nose. He opened the car door for his wife Eugénie, and ushered her in ahead of him.

Eugénie was plump, and had cleverly made up her oval face to look slimmer. Two dangling earrings sparkling with diamond dust ornamented her ears. Her glossy black hair was done up in a knot.

The old woman greeted them affectionately, and admired Eugénie . . .

Once seated in the sitting-room, the two sisters-in-law began to talk about their children and their unsatisfactory results at school. Eugénie contrasted with Fatimata by her copper-coloured skin and the frequent smiles that brought a dimple to each cheek. The two brothers, seated facing each other, exchanged only a few inconsequential remarks.

Joom Galle, in a dark suit, made his appearance. A patriarch, he opened his arms wide to greet them. His forehead gleamed in the light.

'You both look very pretty. As does my wife, of course!'

The two women came up to kiss him. He shook hands with the two men.

Ly brought a bucket containing two bottles of 'Cordon Rouge' champagne, and crystal champagne glasses.

'Badou, you officiate.'

He gathered together the folds of his white robe and picked up a bottle, protecting his hand with a white napkin. Everyone leaned back, watching his hands at work. The cork popped . . . A fine spray rose from the open bottle. They all applauded. Badou served his

66

mother first ... then Eugénie, his wife, *Joom Galle,* his elder brother, and himself last.

'Let us drink to the health of all the family, children.'

They drank. Conversation became general, divided, then merged again. It became lively, exciting, intoxicating: touching upon music, modern, classical, traditional; literature, European; films; education; television; women; children ... The two young couples were tactful with each other, not pursuing remarks beyond their surface meaning. The mother was alert. She held the conversation firmly in hand, like a skilled metal-worker, catching a remark, twisting it, flattening it out and rounding it off before putting it back in circulation.

They went in to dinner.

The Saint-Louis-style dinner, couscous with raisins and young pigeons in a groundnut sauce, was praised by all.

Old Cheikh Tidiane called for a moment's silence after the steward had cleared the table.

'Children, I want you to be the first to hear the news. I've resigned from the Ministry of Justice. As of today, I've retired from the political scene.'

(They had not heard about the European Press Agency's dispatch.)

Djia Umrel, seated at the opposite end of the table from her husband, was watching to see how Dioulde, on her right, and Badou on her left would react. Hesitatingly, she began to speak.

'We must give thanks to Allah ... So many African politicians, the fathers of our Independence, are mouldering in prison, or dead, or surviving as mere wrecks in Africa or Europe. But we, the Sall family, father, mother, sons and daughters-in-law, are gathered this evening at one table to celebrate *Joom Galle's* well-deserved retirement. Let us thank Allah for this favour, and drink the doyen's health ...'

They drank.

Eugénie said with a smile:

'Mother is right! Politics is a devourer of men. I'm glad that *Joom Galle* is retiring.'

She leaned over the table to kiss her father-in-law, and blew a little-girl kiss to her mother-in-law.

Fatimata followed suit.

'Who's going to take your place?' asked Dioulde.

His dark glasses glittered in the light. Although he had responded with a discreet nod of the chin, he was not pleased with this sudden withdrawal.

'I don't know.'

'Didn't you suggest anyone to the Venerable One? Attorney Ndaw was expected to succeed you.'

'That is my wish.'

'What did the Venerable One say?'

Djia Umrel sighed. The danger was at hand. She gazed steadily at her husband.

'Oh! I handed in my letter of resignation a long time ago. Léon and the Prime Minister will have thought things over. They'll have chosen someone in a few hours' time from now.'

'Your departure may bring about a crisis.'

'A race for the missing portfolio,' mocked Badou.

'There's no lack of competent younger men,' intervened the mother, to ward off a quarrel. 'The question is how *Joom Galle* is to occupy his time now.'

'Why doesn't he write his memoirs?' suggested Fatimata, seeking complicity with the old woman.

'That's a very good idea, Fatimata.'

'I've rarely written anything. Even my speeches – I just rehearsed them in my head.'

'We can help you . . .'

'Our reading circle's book this month is *Femme d'Afrique* by Aoua Keita. You should read it,' urged the old woman.

'And there's Doctor Birago Diop's book, *La plume raboutée,*' said Eugénie.

(She would not admit not having read it.)

'That's worth reading too.'

The shrill ring of the telephone assaulted their eardrums.

'I'll get it,' said the old woman, just as *Joom Galle* was beginning to extricate himself from his chair.

'I propose a toast: the honourable close of a long political career, started early in this century and ending just before the dawn of the twenty-first century. Father, your health.'

Badou raised his glass. The others imitated him . . .

'Mother! We're drinking *Joom Galle's* health,' said Fatimata as the old woman returned.

'It's for you, Diouldé,' said the mother, taking her glass from Fatimata's hands.

Diouldé pushed back his chair and left the room.

'I drink to your health, *Joom Galle;* may our children, our grand-children, our great-grandchildren live longer than we do.'

'In peace and brotherhood,' added Eugénie.

She was gay. The champagne was discreetly taking effect. The black mascara on her lashes made her eyes shine.

Diouldé came back hastily buttoning his jacket, scowling.

'*Joom Galle,* a press agency has revealed the news. Furthermore, they insinuate that the President is dying. What's going on?'

'Nothing serious . . . Nothing serious . . .'

Between the question and the answer, Djia Umrel had closed her eyes. She said to herself: 'The evening won't be the same any more.' She met her husband's gaze.

'I must go, mother. Thank you for the *Ceere.*'

'At least wait for the cheese course . . .'

'I'm expected . . . It's a meeting, Eugénie!'

'I'm sick and tired of these so-called meetings. Day and night, it's always the same thing. An excuse! I can't even go out with my husband for one evening.'

In a temper, Eugénie had flung down her napkin and burst out with this angry tirade.

'Enough!' snapped Diouldé with a side glance at her. The sunglasses concealed the ugly gleam in his eyes.

'She can stay . . . Badou will drop her off later,' suggested the mother with a pleading look.

'She can do as she likes.'

'One more ruined evening. I'll go home now, Mother.' She addressed her husband:

'At least you can drop me off before going to your – meeting.'

Standing, they confronted each other. Diouldé was incensed at the way his wife had behaved in front of his parents.

The couple said their goodbyes.

Cheikh Tidiane accompanied his son as far as the porch. The night had swallowed everything up.

'It's Badou who advised you to resign. Just like that famous speech of yours.'

'Diouldé, I've grown older, but I can still think clearly. Badou has nothing to do with my decisions.'

'*Joom Galle,* don't you know that with you gone, Daouda can't possibly replace the Venerable One . . . nor become President.'

'Why? Daouda is more competent than many of the people in your group.'

'That's not the question. It's Daouda's caste origins. The people won't accept him.'

Outraged, the old man was on the point of abusing his son. He refrained out of self-respect, and controlled himself sufficiently to say:

'Your wife's waiting for you . . . Goodnight.'

They did not shake hands. The father was heartsick with sorrow. He waited. The heavy door creaked in the night . . .

CHAPTER 11

Friday, 10.00 p.m.

They were on time for this secret night-time meeting: the five Ministers of State in charge of Foreign Affairs, the Interior, Information, Finance and Defence, as well as young Soutapha and the Prime Minister. Corréa, the oldest man present, chaired the discussion. He acknowledged that the investigations conducted by his men, with the help of some expatriates, had led nowhere:

'It's a very difficult situation! And now the international Press [in fact, by international Press he meant the European Press] is in on things as well. Tomorrow we may be able to answer questions and dispel suspicions . . . but what about the day after tomorrow?'

For the next few minutes there was an avalanche of words. Each man was eager to display his investigative flair. Yet when the Venerable One was present, they all kept quiet. Today, each of them had found his voice.

'The army is the bulwark of legality,' remarked Wade.

'Our government must continue to rule the country. We must stand together, support each other. The people rely upon us,' advised Corréa in his elder-brother role, encouraged by the Minister of Defence's remark.

'Why don't we all hand in our resignations, right now?'

Mam Lat's query astonished them all. For a moment, they stared at each other in silence.

'You must be crazy!' exclaimed Corréa, rising from his chair.

'Why do you say that?'

'You can't ditch a government just like that, on impulse,' asserted Corréa, adding: 'To whom would we surrender power, anyway?'

'First, to the Speaker of the National Assembly; secondly, to the people.'

Corréa shifted his gaze towards Daouda. The latter, behind the shield of his dark glasses, felt psychologically protected.

'Mam Lat must be joking,' said Mapathé. 'Nevertheless, it would be more honest for us to tell the people the truth.'

The Minister of Information was worried about tomorrow's Press conference. All the agencies had taken up the alarming dispatch about the President's health.

'What truth?' asked Haïdara, seated on Daouda's left.

'We can't keep on manoeuvring like this. All the journalists are on the look-out. By keeping quiet, we're only making things worse and we'll be seen as accomplices.'

Mam Lat seized upon the Minister of Information's words.

'I agree with Mapathé. We must inform the people, and soon. Our present situation is dangerous. To try and maintain it would be a political error.'

'We must evaluate our responsibilities, and conduct ourselves as men worthy of the Venerable One's trust.'

'Who is responsible for this state of affairs, Corréa? Take the dead driver's family. His wives and children must be searching for him right now. The Venerable One has disappeared ... Is he dead or alive? For how long must we conceal the truth? In whose interest.'

'No one has anything to gain from the present situation.'

'That's not true, Haïdara,' interrupted Mam Lat Soukabé, his thick moustache lending his face a look of brutal aggressiveness. 'The Venerable One has taken off and left us in the shit ... Yes, in the shit ... economically speaking. What do we do now? Wait for his return, or accept the status quo? Why is the old man behaving like this? What's he after? What respect has he shown us? Or the people?'

'Spoken from a truly kind heart.'

'Shit, Corréa, don't go all sentimental on me.'

'He may have been killed too,' suggested Haïdara, trying to bridge the gulf between the two rivals.

'That may be true, Haïdara! The Venerable One isn't immortal. But he may also have skipped town. The reason being bankruptcy. The country's future is mortgaged for the next two generations. That's not just speculation. I know it's so, damn it!'

'You surely can't believe that the Venerable One killed that wretched driver? Why would he do that?'

'All African Presidents have the blood of innocent people on their hands.'

The sharp, terse reply disconcerted them.

'You're exaggerating, as usual,' said Wade as if to brush off the accusation.

'I say no, Wade! It's the truth. What are we afraid of? If the Venerable One has fled, the people must be told,' he thundered, using his voice to good effect.

With two fingers, he began to loosen his silk tie ...

'You're very discourteous. Remember you're speaking of our Number One.'

'I've never crawled in front of the Venerable One.'

This phrase stung them to verbal violence. They began to fight and quarrel, like birds of prey over a fat carcass.

Daouda had to keep a hold on his emotions not to cry out with indignation. Knowing that Mam Lat Soukabé was having it off with Madame, increased his hatred for him. He rejected Mam Lat's suggestion that they scuttle the ship. He remained vulnerable and on the defensive where Mam Lat was concerned. He didn't have his ready tongue. His opponent's statements were so full of obvious contradictions and wishful thinking, that he refused to take up their challenge. He would wait until Monday ... when the Venerable One might return, and he would confront him: 'It's him or me.' He would have to choose. Until then, he wouldn't leave the sinking ship.

Corréa, in his role as elder, managed to quieten them all down.

'We're all agreed on the first thing. We'll wait until Monday to decide what to do. As for the problem of Siin, the driver, I'll ask Haïdara to speak first.'

'There's nothing unusual in what I'm about to suggest,' he began. 'Diplomacy requires measures which are not always orthodox. We can return the dead man's body to his family. For that, all of us here will have to agree on how it should be done. Professor Fall, doyen of the medical corps, will deliver a death certificate and burial permit.'

Haïdara fell silent. He had spoken haltingly; he wasn't happy with what he had come up with.

'Does anyone have any other suggestions?' asked Corréa.

'I don't go along with that brilliant idea,' replied Mam Lat.

'Nor do I,' said Mapathé.

Wade tried not to stare at Daouda, whose dark glasses disconcerted him.

'What's this? Is an entire Cabinet to be the accomplice of a murder, committed by whom? and why? I'm shocked. I'm shocked to the core. You mentioned the dead man a while back ... Never mind him, anyway! What you didn't mention is the number of wives and children this driver – this dead driver – leaves. Three wives and twenty-five children. With money, a substantial pension, we can shut all those people's mouths, can't we, Haïdara? That's your high-level diplomacy, isn't it?'

By attacking him personally, Mam Lat hoped to shake the self-possession of the Minister of State in charge of Foreign Affairs, and win him over. He already had Mapathé and Wade on his side. A third man would be useful, in order to have a majority before dealing with the Prime Minister. Sardonically, he lit a cigar while observing Daouda's reactions.

'I didn't say anything like that,' objected Haïdara, not wishing to compromise himself too far.

You never know which way a fruit will fall, when a monkey picks it.

'True, I didn't hear it from your own mouth,' Mam Lat said meditatively in Wolof.

72

'Glad to hear you say so!'

'What you're proposing is worse. The father of a family has been murdered, and we're trying to cover up the facts. Who are we protecting? And why? The worst thing about the whole set-up is the deliberate complicity of the Minister of the Interior.'

'You seem to forget that the case has political implications. The higher interests of the state impose this sad ... require us not to reveal the truth about this sad situation.'

'Corréa! that's just low political manoeuvring.'

'Resign, then.'

'Now we have it! That's what you want! And you're not the only one who wants me to go, either! ...'

Corréa refrained from replying. The decision was irrevocable. He suggested:

'A delegation led by the Minister of Information should inform the family of the deceased.

'Who, me?' asked Mapathé nonplussed. 'I've a press conference on tomorrow. What about you, Corréa? As our senior, you're an appropriate person to impart the news.'

'Maan? Me?' he exclaimed.

'Yes!'

'I'm a Catholic,' objected Corréa, caught in the net of the others' glances. 'I don't know how Muslims express themselves on such occasions.'

'That's true,' remarked Mam Lat, tapping his cigar over the ashtray.

He smiled disdainfully.

'Am I not right?'

'Quite right, Mr Corréa ... Let us respect our ancestral customs, our Authenegraficanitus. The proper person to bear such a message is a man of caste.'

The word 'caste' had the effect of a cold shower. Disconcerted, no one knew where to look. Haïdara bowed his head. Corréa's ears began to twitch. Wade suddenly noticed his fingers, and began moving them about. Mapathé and Soutapha remained spectators. The latter was disappointed by his elders' childish behaviour.

Daouda was taken aback. His precise feelings can only be compared to the pain a rape would cause a novice who had just pronounced her religious vows. His thumb was twitching.

'You're irresponsible,' declared Haïdara, addressing Mam Lat. 'We're all equals here. I volunteer to be your messenger.'

'We've outgrown "village democracy". Africa is modernizing, we must be of our time,' added Corréa to smooth things over.

'You have both shown our disapproval of this topic,' said Wade distancing himself; to show his objectivity, he added: 'Mam Lat expressed himself in an unfortunate manner.'

'No!' barked Mam Lat, interrupting the Minister of Defence. He was seeking to regain his hold over them. 'All of you here know that I'm speaking the truth. Daouda knows it too. We grew up together.'

This time Daouda leapt up, cut to the quick by this second taunt. He tore off his glasses. Standing tall as a giraffe above the others, his arm, quivering with nerves, like a branch stretched over the table, his index finger pointing at Mam Lat, he shouted at him in Wolof:

'If you say that again, with this finger here I'll screw your mother. Child without a father, bush foundling . . . Bastard . . .'

Carried away, Daouda knocked over the heavy chair, that fell on the tip of Haïdara's shoes. His brain felt as if pierced by a swarm of burning needles. White lights flashed across his eyes. Limping, Haïdara grasped the Prime Minister's outstretched arm.

Each of the two protagonists showered the other with highly seasoned insults. The others restrained them from coming to blows.

'You're a man of low birth, less than a slave. And you can't do anything about it . . . You, the leader of this people – my arse . . .'

'I'm the PM, and you can't do anything about that, either. Your whole family depends upon me . . . Son of a bitch.'

'You're my slave . . . You should be singing my praises,' rapped out Mam Lat, and he turned towards Corréa who was clinging to him. 'Let go of me, you! I don't like arse-lickers. Get away!'

The two men were separated.

Corréa, who dreaded a blow or some other impulsive action from Mam Lat Soukabé, stepped back. When he was near Daouda, he said:

'Calm down, David-Daouda. It's a provocation.'

'I'll make you resign, caste or no caste.'

'You'll never be head of this country. A man of caste . . . Hell, no!'

With great difficulty, a momentary peace was restored. Haïdara took off his shoes and began rubbing his toes.

Mam Lat Soukabé maintained an arrogant silence. He had relit his cigar stump. Daouda's outburst of fury, that he had deliberately provoked, did not displease him. In fact, it favoured his plan of attack . . .

'We're all nervous and irritable! We need rest . . . Let's all go to bed, gentlemen.'

Corréa thus brought the meeting to an end.

Daouda, prostrated, was struggling against the first stings of adversity. The Cabinet was falling apart. The chasm was a deep one. Who were his allies? his friends? He put his glasses back on, and gamely lifted his head. Blue, yellow, red flashed across the lenses. He decided to strike a harsh blow at Mam Lat . . . to eliminate him, to reduce him to silence.

The Ministers of State in charge of Defence and Information were gathering up their papers. Mam Lat Soukabé was shutting his Samsonite case. 'Goodnight,' he said, leaving.

'You can go home too, Soutapha,' ordered Corréa in elder-brother tones.

'Good night, Messieurs.'

'Soutapha!'

'Sir?'

'Be here tomorrow before the usual time,' ordered Corréa.

'Yes, Sir,' he assented.

Daouda, Corréa and Haïdara remained silent, meditating the future. The strife within the ruling body alarmed them. It threatened a catastrophe that could bring about the country's ruin.

'Let's sleep on it . . .'

At this suggestion of Corréa's, the trio began to move . . .

CHAPTER 12

As far back as the tutelary spirits of the Cap-Vert peninsula could remember, there had never been so sinister a night. From twilight on, the subtropical atmospheric pressure of the daytime triggered off a high-flying saraband laden with warm air. The whirling trade winds wound about tall buildings and television antennas, probing and whistling. A cool wind moaned, heavy with moisture. Cars parked outside were covered with a thick layer of dew. Large drops of water fell from the leaves of tall trees.

In two of the city's top hotels, two gatherings were taking place. At one, two native born citizens of the country, belonging to high society, were being dubbed 'chevaliers du taste-vin.' Proud of becoming members of this order of connoisseurs, they were initiated into its ritual. In the other hotel, at the very westernmost tip of the continent, an evening's entertainment was being offered under the aegis of 'cultural tourism'. A fading French singer was bawling his lungs out in an effort to revive his hits of yesteryear. His audience, more interested in dividends than in sentiment, were busy totting up the profits today's herd of tourists would bring in. The repressed and frustrated, and women on their own, were eyeing the folklore troupe, made up of gazelles with jutting breasts and wriggling bodies and youths with solid biceps and muscular thighs, all exuding a salty scent of perspiration.

This very night, three people did not fall asleep . . . easily.

The residence of the French Ambassador was drowned in a mass of dark greenery. All the lights were trained on the bougainvillea hedge.

The usual security arrangements had been reinforced by armed soldiers. The garrulous old native watchman, happy to have company, was recounting his many billets in France and her former colonies. He admitted that he preferred the colonial system to this Independence.

In his dimly-lit, milky-white sitting-room, Jean de Savognard was listening to a Richter recording. At fifty-six, he no longer had sexual desires. Classical music gave him as much pleasure as the act of love. He no longer shared a bedroom with his wife. This evening's Richter concert stimulated his thinking. 'Will everything go as planned? All the pieces are in position.' This temporary vacuum was causing him considerable anxiety. Léon Mignane had been an asset to the West's political manoeuvres in Africa. His presence ensured that the continent was equally divided. His influence was beneficial . . .

Last night, when Adolphe had informed him that 'things had been set in motion', he had ordered him to keep a close watch on developments. Léon Mignane's personal adviser suggested that 'in the event of a slip-up', there was always the possibility of economic reprisals.

'Whatever the régime that finally emerges, we won't be able to cut off aid to this country . . .'

He added nothing more. He began a monologue: 'The Cap-Vert peninsula is a strategic location for NATO, and an important base for France. We must avoid the successive blunders of Bénin, Togo, Chad, Bangui and Mauritania,' he declared.

'This country must remain within our orbit, at whatever cost.'

'If things go wrong . . . we can always do the Bangui bit again.'

'If necessary, yes. The Chief of Staff is still a good candidate.'

All the arrangements had been made. As soon as he gave the word, a foreign intervention force would land to protect French nationals. Jean de Savognard was betting on Daouda. Would he win through in the end? Adolphe's presence would ensure continuity. 'Why did Daouda not want Adolphe to attend tonight's meeting? How can I find out what they've decided?'

There was a sudden click. Jean de Savognard had pressed a knob to turn off the hi-fi; he went out on to the verandah.

The darkness was rent by flashes of light . . .

After the departure of his children – his guests – Doyen Cheikh Tidiane Sall remained silent. 'The evening went well after all,' said old Djia Umrel Ba, pleased at having managed the dinner. 'Yes,' he murmured, ruminating the words of his elder son. The more he thought about it, the more the idea of castes was repugnant to him. Throughout his life, he had never given any consideration to such things. He had remained aloof. Alarmed, he wondered: 'Was my resignation at a time like this a breach of duty?'

He joined his wife in bed.

'Turn the lights out, *Joom Galle,*' she said.

He obeyed.

Djia Umrel snuggled close to him. Her breath brushed his naked chest.

'Do you think this was the right time for you to retire?' she asked, even though she knew he had struggled long and hard with himself before reaching this point of no return.

'*Debbo,* I didn't choose this particular moment as such,' he replied in the dark of the bedroom.

They did not exchange another word. They listened to the big branch of the flame-tree overhead, swaying in the wind and rattling on the tiles of the roof.

Daouda went back to the Little Palace, the Prime Minister's official residence.

His wife Guylène, after the morning's 'phone call, had undertaken a number of tasks. As president of various women's associations, she had to organize and direct their charitable activities. She was passionately fond of bridge, and played twice a week for three or four hours at a stretch. This Friday she had taken part in a tournament, and lost ... a trifling sum: one hundred thousand — CFA — francs.

At nine in the evening she went alone to the cinema to see an Ingmar Bergman film, *Scenes of Conjugal Life.* Her husband was still not back when she returned. She wasn't worried about it.

'You had a long day,' she said without acrimony when Daouda came in.

'Yes.'

'You didn't forget your pills, did you?'

'No.'

'I'll heat up your dinner. The cook's gone home.'

Wearing a dressing-gown, she moved towards the vast kitchen.

'I'm not too hungry. Some soup and vegetables would do me fine,' said Daouda, following her.

Guylène moved about the gas stoves. Going from one corner to the other, she turned to talk to him:

'I went to see a Bergman film. You should go too.'

She began to comment on episodes from the film.

'You could have asked for a private showing here.'

'I wanted to see it along with the public.'

'It's sometimes necessary. Did you pay for your seat?'

'The manager didn't want me to, but I insisted.'

'That's good. If you'll excuse me, I'll go and have a bath.'

Daouda strode off on his long legs.

In bed, Daouda was troubled by visions, and sank only fitfully into the arms of Morpheus. A procession of dancing limbless *tyiwarras* leapt after him, shouting. Disguised as a warrior, painted, armed with a rifle with telescopic sights, Mam Lat Soukabé was hunting him down, firing at the ground between his feet. He hopped about, howling.

Guylène lit the bedside lamp.

He woke up.

'Are you ill?'

'A nightmare,' he answered.

He was perspiring, although the air-conditioning was on. He got out of bed.

'Where are you going?'

'To drink some water.'

He came back to bed. Guylène took his head and with a motherly gesture laid it between her breasts.

Outside, the wind gasped.

CHAPTER 13

Saturday

The dew of the night just past had rinsed the trees of dust and deposited it on the ground. Heavy slow-moving clouds coming in from the sea to the west, blotted out the youthful sun.

The President's momentary indisposition and the 'disgraceful assault on the driver, a family man, a government employee', skilfully presented, filled the first news broadcast of the day. Transistors spread the information in all the languages of the country. The front page of the *National Daily* juxtaposed the two news items, with accompanying photographs.

Before dawn of this new day, the police had established themselves at every intersection. The operation was well conducted; not one intersection was omitted as they checked and searched all vehicles, even horse-drawn carts.

The streets were choked with long queues of vehicles; employees, workers, schoolchildren and housewives were all held up. People were shouting, storming, cursing, complaining. A deafening concert of hooting horns drowned out the shouts and cries. Annoyance was the dominant feeling. The big public transport buses were left standing empty as their users set out on foot, with caustic remarks cursing the police and calling the government a set of leeches.

In the Plateau area, the commercial centre of the city, you couldn't help noticing how many policemen there were. The presence of so many armed men, coming and going and observing passers-by, was frightening. As the morning wore on, all cripples, beggars, pedlars, itinerant fruit and flower sellers, car-washers, boot-blacks and vendors of lottery tickets all melted away.

The Plateau was ominously empty.

CHAPTER 14

Haïdara woke with a splitting headache. Remembering last night's secret meeting, he regretted having been so impulsive. He upbraided himself for having so hastily volunteered to impart the news of the death. Now he couldn't get out of it. He erected pyramids of consoling phrases presenting the death of the driver Siin as an accident. He would adopt a sorrowful countenance and compassionate voice. He would begin like this: 'Each must accept his fate . . . Allah gives, then takes back what he has given. Your good, loyal and generous father, whom I as a minister numbered among my . . . No! No!' he thought. The thread of his monologue was broken. He changed tactics, and decided to try a more circumstantial approach. It was a long time since he had used prayer-beads in public; but tomorrow he would carry a string of beads. And he would start the palaver by reciting two verses of the Koran — the easiest ones. But he soon ran out of such soothing, soporific thoughts.

He tossed and turned in bed. His wife was as fast asleep as the stump of an ancient baobab. He left her to go and make himself some coffee. He liked its strong aroma . . .

In the bathroom, he bathed his eyes with an eye-cup. His eyes were becoming greener every day. The narrowing of his field of vision worried him more and more. He thought of going to Europe for treatment, but he would risk losing his position in the ruling-class hierarchy.

He took his medicine.

Sipping his strong coffee, he examined the various messages he had received from ambassadors, asking for news of the President. He would have to calm them down. The same message for all. This Saturday he had two dispatch-bags to send off.

His mind reverted to this morning's mission. His aches and pains were beginning to make him regret it.

On the radio, the announcer spoke of the press conference to be held by the Minister of State in charge of Information and Parliamentary Affairs, and of the momentary indisposition of the Father of the Nation. None of this was news to him. He started when the announcer spoke at length of the attack on Siin, the old driver. He muttered to himself: 'They're crazy! Why did Daouda decide to do it that way without letting me know?'

He quickly set out for his ministry.

The guard recognized him, and opened the gate.

From his office, he rang up Daouda. The latter didn't know what was going on, and suggested he ask Mapathé. He rang the Minister of Information and demanded to be told what was happening: 'It's a breach of trust.' Mapathé referred him to Corréa. Corréa had left his residence for the Ministry of Foreign Affairs. At the moment, everything annoyed him. They didn't trust him.

There was a knock at the office door.

The guard opened the door; behind him was Corréa, cool, newly shaven.

'I rang your home. But you were here. What conscientiousness!' said Corréa, shutting the door.

'I have two dispatch-bags to send off today. And I have to calm down the ambassadors.'

'That's true,' remarked Corréa, speaking naturally so as to lull suspicion. 'We forgot about them. By the way, weren't you going to call on Siin's family?'

'Exactly. What's going on? The PM doesn't know anything about it. Mapathé told me to contact you. I heard the news on the radio ...'

'I understand,' began Corréa to appease Haïdara's disappointment. 'It's not that we didn't trust you. I quite understand,' he repeated, looking him full in the face, to sooth his wounded feelings.

Haïdara made no objection. He was relieved of an awkward chore.

Last night, after escorting Daouda home, Corréa had gone back to the 'Coffin House.' Although it was past midnight, Diatta, the mass-psychology specialist, was waiting for him. He had found a way of 'distracting people by focusing their attention on a secondary issue'. Together they drafted the newsflash and an article for the *National*

Daily. Mapathé yielded to Corréa's injunctions.

'I had an inspiration last night. Everything's been taken care of. The deceased's eldest son has been summoned to identify the body. The driver was attacked by thugs. The doctor in charge has delivered a death certificate. The PM in person will represent the Venerable One at the funeral this afternoon.'

Haïdara's face was clouded by conflicting sombre thoughts. Corréa frightened him. He toyed with his steel ruler. He wondered: 'Why didn't he keep a closer watch on the Venerable One's security? Did he plan to let things deteriorate to the point where he could stage a coup?' The Minister of the Interior's coldly logical reasoning left a bitter taste in his mouth.

'An excellent idea. You've saved us all. What if the Venerable One has disappeared for good?' asked Haïdara suspiciously.

The art of politics is always to hold something in reserve.

'The country will still exist! As far as you and I are concerned, the PM will assume the responsibilities of his position,' answered Corréa with a sly half-smile.

'Don't you find the Venerable One's absence strange?'

Haïdara had not dared pronounce the word 'flight'.

'Yes!' Corréa stated unhesitatingly, looking Haïdara full in the face.

The direct reply numbed his senses. A keen flash of pain, like heat lightning, struck the nape of his neck. His entire body shivered. He took out his handkerchief to wipe his eyes, turning away from Corréa. Haïdara could not adjust to the idea that the country could outlive Léon Mignane.

'We must wait until Monday before deciding anything,' Corréa pursued in the tone of an experienced man helping his youngest son cross a decaying rope bridge in the jungle. Knowing Haïdara, he changed the subject: 'We should be thinking of the future, you and I. We're older than the others. Even the PM, Daouda, would be a good President. We should support him. Doyen Cheikh will be replaced ... As for Mam Lat Soukabé, it's just a matter of days. The most delicate question will be deciding who should head the Cabinet. Who do you see as PM once David's taken his place on the throne?' he asked circumspectly.

At this question, Haïdara was as deeply stirred as a consenting virgin at the first carnal contact with her beloved. He had too long dreamed of, waited for, this promotion. A fraction of a second later, he declared:

'As the oldest member of our team, the most experienced, you'd be best for the job. You're the only one who could continue to carry out the Venerable One's policies.'

'You know very well I'm not the right man for such an important

81

post,' replied Corréa with a show of surprise, adding: 'On the other hand, I can see you in the job.'

'Who? . . . Me? . . .'

'Yes, you. Why not,' pursued Corréa. 'I can see you very well as PM. You've been known as Minister of Foreign Affairs for a long time. That counts. By becoming Prime Minister, you'd help David-Daouda consolidate his authority.'

To be Prime Minister! The second-ranking man in the nation! Haïdara had thought of it. He considered himself the best man for the post. He knew that he was well thought of in the West. Yesterday Jean de Savognard had asked him: 'If Daouda were to become President, who do you see as Head of Government?'

'It's too soon to mention names! . . . But there are competent people,' Haïdara replied once more.

'For instance, someone like you.'

His black skin concealed the rush of blood to his face.

'I don't know about that that,' said Haïdara out of political prudery. 'If my party should require it of me, then of course I would have to . . .'

'Of course, it would have to be endorsed by the higher echelons of the party. For the moment, let it be just between the two of us . . . So . . .'

Corréa deliberately left his sentence unfinished. He rose. Haïdara followed him. At the door, Corréa added:

'The driver's funeral is this afternoon.'

'I'll be there.'

'I'll see you there, then! I'll leave you to work now.'

Haïdara, drawn by the idea of becoming Prime Minister, agreed with the Minister of the Interior's decisions. A man's death must not obstruct the functioning of the machinery of government. He began to work out whom he would have on his future staff. There were competent people from his clan, his region . . . Highly competent, even. He'd call on them, for greater security.

Back at his table, his mind relieved of worry, he felt powerful as he ordered the ambassadors to behave with dignity during the sad hours of the Venerable One's illness.

CHAPTER 15

Doyen Cheikh Tidiane Sall had risen early as usual, this Saturday morning. What his elder son Diouldé had said last night remained stuck in a corner of his mind. He had served under Daouda without reservations; the question of caste hadn't come into it. While breakfasting copiously, he was thinking.

'You've nothing to do this morning, you could have stayed in bed a bit longer,' said the old woman, who was wearing a dressing-gown.

'Apparently the first few days are the most difficult for a retired man.'

'Come with me . . . We'll visit our grandchildren.'

She poured herself a cup of tea. She drank it with milk and lemon.

'I don't know yet how I'll kill time today, but I'll manage somehow . . .'

'Listen . . .'

Both listened carefully. The old woman turned up the volume of the radio. In measured tones, the speaker announced the press conference to be held by the Minister of State in charge of Information, for journalists of the national and international press, at ten o'clock this morning. He added:

Cheikh Tidiane Sall, Minister of State in charge of Justice, no longer occupies this post. In view of his advanced age, Cheikh Tidiane Sall, born with the century, has chosen to hand over responsibility to the younger generation – the Second Generation of Independence. The Prime Minister told the National Press Agency: 'Cheikh Tidiane Sall, whom we called doyen out of respect for his great age, will be sorely missed. He was the most faithful and devoted companion of the President of the Republic, the Venerable One. He has had a considerable influence upon our judicial system.' End of quote. The Father of the Nation, His Excellency Léon Mignane, President of the Republic and founder of our idealogy of Authenegraficanitus, stated in his inimitable poetic style: 'Yesterday I saw fade away the morning star of the dawns of yore, of our twentieth year. That star beyond compare, that rose in the east above our Senegal River, then shone over Saint-Louis-du-Sénégal, cradle of the enlightened minds that once made their grievances known to the *Etats Généraux* in Paris. Cheikh Tidiane, my elder, is a model, an example for generations to come . . .'

Cheikh Tidiane Sall was seething with anger, his mouth drawn tight.

'Lies! Nothing but lies,' he groaned.

'Perhaps Léon is back.'

'Do you think so?' he inquired sceptically, raising his eyebrows. He was asking himself as well as her.

'I suppose so,' she replied in a deliberately soothing voice. She examined the old man's countenance, stiff with annoyance. She said things to appease him: 'Nothing humiliating was said, you're here safe and sound and that's the main thing. I've always heard you yourself say that facts must be presented in such a way as to favour those who are in power.'

She reached over and turned off the radio. She wanted to ward off his growing disillusionment.

No wife wants to see her husband in the throes of failure and self-reproach.

Cheikh Tidiane slowly sipped his coffee. He was breaking with an active life, wholly devoted to a cause he had made his own. For three-quarters of his life, he had considered himself French ... a French citizen. He had fulfilled his contract with what was then his mother country. When his country became independent, he shed his skin like a snake. He had seen himself playing a salutary role in the functioning of the new state. His youthful illusions of the 1920s, 1930s and 1940s, like those of his years of maturity, the 1950s, 1960s and 1970s, had vanished overnight. His beliefs had cracked and fallen away, like an accretion of stalactites, made of the successive layers of education he had received – African, Arabic, European. While the country was recovering its personality (which for him was mingled with his own) he had pruned the parasitic shoots sprouting from each of the cultural branches which sustained his life ...

'*Joom Galle,* there's a visitor for you,' said the old woman.

She had narrowed her eyes to see who it was: Attorney Ndaw.

He raised his spectacles to look at his disciple, who was being shown in by the servant Mamadou.

'Good morning, Madame! *Tonton,*' said Ndaw, taking him by the hand.

'Sit down ... over here,' he ordered, moving his chair and feeling the coffee-pot. 'This coffee is cold ...'

'I've just had some at home ...'

'No ... No ... Just a little ...'

'Mamadou, tell Ly to heat it ...'

'Yes, Madame,' said Mamadou, removing the coffee-pot.

'Excuse me, I must get dressed ...'

'Certainly, Madame ...'

She left the room.

'*Tonton,* did you hear the news?'

'Yes. Where on earth did they dredge up that rubbish? I have the feeling that they're entangling themselves in a web of lies. And that's very serious . . .'

A shadow of worry spread over his face.

'. . . Even if Léon has come back, there's still the dead man.'

'As of this morning, his death has become a banal news item. The PM has asked to see me this morning.'

'Maybe he'll offer you the justice portfolio.'

'Maybe,' replied Ndaw, observing Ly moving towards them with the coffee-pot and another cup.

The steward served the two men, and moved the sugar-bowl and milk-jug nearer.

The presence of the young attorney moved the old man to confide in him, in order to justify his resignation.

At all levels of the executive branch, decisions eluded us more and more. Surrounded by expatriate advisers, Léon Mignane decided everything on his own. The young ministers went along with everything. Meeting after meeting, I was being attacked, almost assaulted. In the end, I kept quiet, while still taking part in Cabinet meetings once a week.

That evening, Umrel and I were in the sitting-room. Events at Kolwezi, in Shaba — formerly Katanga — then loomed large in African current affairs, just as they had almost exactly a year before.

The announcer's voice was reading out the news. The Vth Franco-African Conference was taking place in Paris, under the aegis of the French President . . .

The Franco-African Conference of Heads of State has just ended. We have heard from well-informed sources that some of the delegations present are in favour of setting up an Inter-African Armed Intervention Force within the next few days, in order to reinforce the Non-African Force of Intervention, made up of Belgian and French paratroop commandos.

'It's not possible! No! They've gone crazy,' repeated Cheikh Tidiane over and over.

The announcer continued:

Léon Mignane, President of the Republic of Senegal, as spokesman for his peers made a brief statement as they left the Elysée.

A distant mechanical crackling was heard. Over the air, Léon

Mignane spoke in carefully articulated, refined tones.

If Western Europe does not arm the moderate states, to enable us to defend ourselves against the subversive activities of Cubans and Soviets, African states will be destabilized. The dispatch of an expeditionary force from outside Africa is a humanitarian duty.

Cheikh Tidiane became more and more angry. He started up and asked:

'Did you hear your "friend"?'

'Yes,' replied Djia Umrel.

'What the hell are we going to do down there? He's talking rubbish. Send soldiers to defend whom? And then what?'

'You know he can't hear you.'

'Are you insinuating that I wouldn't dare speak the truth to his face?' he retorted sharply.

His harsh tone of voice startled the old woman. She swiftly adjusted her spectacles to examine her husband. She choked back the reply that was tickling her throat. To challenge him would make him defy Léon just to prove his own courage to himself. Ever since his birthday speech, relations between the two old men had been cool.

'Just listen to him! He's calling for an anti-communist crusade. He reminds me exactly of Pascal Wellé in the 1920s and 1930s. More European than any white man.'

'If anyone heard you, they'd think you were a communist.'

'Me?'

'Yes, indeed!'

A hoarse but light-hearted peal of laughter rose from his chest. He slapped his thigh, laughing until the tears came to his eyes. His spontaneous gaiety spread to the woman.

'Léon is too much for me. What goes on in his head? Can you tell me?'

She did not answer.

He continued his grumbling monologue.

'The French are intervening directly all over the continent: Chad, Zaïre, Mauritania, Central Africa. Not to mention their bases.'

'Léon is acting in accordance with his norm. And you're just preaching,' she remarked, to voice an opinion.

'How's that!' he exclaimed, lifting his chin.

'Léon is acting in accordance with his norm,' she repeated, to explain herself. 'Léon is consistent. He's never changed. The precedent of Zaïre is part of a long-term strategy. Your government – for you belong to this government – has been the accomplice of every piece of back-handed business done on the continent. From the Algerians' liberation struggle to the Polisario's, you've always been on the losing side. You held talks with Salazar, Espinoza and the propounders of apartheid. In Angola, you support a faction financed by the CIA. I could mention other instances. Léon is being consistent. And you're just letting off steam . . .'

Speech is as deadly as a firearm. But it kills only those of noble character.

Joom Galle was stunned by this diatribe. What she said was true, and he perceived it as something more than criticism: as an accusation. Had he not, indeed, taken part in every successive government since 1960? A man of honour, he became aware of his responsibility. Abashed, dumbfounded, he lowered his gaze to conceal his growing unease.

'. . . If a man can't express himself in his own home, where can he do so?'

Djia Umrel Ba regretted having expressed thoughts she had had for a long time. She had not intended to shock or provoke him, nor to display her own opinions. Knowing that few husbands are fond of hearing the truth from their wives, she broke the oppressive silence by chatting about what she had done during the day.

They had dinner as usual.

The following day, at his ministry, he received a call from the Prime Minister, advising him that the Venerable One would be arriving back that afternoon.

He did not go to the airport. The fact that he was not there to welcome the Head of State, did not pass unnoticed. This breach of etiquette was commented on in ruling circles.

That night, Léon Mignane sent a messenger to inquire about his health. He invited him to breakfast the next morning, specifying: at seven o'clock sharp.

These early morning invitations to the President's table were like an official stamp of approval, reserved for the privileged few.

Cheikh Tidiane arrived punctually at the palace. A guard was awaiting him. A servant led him into the small dining-room. The table was already set . . .

On the threshold, the two old men shook hands cordially, and said 'Good morning' in chorus. They were like schoolboys at break, concealing some prank of the previous day. They exchanged courtesies as they sat down. Each performed the same gestures: spreading the white napkin on his lap, unbuttoning his jacket, sipping his orange juice.

'How was your trip?' asked Cheikh Tidiane, putting down his glass.

'It went very well! The Franco-African summit was very useful. You must have heard about it . . .'

'I've been following it closely.'

'By the way, is it important to own a house ...'

'What?' asked Cheikh Tidiane, his forehead wrinkled with perplexity.

'Once again, I've come across an attack from the crypto-personal opposition. In their rag, they've encroached on my private life. They've had the cheek to write that I haven't so much as a burrow of my own in this country.'

'Do you want to sue them for libel, Léon? ...'

'To gratify them? No. God, no ... I just want to know whether it matters to own a house here?'

'In the old days, a chief's prestige was measured by the number of huts clustered in his compound. Come to think of it, I wonder how you manage to reconcile your Authenegraficanitus and your personal conduct.'

'Do you agree with my opponents, then?'

'Léon, stop considering yourself affronted every time someone tells you the truth. It's true, you don't even own a thatched hut in your own country. And you hold the position of First Citizen of the Republic.'

'I haven't any savings, Cheikh!'

The latter drew his white-haired brows down into a frown. His incredulous gaze was heavy with disapproval.

'Don't you believe me, Cheikh? Say so, instead of looking at me like that.'

'Léon, who do you think you're fooling? You own an apartment in Paris, and a house in the country, in France ... And in your father's country you own nothing. Don't give me that womanish nonsense.'

'But Cheikh, I have expenses! I'll borrow from the state to build a house here.'

'That's not honest of you ... But it's better than nothing, Léon. Could you pour me some more orange juice?'

Léon Mignane paused, his arm outstretched to grasp the china jug, and raised his gaze to Cheikh Tidiane's frowning brow.

'That's good fresh juice. Perhaps the oranges came from Morocco, or South Africa? ... But not from our Casamance,' uttered the Minister of Justice, without deflecting his gaze from the President's.

He held out his arm.

Léon Mignane overcame his annoyance. He poured the juice, asking in a constrained tone:

'Will that do?'

'Yes, thank you, Léon.'

Cheikh Tidiane emphasized his use of his first name, to dispel all protocol from the breakfast table.

The steward approached in silence.

'How do you like your eggs? An omelette, or fried eggs and ...'

'Fried. But just one egg, please,' answered Cheikh Tidiane, turning towards the steward.

'I'll have two eggs, with ham.'

'Yes, Your Excellency.'

Léon Mignane glanced after him as he left.

They broached the subject of digestion, often slow and difficult for elderly people.

'How is your health, Cheikh?'

'I've seen my doctor, and all is well. Touch wood.'

Thus saying, he rapped his bald head.

'I've a few problems, of course. But nothing serious.'

Léon Mignane exercised sedulously, to combat muscular weakness and mental senility. He was driven to it by a terror of old age.

'I'm told there's a shortage of coffee in town,' remarked Léon Mignane, to introduce a new and lighter topic of conversation.

'It's the deterioration of the terms of exchange,' said Cheikh Tidiane non-committally.

He remembered his wife's accusations.

'That's what I said in my speech, when I visited the European Assembly,' responded Léon Mignane. The theme was a favourite of his. Ever since in 1953 he had read the book: *Africa, Complement to Europe* by Anton Zischka, published by R. Laffont, he had asserted its thesis. He splashed about happily in the idea of complementarity, of Eurafrica. Pausing in his flow of rhetoric, he noticed Cheikh Tidiane scrutinizing him. He fell silent.

'Eurafrica is an association between horse and rider. And we're the ones being ridden, Léon.'

'We can't do without Europe,' he said, with a wry smile.

'Is it to defend us that they're sending us mercenaries, otherwise known as a foreign intervention force? Are we independent or not?'

'You're getting things mixed up, Cheikh! Those lost soldiers have nothing to do with their countries of origin.'

'Léon! Léon! Come now!' he interrupted, after finishing his second glass of orange juice. He wiped the corner of his mouth ...

'Don't take me for a fool! Those mercenaries don't kill blacks just for the money ...'

'You can't expect me to believe they have ideals, Cheikh.'

'Yes, they have. The action of these pretorians is based on an imagined superiority complex. Whether they fight on behalf of a tottering African régime, or to protect the nationals of a European country or Judeo-Christian civilization, it's always in the interests of the Hexagon, of metropolitan France ... The centre of the circle. Reread, or read, the articles written about them, or have yourself shown some films. The "Hexagonians" – I don't know if one can say that, but you know what I mean – see these men as the latter-day counterparts and heirs of the epic empire-builders of yore. Debased and bitter, full of nostalgia for former glory, these lost soldiers are the last dying embers of colonial power.'

Léon Mignane's half-smile had turned into an ill-tempered grimace. He refrained from speaking.

The steward reappeared, pushing a trolley laden with dishes. They watched him officiate.

They began to eat in silence. From time to time they caught each other's eye, then looked away. They chewed methodically. They watched each other, as old hands . . .

'You're becoming political, Cheikh. Very much so. Isn't it rather late . . .'

'Better late than never, Léon. Our Independence is being usurped.'

'I can't see how. If you mean France, they're very loyal partners.'

'They're also partners with South Africa; providing them with arms, instead of sending soldiers to free the country from apartheid . . .'

Léon Mignane smiled, playing along, and remarked:

'France is the country that gives us the most aid by far. You know that.'

'Of course,' shrugged Cheikh Tidiane. 'Of course. We pay too high a price for that aid, Léon.'

'If I didn't know you, I'd say you were going through a difficult phase.'

'It's true! It hurts me here [he tapped his chest near the heart] to see you all behaving like children in front of foreigners. France is now a second-rate power, behind Federal Germany, Japan, Canada and the USA. When an African state is classified as friendly or moderate, it's subsidized to the extent that it grants their industries and banks privileges. And those bankers and industrialists, together with their government, make up for their economic inferiority by military intervention.'

This open attack on his beloved country was like an assault on his own person. Léon Mignane felt European. It was a diffuse feeling, like an ocean current pulsing in his veins, disseminating soporific vapours. He repressed his reaction of hostility towards Cheikh. If he had been in a public place, he would have walked away. He ate calmly, his eyes fixed on his plate.

'Over twenty years of Independence should have taught us something . . . unless it's merely confirmed our state of dependency,' continued Cheikh Tidiane.

He drank a glass of water.

'I've made a discovery.'

'What's that?' asked Léon Mignane with curiosity, glancing at the older man's face.

'Our French "cousins", to keep it in the family, are a hard-working people, healthy in mind and body. For them, democracy means "yes" or "no". They repeatedly hold elections to provide themselves with a "great leader". They remind me of the Diola, with their *beekin*. The *beekin* is a king-fetish. When it no longer incarnates the totem, the Diola beat it and throw it away. They then search for a new *beekin,* chosen in the same wood, grown from the same soil. They ask this new *beekin,* with the same insistence, to provide them with the same spiritual effluvia as the former *beekin.* And if this second king-fetish doesn't give satisfaction, they'll cast it away, insulting it and spitting on it. They will then prepare the same ceremony to welcome a third *beekin.* Do you know where they fetch it from?'

'No,' said Léon Mignane.

'From the *beekins'* ash-heap. French democracy is fetishism! They always vote for the Right.'

Léon Mignane, admiring the comparison, repeated each word to himself in order to remember it, and repeat it in public as his own.

'I didn't see you at the airport yesterday,' Léon Mignane suddenly remarked in an inquiring tone.

'For the simple reason that I wasn't there,' said Cheikh Tidiane casually, while thinking: 'Here we are at last.'

'The entire government was there, as well as the religious leaders.'

'The religious leaders are there because they have to be . . .'

Léon Mignane frowned, annoyed. However, feigning non-chalance, he pretended not to have heard the sharp reply.

Once a year he received the religious leaders in his palace. The persistence of the feudal spoils system, in a renovated guise, enabled him to oversee the appointment of imams and traditional chiefs, thus ensuring their support. These honourable spiritual leaders acknowledged him as their one and only leader, above elected representatives and the Constitution.

'It is the duty of all ministers to greet the President on his return. Weren't you informed of my arrival?'

'I was, Léon. The PM rang me up. I didn't want to come. That's all.'

Accustomed to end Cabinet meetings, bring conversations to a close, or reduce a subordinate to silence with the words 'That's all'. Léon Mignane was offended, this morning, to hear the expression from someone else's lips. However, he calmly finished his eggs, deliberately refraining from speaking. He knew that his old companion did not act without reason. He inquired into his motives.

'Perhaps you have reasons?'

91

Cheikh Tidiane pushed his plate aside before replying in a confidential tone:

'Here in Dakar, on the occasion of the Vth Franco-African summit, you questioned me and I told you how I felt. I did not agree with setting up an Inter-African Intervention Force, as was decided at the Vth summit. Such a force is nothing but an insidious device for crushing emergent young shoots. An oppressive cover for maintaining in power individuals rejected by their people. Your inter-African army is a police force designed to watch over foreign interests. I resign from the government and from my position.'

'Blackmail! He's threatening me with blackmail!' Léon Mignane thought to himself, his face like a fierce funeral mask. Ever since his seventieth birthday, Cheikh Tidiane was in rebellion against him. What was behind this departure? What financial lobby was backing him? Had he become pro-communist? Léon Mignane took every contradiction as a personal attack or a sign of a plot.

'We'll discuss the advisability of such a force within the government,' objected Léon Mignane defensively.

Taken by surprise, he was trying to defer a resignation that might discredit him and his policies.

'Nothing's been decided yet,' he pursued, forcing himself to produce a tortured smile. 'We are a democratic people! Everything is discussed at the highest level. You know that.'

Léon Mignane toyed with his spoon, his eyes lowered. He was suspicious of Cheikh Tidiane. Nevertheless, he made a deliberate attempt to touch him.

'Do you really want to "forsake" me, Cheikh, and leave me all alone?'

'Léon, you're the first person to whom I've said this . . . Even my wife doesn't know about it yet,' confided Cheikh Tidiane sentimentally, filled with compassion for his old comrade.

The current had changed. Léon Mignane, obsessed with the idea of his historical role, an idea he brooded over day and night, did not take advantage of the opportunity offered him by the other man. Thus he missed his Minister of Justice's moment of greatest weakness, because of his lust for power.

'Do you want to be PM? With clause X, you'd be my successor. You deserve it,' he suggested, eyeing him from behind lowered lashes.

Cheikh Tidiane Sall was exasperated. Léon was mocking him. The sudden silence annoyed him. He regretted his moment of weakness.

'Léon,' he began, gazing at him steadily . . . 'Léon, I talk to you of resigning, and what do you suggest? You must know that I've never gone in for political adultery. That's petty-minded of you, really petty-minded . . .'

92

Léon Mignane reacted angrily to the insult. His eyes flashed with exasperation. Blood rose to his head in hot seething waves. Sharp pains shot through one half of his brain. His head was on fire.

'They're trying to destabilize Africa . . .'

'Léon,' interrupted Cheikh Tidiane, sitting up straight, 'spare me your line of patter on the threat facing Africa. All these Franco-African summits always remind me of my father. He took part in all the colonial campaigns to "pacify" the natives. They told him he was "the bearer of civilization". They removed from office a true native chief who had resisted conquest, and appointed him instead. He had been told he was accomplishing "a humanitarian duty". I remember my father. He was proud of what he had done, and of being an auxiliary. He was even rewarded for services rendered to France. What difference is there between my father and you? My father used force to enslave people . . . out of ignorance. One can forgive him . . . But what about you, or me? . . . Are we auxiliaries? More like accomplices of neo-colonialism. Léon, enough is enough. Well and truly enough,' he repeated.

He folded his arms across his chest, breathing heavily . . . His gaze fixed upon Léon's pendulous lower lip.

Léon Mignane was furious, his mind in a whirl. He repressed his rising anger, and reminded him:

'So far as I'm aware, you've taken part in each successive government since Independence. So don't come at me today with your sudden fit of thirty-second hour revolutionary spirit. For my part, I've never concealed my opinions. This evening, there will be a special meeting of the Cabinet.'

'I'll be there, Léon. And that's all,' said Cheikh Tidiane, beating him to it. He buttoned up his double-breasted suit before leaving the room . . .

Left alone, Léon Mignane fumed with anger. Rising pressure sent waves of blood surging to his head. His head, as if caught in a vice, seemed about to burst. With an almost superhuman effort, he called out, 'Gaston!' and his hand gripped the table-cloth.

Someone rushed from behind the mauve velvet hangings, and caught him before he fell.

Saturday morning

Attorney Ndaw lit a cigarette and re-crossed his legs. He glanced at his watch before saying:

'That was a difficult situation, *Tonton!* The trouble with Africa is that politicians aren't told the truth often enough.'

'Léon's been spoiled! I couldn't say in public what I said to him in private. African-style democracy is public. European-style

93

democracy is kept under control. The latter method suits me, and I was determined to resign my post, without slamming the door as I left . . .'

At nine o'clock at night the door of the Cabinet conference room opened. Léon Mignane, followed by Soutapha, made his appearance. He had changed suits. The gaze that swept the twenty-two ministers was laden with the weariness that comes with old age.

The rumour of conversation dwindled. All the ministers rose or took a few steps toward him to shake his hand. Nafissatou, Minister for Women's Affairs, curtsied slightly before grasping hold of the Venerable One's hand. Talla, Minister of Higher Education, was finishing his prayers on the wall-to-wall carpet. He hurriedly slipped his shoes back on:

'I've finished, Mr President,' he stammered, his prayer-beads in his hand.

'I trust, Mr Talla, that you did not forget us in your prayers to Allah.'

Uttering these words, Léon Mignane drew near his throne. He signalled to Nafissatou – six places to his left – to be seated first.

The men took their seats in silence.

Soutapha read out the agenda. Daouda summed up the current state of affairs. The President gave an account of the Vth Franco-African Summit. He explained the reasons for the creation of an Inter-African Intervention Force. As he spoke, his flat forehead turned from one side of the table to the other. After scrutinizing each face, he concluded:

'The government must agree on this, so that the PM can defend the plan before the deputies. It is our humane duty as black Africans to send an armed force to preserve the territorial integrity of Zaïre. That country has suffered an attack by forces backed by an ideology alien to our Authenegraficanitus. The debate is open.'

The ministers looked at each other. A reverent fear of making a mistake, of saying something that might not be compatible with the patriarch's ideas, reduced them to silence.

'Mr President . . .'

'Ladies first!'

Nafissatou leaned forward, as Mam Lat Soukabé sat back.

'Mr President, the PM is to present the government's proposal before the National Assembly. Does that mean the party will not be informed? Also, how many units will there be in this Inter-African Armed Force? I've heard that you'll be out of the country. Will your trip have any connection with the creation of this force?'

Léon Mignane glanced at Badara, Minister of Culture.

94

'If I may, Mr President,' began Badara, addressing Nafissatou: 'an American university is honouring our country in the person of the Venerable One, by awarding him the title of Doctor *honoris causa*.'

'As you know, I don't attach great importance to such distinctions. In fact, during my stay in the States, I'll be conferring with the American Chief Executive, as well as with various bankers and industrialists.'

Disrespectful tongues had labelled him 'the black with the biggest haul of European distinctions'. A law had been voted against such denigration, defined as libel.

'The PM is to defend before the deputies the government's proposal to raise troops from our Armed Forces. It would be advisable to enable the people to follow the debate ... by a public broadcast. We are a democratic country ...'

'That was my intention, Mr President,' inserted Mapathé, who could take a hint.

'Mr President,' began the Minister of Hydraulics, 'a few months ago fellow-countrymen of ours were expelled from Zaïre, without compensation. Many of them had contributed to developing that country. They left behind families, children and property. We – our government, I mean – were obliged to come to their assistance. As of now they have received nothing ... from that country, to compensate for the expropriation of their property. And now we're going to send our soldiers to defend that very same country ... Mr President, will the people not be hostile to such a step?'

With a motion of his wrist, the Prime Minister raised his index finger. The Venerable One, on his left, invited him to speak.

'The Minister of Hydraulics has outlined the problem clearly. It's true that we're torn between two alternatives: either we assist an ally invaded by foreign elements, or we selfishly deny that ally our help because in the past it treated some of our fellow-citizens badly. Our emotions and reasons swing between these two poles. Nevertheless [he had borrowed this word from the Venerable One's style of speech] we must acknowledge that sending part of our army down there is a humanitarian action on our part. In the short term, those who refuse to lend such assistance may seem to be in the right. But in the future ... in the long term ... they'll regret it. Zaïre this year is more or less what Spain was for Europe in 1936–9.'

'What side will we be on? The Republic's, or Franco's?'

Mam Lat's sudden, sharp intervention disconcerted the Prime Minister. He began to stammer.

Mam Lat Soukabé, pleased with himself, leaned back with a satisfied air, waving away the smoke of his cigar.

Doyen Cheikh Tidiane Sall laughed harshly amid an ominous

silence. They all looked at him. He could take such a liberty . . . Just as this evening he had taken the liberty of wearing African clothing, a loose tunic over trousers. That was a provocation. Léon Mignane had officially vetoed the wearing of native dress at meetings or official ceremonies.

The Prime Minister overcame his confusion, and continued:

'A promise to send troops has been made in the name of our country. It would not be African to go back on the Venerable One's word, and abandon an ally in distress.'

His long doe-like eyes shifted from face to face, in search of a consensus.

It seemed as if no one wished to oppose him.

'Good! Good!' he hurriedly said. 'We've agreed to send soldiers to take part in this Intervention Force, along with other African countries.'

'Which African countries are going to participate?' asked Mam Lat.

'Mam Lat, everyone is entitled to speak. But you might at least ask permission,' Léon Mignane remarked, to keep his two protégés apart.

'Mr President, I asked a question. I maintain that question.'

'Very well! All the Francophone governments which took part in the Vth Summit are now debating the question back in their respective countries. For the moment, we're discussing the principle . . .'

'Léon, what principle?'

Doyen Cheikh Tidiane Sall had intervened. He had judged the time was right. His gaze had twice met that of Léon Mignane, Daouda, Corréa and Haïdara. Each man's face wore a mask of wary alertness, which showed they were waiting for the right moment to confront him.

Léon Mignane, tiny on his throne, reacted listlessly. Corréa and Daouda noticed this; the latter unwillingly gave an obsequious glance towards the Venerable One, and spoke:

'Doyen! It's a matter of sending soldiers to Zaïre . . . for a start . . .'

'We've committed ourselves to it in the eyes of history,' added Haïdara to help Daouda out.

'I'm asking for the reason, or reasons! Let me make myself plain: I want to know what motivates involving our army, even a single soldier, in such an operation . . . Is that clear?'

The old man's determined tone of voice cast a pall over the gathering.

'We'll put the principle to a vote,' suggested Wade, Minister of Defence.

'Mr Wade, one doesn't put a principle to the vote,' objected the doyen, turning towards him.

Embarrassed, Wade tried to make himself unobtrusive.

Mam Lat Soukabé whispered in Nafissatou's ear: 'Two old chiefs settling scores.' From time to time he fondled the woman's thighs, winking at her. She was making sounds of disapproval.

'Doyen, why are you against this plan, put forward by the President of the Republic, Secretary-General of our party?'

Corréa embarked on a sermon full of goodwill and noble sentiments. Then he yielded to Talla, seated at the end of the table: 'We all belong to the same party. Discipline requires us to fall in line when the interests of the nation are at stake. The doyen knows that.' The Minister of Higher Education spoke in a courteous tone of voice. Badara, seated towards the middle of the table, approved each phrase by exclaiming 'Un-hun! Un-un!' His close-set eyes did not stray from the speaker's profile. He added: 'What you've just said is truly African. We must preserve our Authenegraficanitus,' delighted to be able to remind everyone that he was the guardian of tradition.

'They take me for a fool,' Doyen Cheikh Tidiane kept telling himself.

'Everything's settled now . . . We all agree, don't we?'

They were slow to reply. The Prime Minister looked about inquiringly. One by one, they nodded. Mam Lat Soukabé made no sign, looking Daouda full in the face.

'I don't agree,' declared the doyen, turning his old face towards each in turn.

He commanded their attention.

Mam Lat started, overjoyed. He gave Nafissatou two playful smacks. She murmured:

'Please, Lat!'

Léon Mignane, like a patient schoolmaster, changed position and rested both elbows on the arms of the throne. He gazed gloomily at the two rows of ministers. Talla, at the opposite end, was telling his beads under the table. Soutapha kept an eye on the Venerable One, hoping he would not have an attack. Only his intimates knew of the Venerable One's health problems.

'Why didn't we send our soldiers to fight on the side of the nationalists of so-called Portuguese Guinea, at the time? And why are we sending our soldiers to Zaïre now? For what glory? For whose benefit? Every soldier who dies in this expedition will have died for the sake of capital: of the multinationals. Instead of training our youth as competent technicians, we turn them into cannon fodder. Unless Léon is keeping something from us . . .'

This lack of respect in front of the 'young ones' deeply hurt Léon Mignane.

After having liquidated his companions during the years 1963 to 1970, Léon Mignane had surrounded himself with docile young technocrats. Knowing them to be avid pleasure-seekers, eager for rank and honours, he kept them plentifully supplied with all the little things that deaden a man's will to react, to refuse, to disagree with the Father in charge.

Anyone's dignity can be destroyed by sedulously fulfilling his every desire. Léon Mignane showered them with benefits: luxurious staff housing, cars, appointments to the boards of mixed-economy companies — with honoraria. Better still, he turned a blind eye to the embezzlement of public funds.

Facing Cheikh Tidiane, he felt isolated. In the presence of his protégés, Léon Mignane did not want to seem to avoid confrontation, lest his halo be tarnished. He met the challenge.

'Our doyen is deliberately disregarding the aggression being perpetrated on a friendly country. The destabilization of our continent has begun. Are we to stand by with folded arms? I'm not anticommunist. It's true there are none in my family ... Fortunately! Our country has a legal communist party. What country south of the Sahara can say as much? Our party's ideology is Authenegraficanitus. I advise those who don't know about it to read or reread volumes 1, 2 and 3 of my *Fraternity*, written before our Independence.'

Léon Mignane spoke with all the serenity of an old man nourished and sustained by his own truths. By personalizing the discussion, he reduced it to an assertion of his role as supreme, clear-sighted leader.

Had he not perhaps underestimated Cheikh Tidiane? It was time to get rid of him. As was his wont, he would avoid openly opposing him. Especially now. He would proceed by stages, discredit him to make him unpopular, then isolate him. Whatever his age, a serpent secretes venom. The solitary exercise of power had made him more vulnerable. He had relied on the younger men to counter Cheikh Tidiane. But none of them had the fire, the zeal, the ability to deploy facts, needed to reduce him to silence.

'We must be ourselves, and think for ourselves,' concluded Léon Mignane.

'It's for the West's sake that you want to send troops, Léon. Period! Ever since 1960 you've done nothing but support lost causes ... Enough! Enough!'

As he finished speaking, the octogenarian pounded his fist on the table. He was unrecognizable in this new guise. Mam Lat Soukabé whispered into Nafissatou's ear: 'The doyen is suicidal.' She turned away from him, towards Léon Mignane. Mam Lat made a kissing sound. She kept looking at Léon Mignane. (Mam Lat had it off with her after the meeting, in his 604.)

'Doyen, you're undermining our unity by opposing majority rule.'

'Your democratic majority is a monarchist pyramid, Corréa. The President is in the wrong. And he's dragging us after him . . .'

'Doyen, it's not a constitutional question, but . . .'

'Yes it is, Corréa! . . . Yes it is,' asserted Mam Lat Soukabé, who had his own reasons for introducing this topic. He was pleased at this involuntary digression. He proclaimed loudly: 'The Presidency isn't a piece of property to be handed down.'

'That's what I was afraid of,' objected Corréa in an inflated, aggressive tone of voice: 'The doyen's demagogy is taking things too far. Not one of us here, except for the Venerable One, was elected to his post.'

'All the more reason for his successor too to receive power from the people,' thundered Mam Lat.

Soutapha, like a good shepherd, was watching the Venerable One out of the corner of his eye, ready to assist him if he should feel unwell. Léon Mignane kept silent, his eyes closed. He could not afford to let Cheikh Tidiane Sall go just yet. To be disowned by his old companion, nationally and internationally respected, could be awkward for his trip to the USA. He said a few words to the Prime Minister, who in turn signalled to Mapathé who came over to confer with him. The latter returned to his seat and called for everyone's attention:

'To bring this special meeting to an end, I suggest the following announcement. I'll read it out: "The Cabinet meeting, chaired by the Head of State, after carefully examining the agenda placed before it, agreed unanimously less one dissenting vote to submit to the National Assembly the plan to send some of our troops to reinforce the Inter-African Armed Forces in Zaïre. The Prime Minister, Head of Government, will explain the government's motives to the deputies."'

'That's all, lady and gentlemen,' said Léon Mignane, rising.

Saturday morning

'You know the rest! It's public knowledge. Léon took off for the United States. The PM got the deputies to approve the dispatch of troops. One of the main supporters of the plan was my son, Diouldé Sall. Strange, isn't it?'

Cheikh Tidiane was gazing at a blue-scaled lizard crawling up a tree-trunk.

'*Tonton*, I must go. It's nearly time for my appointment,' said Attorney Ndaw, looking at the old man's face in three-quarter profile. He felt a vague but painful compassion. To dispel the oppressive silence, he asked: '*Tonton*, how are you going to spend the time now?'

Cheikh Tidiane revived.

'I don't know yet. Yesterday the children suggested that I write my memoirs.'

'I agree with them. You've lived through colonialism, the period of assimilation, Independence, and you've taken part in all the different governments.'

Cheikh Tidiane remained silent for a moment, bemused, toying with the idea of talking about himself. Had he not been a prominent figure among his people during the 1920s, 1930s, 1940s? This morning, he thought of evoking that period. A violent, vengeful idea took hold of him. He would fight against the anonymity of death! For years he had suppressed all rebellion towards Léon Mignane.

'Do you really think it would be useful?'

'Indispensable, *Tonton*. All the youth of Africa should know the story of your life. I'd even say it was your duty,' said Ndaw, rising.

They moved towards the door.

'I'll be back to convince you to write that book, *Tonton*.'

'I'll be here.'

Cheikh Tidiane returned to the rocking-chair. It was his first free Saturday for as far back as he could remember. Like the *Xun*, the mystical beast of his culture's legends, a generous mother and the saviour of the race, he had believed that was his task in life. He had performed it with faith and fervour. He had suffered affronts and humiliations. Meditating on his past, he rocked gently to and fro . . .

CHAPTER 16

Saturday morning

Prime Minister Daouda arrived at the President's palace. Soutapha was waiting for him.

'Good morning,' he said to the President's personal assistant. He told him to sit down, remembering the years when he himself was a novice in that same post. He sat down himself. The walls had been redecorated since his time.

Soutapha hurriedly rearranged a few files spread out on his desk.

'You're up early,' remarked Daouda.

'Yesterday, you said I should be here early this morning.'

'Yes! Yes, that's true,' admitted Daouda in a cordial tone of voice.

Soutapha politely showed him his agenda. 'For the press conference, we've arranged for a direct transmission.' He finished, adding:

'I think that before receiving Attorney Ndaw, you ought to see the ministers.'

'Oh?' said Daouda, gazing at him without further comment.

Soutapha remained silent. He had already taken the initiative of directing all calls to the Prime Minister's office. He was reluctant to speak, but Daouda made it necessary.

'I think the ministers would like to have news of the Venerable One.'

'Quite! Quite!' repeated Daouda gravely. His face bore the traces of a troubled night. He had forgotten about the ministers. 'I'll receive them here.'

'I think,' said Soutapha in deferential tones, 'that it might be better to receive them in the Prime Minister's office. If they see you here, they may think . . .'

Soutapha's hints were quite transparent.

'How old are you?'

'Me? . . . Fifteen years younger than you,' answered Soutapha.

'The Third Generation of Independence,' said Daouda to himself. He thought of the Venerable One, and the great difference in age between them.

'I'm going over to the Prime Minister's office.'

Walking across the garden, he met the police sergeant on duty, who saluted and inquired after the President's health.

'He's better this morning.'

'*Alhamdulillahi* . . . We pray that God may grant him a long life, and you too, Mr Prime Minister.'

'Thank you, sergeant.'

The policeman felt it necessary to escort him across the street.

On the ninth floor of the government building, Daouda was at home in his lair: a huge office, with armchairs. He settled in, his long legs lodged comfortably under the table. 'Power is exercised in solitude,' the Venerable One had taught him. This morning, alone, he was terrified of the unknown future. He was afraid. Like a minor left without a guardian, he clung to his guardian's shadow. He struggled to overcome his inhibitions and measure up to his present responsibilities.

He had been astonished to hear the first news bulletin commenting on the attack on the Venerable One's driver, and announcing the funeral this afternoon. Haïdara had been surprised. He had told him over the telephone: 'I don't know anything about it! I'm waiting for an explanation from Corréa and Mapathé.' Jean de Savognard, the French Ambassador, had rung him too to make inquiries. Daouda had merely evaded his insidious questions, by repeating: 'Nothing has changed . . .'

'Oh! excuse me, Sir,' exclaimed his private secretary, closing the door.

'Come in, Victorine!'

She was wearing a long red skirt, slit to the knee, and a blouse with ruffled sleeves. Thin gold bracelets clicked at her wrists.

'Good morning, Sir. How is the Venerable One?'

'Better.'

'Here is the post, and a list of the people who've called. I took the liberty of saying that you would make appointments to see them.'

With a graceful gesture, she picked up the receiver and pressed a button.

'The Prime Minister's office. This is his secretary speaking. Yes. Good morning, General. Excuse me, General . . . I'll see if he's free. There's someone in his office . . .'

Her ringed fingers covered the mouthpiece.

'. . . it's General Ousmane Mbaye, Army Chief of Staff,' she whispered, raising her kohl-rimmed eyelids.

Daouda took the call.

'General? I'll put him on.'

She held the receiver for a moment, looking towards the door, before handing it to Daouda. A light was flashing on another panel. She repeated once more: 'The Prime Minister's office. The President's office? Soutapha. Good morning, young man. He's on the line, hold on . . . ' She signalled to Daouda that she was returning to her desk.

'Good morning, General. Yes . . . The Prime Minister speaking. You rang the palace? He's resting, and not to be disturbed. I saw him this morning. I'll tell him you rang. Besides, he's being given a list of the people who called. Good! Good-day, General.'

After the telephone call, the ministers arrived *en masse*. He put on his dark glasses to receive them. Behind that glass wall he felt another man, more self-confident. He lied to them all: 'The Venerable One is recovering. It was a temporary indisposition. Although confined to bed, he's taking part in the government's activities.' Daouda gave advice freely: loyalty, gratitude towards the Father of the Nation. Carried away, he repeated his lies with conviction. He said the same things to the Cardinal, the Muslim religious leaders, the Grand Imam.

The growing weight of his brand-new position oppressed him, yet flattered him. To be the one who decides! The centre of the circle. The only card in his favour was his respect for the rules of the game laid down in the Constitution.

Victorine reappeared to tell him that a car was waiting to take him to the President's office. She added: 'Soutapha thought it would be better to go by car.'

He went back by the path he had taken earlier, but this time by car.

'There are journalists hanging around outside the palace,' said Soutapha when he arrived, and warned him of the danger of being seen in the street.

'By what right does this young man tell me what to do?' This thought was soon drowned in an ocean of unformulated thoughts. He returned to the President's office. Corréa was waiting for him, while reading the *National Daily* for the nth time. He handed him the paper. A headline in heavy type announced the official denial. Centre page, an old photograph of Léon Mignane. To the left, two columns of editorial on trouble-makers. Lower down, a photograph of Siin, the driver, with two colleagues, framed in black. The association of government drivers called on all workers to attend the funeral.

Corréa informed him briefly about Siin. Daouda paced back and forth. He stopped to examine a signed photograph of General de Gaulle, dedicated to Léon Mignane, and asked:

'Corréa, tell me the truth. The real truth. What is it? ... What's going on?'

'He must have been kidnapped! The police are still investigating. They want us to panic. It's a war of nerves. In any case, a vacancy at the top could lead to anarchy. You must attend the driver's funeral this afternoon.'

'Do you think the Venerable One has fled the country?'

At Daouda's question, Corréa inserted his index finger into his ear. The newly sprouting hairs tickled him. Memories of yesterday's meeting came to his mind.

'I can't believe it.'

'But it's occurred to you!'

'Yes,' he answered bitterly. Daouda had forced him to say what he had been concealing from himself. He hastened to add:

'I don't see what the reason would be.'

'The bankruptcy of the state. Mam Lat told us so. If he's deserted, what's behind it all? Hasn't he, the Venerable One, been ruling the country since Independence?'

Corréa couldn't think of a reply; or perhaps he thought of some, and discarded them. He ventured to say:

'You have the Constitution on your side. You must ensure that it's respected.'

'A state without financial resources.'

'Today is Saturday. If the Venerable One isn't back by Monday, we'll decide what to do.'

'Do you have a miracle cure ready to hand?'

'Who knows . . .'

Soutapha knocked and entered, interrupting Corréa. He brought the Paris newspapers, *Le Monde, France-Soir, Le Matin, La Croix* and *L'Express*. He put them on the desk, and said:

'Attorney Ndaw is here.'

'I'll be off now,' said Corréa.

'Show him in, Soutapha.'

Ndaw entered with an athletic stride. He was surprised at the Prime Minister receiving him in the President's office. 'He's already assumed the succession,' he thought. 'Sit down here, *Grand*,' said Daouda, pointing to the armchair. (By addressing him as *Grand*, he referred to him as to an elder.) In spite of his glasses, or maybe because of them, Daouda had the uncomfortable feeling that he was depending on Attorney Ndaw ... This lack of self-confidence was compounded by a feeling of guilt ... 'Was this the right place for him?'

They soon exhausted the preliminary courtesies. Braving his first trial, Daouda tried to assert himself:

'*Grand*, as you will know, Doyen Cheikh Tidiane has resigned. He was an honourable man. One generation goes, another comes. I thought of you for the Ministry of Justice ...'

Ndaw was listening. He had lifted his chin. He couldn't see Daouda's eyes, trapped behind glass. He tried to catch his gaze.

'*Grand*, a competent man is required for that post. I informed the Cabinet that I would ask you to join us.'

Ndaw looked at him. His gaze slid over the polished lenses. He remembered the words of a European magistrate, whose name he had forgotten:

'However lenient judges are, nothing will really have changed so long as society – whence proceeds the law – has not been altered. How does our people intend to achieve this? Our leniency as judges serves only to appease our conscience. That which eases our conscience, merely serves to cover up the corrupt society of which we are a part, as representatives of those who govern us. For those intriguers, to rule is a way of earning a living; as for their political party, it's a brotherhood of usurers dealing in conscience.'

After reciting this tirade to himself, he smiled inwardly, gazing at a pottery vase filled with faded red roses.

Encouraged by Ndaw's silence, Daouda continued:

'*Grand*, your answer can wait. Until tomorrow.'

'*Petit*, you'll have to find someone else for the job.'

'Why, *Grand*?'

'I don't want it.'

Daouda had lost control of the operation; he could no longer compel the other man to comply with his aims. Attorney Ndaw would have been a major asset; he was known as an honest man, incorruptible.

'*Grand*, do you know the situation the country is in?' asked Daouda, with the virulence shown by the weak when they want to

104

compel others to agree with them.

'*Mon petit,* Léon Mignane is nowhere to be found,' answered Ndaw gravely, gazing straight ahead. He continued in a firm tone of voice: 'You have a dead body on your hands. It's been done up to look like a banal incident. We have laws to punish all those who have taken part in this travesty of the truth, this obstruction of justice.'

His brutal tone made Daouda ill at ease. His upper right cheek began to twitch, a tic that affected him when he was annoyed.

'*Grand,* it's in the people's interest. Reason of state. The general good is worth more than one man's life,' said Daouda.

'*Petit,* I don't understand that jargon. The law applies to everyone. Power is a citadel; to live there, you must be granted admittance. If you force your way in, you'll have to use violence to remain there.'

Touched on a sensitive spot, Daouda reacted angrily.

'As far as I know, it was you and Doyen Cheikh Tidiane who drew up the Constitution that makes me . . .'

'A replacement.'

'Maybe so, but I'm acting legally.'

'What you say may appear to be true, superficially. But it was your deputies who legalized that bastard Constitution. A people's spirit is above laws.'

'How do you mean?' asked Daouda. His tightened jaws hardened his face.

'You and I may have overcome the imperfections of village democracy, thanks to our European education. But our people live by their spiritual traditions. Those traditions are still alive, even among high-ranking officials within your own party.'

A flurry of sharp words rose and died away within Daouda. Offended in his dignity, he was paralyzed by indignation. Ndaw was implying that his role was not legitimate. Troubled by the handicap of his birth, he himself had doubts about his legitimacy.

Until Attorney Ndaw's departure, subjugated, he held a dialogue with himself. He had never learned to use his connections to advance himself. He was supported by a tiny minority, a handful of men more interested in retaining their privileges than in placing him on the throne. The Venerable One had confided in him: 'A leader must never doubt his own will and power of decision.' Comforted by that phrase, he decided to carry on. True, in ancient Africa those of his birth were never more than temporary rulers; but they had shown themselves to be honourable men. Had he himself not proved his capability? What is a caste? Just a trade guild, he told himself.

Soutapha had come in quietly. He coughed, distracting the Prime Minister from his painful thoughts.

'The press conference is about to begin, Sir . . .'

CHAPTER 17

The pavement across from Radio House was thronged with national and international journalists, directors of press agencies, informers, plain-clothes policemen and a few members of the ruling party.

Wild rumours were circulating concerning the President's health and the fratricidal struggles between clans. People's estimates of what was at stake were steadily rising. The withdrawal of the Minister of Justice was a further question mark. Doyen Cheikh Tidiane was staying at home and refused to make any statement.

Two policemen were controlling entry to the conference room, admitting only those who held press cards.

The room was small for so many people. In spite of the air-conditioning, it was overheated. People were fanning themselves, with note-pads or the *National Daily,* and sweating. 'Stop smoking, gentlemen,' ordered a voice. 'What about individual freedom then, you dictator!' someone shouted back. The room rang with noise and the uproar of many tongues.

Fifteen minutes behind schedule, Mapathé, the government spokesman, made his appearance, escorted by the doyen of the Faculty of Medicine, Fall (who was given to wearing suits of English cut, and had on a tweed hat), and his principal private secretary.

The three men took their seats behind a cluster of glittering microphones. They were fired at by photographers, blinded by the lights of television and newsreel cameramen.

'Ladies and gentlemen, we apologize for the delay,' began Mapathé when the noise had died down. 'To begin with, we will distribute the medical bulletin drawn up by Professor Fall, the President's personal physician. For those of you who don't know him, Professor Fall is here on my right. As you will note, the medical certificate has been counter-signed by two other eminent medical figures . . .'

In a few seconds, a wave of disorder swept the gathering. Everyone wanted to secure his sheet of paper. Chairs scraped the tiled floor. Arms reached out, sheets passed from hand to hand.

'. . . In addition to the medical certificates, there is a government statement on the topic which brings us together this morning. We know that your job is sometimes not an easy one. However, yesterday, Friday, one of your colleagues, a certain agency, caused a wave of panic here and abroad. The government objects to certain false allegations, and wishes to reassert the facts. Professor Fall, in his medical capacity, will answer your questions if necessary. I myself am at your disposal. As usual, there is a mobile microphone; please state your name and that of your paper or agency before asking questions.'

Professor Fall had removed his hat. An expanse of baldness prolonged his forehead. His upper lip bore a white moustache.

Questions were slow to come.

'Yes! You.'

'Alassane, Editor-in-Chief and Director of the *National Daily*. Minister, this question is for you. Why have the forces of order been called out on such a scale, and why are cars being systematically searched?'

Alassane relinquished the microphone, and sat down.

'It is quite in order for vehicles to be checked from time to time. Last night, a driver was murdered on duty. Naturally, the Minister of the Interior, who is in charge of security, cannot remain indifferent to such actions. The series of armed attacks recently perpetrated, has made us determined to call a halt. We don't want our capital city to become a tropical Chicago or a Marseilles of the Sahel. The victim of this cowardly attack was the father of a large family . . .'

Mapathé fell silent. He rummaged through his papers before continuing:

'. . . besides this regrettable affair, the Minister of the Interior has informed us that fifty-odd vehicles in irregular circumstances have been impounded. These security measures may be inconvenient for motorists, but they are required from time to time.'

A murmur of disapproval swept the assembly, followed by hostile noises.

'You!'

'Henri, correspondent of *Europe-Soir*. Minister, first of all: why has the transfer of funds to Europe been cut off? Secondly: is this a temporary measure? Thirdly: why are our dispatches being checked? And lastly: who is going to replace the Minister of Justice? Thank you.'

Henri, the representative of *Europe-Soir,* knew how influential his paper was among the African political class. Mapathé, too, knew that people paid attention to that rag. A favourable article by Henri would be a guarantee for investors. He began to speak with great circumspection:

'Ever since inaugurating the BCEAO head office, we've been keeping a check on our supply of banknotes. Like all the countries which belong to this organization, we need to make up our accounts from time to time . . . See what's in the till! There are no restrictions on the movement of funds towards countries belonging to the UMOA. These controls are temporary . . . The Minister of Finance, who is directly responsible, will be able to give you more details. Be that as it may, our European partners have nothing to fear. In our country, the government guarantees investments. Your second question! The government is not in the habit of hindering the free flow of information. Journalists of all persuasions and ideologies come and go here as they like. You must, for once, grant us the right to exercise supervision. An agency, no doubt by mistake, broadcast false news. Enough is enough! Monsieur Henri, you yourself are not censored nor even checked. Just make sure the news you give of us is based on fact. As for your last question: who will succeed Cheikh Tidiane Sall? You'll soon be finding out . . . You next.'

'Kad . . . of the Europress Agency . . .'

When he gave his name, a wave of alertness swept through the assembly. People standing at the door thrust their way in. Everyone was listening.

'. . . Minister, my question is for Professor Fall. Professor, did you see the President this morning? . . .'

'The medical report you've been given is dated as of this morning,' interrupted Mapathé.

'Minister, you said at the start of the conference that we could question Professor Fall. I repeat my question: what is wrong with the President? The name of the illness.'

The Professor saw all eyes fixed upon him. He began to be annoyed.

He smoothed his moustache and said:

'The President is suffering from a temporary indisposition. I've advised him to keep to his room, not to his bed. And I'm not in the habit of making my diagnoses public.'

'Professor, the President of the Republic isn't just any patient. Since you have agreed to take part in a press conference, it is your duty to inform us. Could we know the name of this temporary indisposition? We can only inform the public if we know the truth.'

'What truth! What truth!' repeated the Professor, stung to the quick, as if his competence had been called into question before witnesses. He glared at Mapathé: 'I told you I shouldn't attend. Journalists have no breeding,' he seemed to hiss at him.

Silence was at an end. As if through a crack in a dike, words flooded the room. Mapathé, who knew Kad's perspicacity and his Sioux wiles, calmed down the Professor to keep him from saying too much.

Kad, still standing, microphone in hand, noticed the government spokesman's manoeuvre. Accustomed to rapid deductions, he felt sure his suspicions were justified. Turning his head, his gaze met that of Alassane and Diatta – the cop – seated side by side.

'Monsieur Kad,' said Mapathé to take the situation in hand, 'we cannot make a statement to the Press every time the President has a cold. Your agency has committed a breach of professional etiquette.

I daresay your haste to inform the public occasioned your regrettable dispatch.'

'It wasn't Dakar that gave the newsflash, minister, but a neighbouring country . . . Now, just to get things straight. Why the delay before issuing a medical statement? Thursday afternoon, the President received a delegation. Friday, no more news . . . except that he's ill. What's going on?'

'Your chronology is to the point, but extremely childish. No offence intended. Next! You.'

'Tamba, National Radio Network.'

Kad sat down. 'Something's going on. Their silence about the nature of the illness, the evacuation of his family, conceal . . . the truth.' Alassane was observing him once more.

Once rid of Kad, Mapathé took refuge in vague answers. Professor Fall was happy to be forgotten. Bringing the conference to an end, Mapathé invited them all to call on him whenever they wished.

The recording would be broadcast on the one o'clock news.

Disappointed, feeling cheated, the journalists hung about in front of the radio building. They exchanged tips, adding: 'Best check it out.' The elephant had brought forth a mouse.

Kad was approached by two young people fresh from the School of Journalism: a girl in trousers and khaki jacket, her open face innocent of make-up, and a slightly effeminate young man who blinked and nodded as he spoke. Caught between two parked cars, Kad tried to fend them off.

'I'm neither the director nor the owner of a paper. I'm just a wretched scribe . . . a hack . . . employed by this sodding agency.'

'We know! We want to work with you, as a team,' argued the girl.

'We'll learn all there is to know about the job . . .'

'We want to be free to write: to be independent, in order to be able to write the truth . . .'

'Free journalism, Miss, means freedom to write in accordance with the line taken by your paper, weekly or monthly. Our freedom is held in check by those who control the finances. The only freedom you can have is freedom within the group you work for . . .'

'But you're an independent journalist!'

'Not always, young man. My boss keeps an eye on what I write. In French-speaking Latin countries, a paper is linked with the party in power; and all power is by nature conservative. What you want to do is be writers and sociologists. That doesn't pay.'

'That's just it, we don't care about earning money,' said the girl, putting her hands in her pockets.

'Paper, ballpoints or ink need to be paid for, not to mention a pound of rice, cassava, yam . . . or *couscous*, to keep you going . . .'

Kad fell silent. From a distance, he observed Alassane and Diatta exchanging pieces of paper. The girl turned round, as did her companion, to look in the same direction.

'Do you know those two men over there?'

'The big one is Alassane, the Director of the *National Daily*. Who's the other one?' she asked.

'Professionally speaking, you should photograph him; mentally, I mean. That's Diatta. A cop. Political police. He's good at his job.'

The three looked at each other, before glancing at Diatta, who was walking towards the 'Coffin House'.

Accustomed to air-conditioning like many of his kind – in his office, car, sitting-room and bedroom – Alassane was sweating. At every step he mopped his face and elephant-foot nostrils with his handkerchief.

'Alassane, these two young people are looking for a job,' Kad said in lieu of a greeting. 'They've just finished at the school. My friends, Alassane is the Big Boss of our *National Daily*.'

'Come and see me at the paper,' suggested Alassane to get rid of them. 'Do you know them?'

'I've only just met them,' answered Kad. 'They seem ambitious; that's a good thing.'

Watching them walk away, Alassane suggested:

'Coming for a drink?'

Kad looked him over, without animosity, before accepting.

They crossed the street, dodging the cars that slowed down for the Director of the *National Daily* with his tortoise gait. They went into the cafeteria, the meeting-place of broadcasters, actors, artists, radio and theatre technicians. The racket and chatter irritated Alassane.

There was an empty table under the wooden stairs leading to the mezzanine. They sat down, backs to the wall, facing the room.

'You were rough on Prof. Fall,' said Alassane, sitting well back in his chair, belly to the fore.

'I asked questions! He wouldn't give a straight answer.'

'What are you trying to find out?'

Kad glanced at his profile. The depressed bridge of the nose, beneath a prominent forehead, gave Alassane the look of a Bambara bas-relief representing The Ancestor. Kad had a poor opinion of the Director and Editor-in-Chief of the *National Daily*.

'What's being kept from us? Just what is the President's illness – if there is an illness?'

'You don't believe the minister's statement, or the doctor's.'

'No! And why are you trying to convince me? And what's Diatta got to do with it all? A cop isn't a journalist ... There's too much funny business ... too much.'

The waitress came to take their orders. Kad specified: a

Schweppes tonic with ice and a slice of lemon. Alassane ordered a whisky, cleared his nose with a snort, then asked:

'Who informed the Europress Agency?'

'I didn't know you worked for Central Intelligence too,' replied Kad, keeping his eyes on the other man's face.

Among journalists, Alassane's nickname was 'The Sieve'. He was an active member of the PB, the Political Bureau.

'You're a real anarchist . . .'

'Why not! The agency got it dead right, too. Otherwise, you wouldn't be after me like this. And your friend Diatta wouldn't be hanging around spying.'

'You have spies on the brain, my friend. All the same . . .'

The waitress brought their drinks.

The noise rose to a peak, with applause and shouting. A lively actor, throwing out his chest, recited a Wolof poem by Cheikh Ndao.

'All the same,' continued Alassane, 'you should find other things to write about. You're always attacking the government. In another African country, you'd be in gaol right now.'

'A one-eyed man doesn't like being winked at.'

Alassane whistled at a new arrival: a very slim girl in tight trousers with rows of beads round her hips, wearing a short full top of transparent orange muslin that showed off her jutting breasts. Her arrival was greeted with a round of applause. She whirled round, arms outstretched, like a black swan taking flight. She began to dance, undulating her slender body to the rhythm of drummers improvising with hands, spoons and glasses. Like a startled animal she leapt, bounded, gracefully retreated and advanced. A silhouette bursting from darkness into light, she strutted and pranced. Miming the act of love, she caught hold of a customer sitting in front of her, and thrust her hips suggestively to echoing cries of Huh! huh! huh! The applause grew louder. Exhausted, she flung herself into another man's arms.

Alassane would have invited her to his table if he had been alone. He signalled to the waitress, who informed him 'She's a dancer from the theatre.'

'She's got a nice figure,' he said to Kad.

'Yes. Thanks for the drink.'

'Can I contact you?'

'I'm still at the same address.'

'At Madjiguéne's.'

'You know everything.'

Kad was a singular character. Whether in African or European clothes, he always wore a bow-tie. He had quantities of them, in all shapes and colours. Day or night, he was always neat and tidy. He had won twice running the 'Golden Pen' prize for the best African journalist of the year, awarded by his colleagues. Working as a freelance, he analyzed the most prominent and the most banal-seeming events taking place on the continent. His work was sacred to him. He had a bent for investigation. He had interviewed Nkrumah, Lumumba, Amilcar Cabral, Mondlane, Neto, Nasser, Sékou Touré etc. . . . .

Dakar was his base, his birthplace. For the past four months he'd been working for the Europress Agency, and had seen the newsflash. For the past twenty-four hours, a series of facts had provoked his professional curiosity. He felt there were too many contradictory elements, one after the other. What was going on?

Upon leaving Alassane, he went to have a look at the neigh-bourhood of the 'Coffin House'. He kept an alert eye on the main entrance. Ordinary people went in and out. He was greeted by a man he had once called upon, and walked round the block with him voluntarily. The armed sentries paced to and fro in front of their concrete sentry boxes.

He took leave of his acquaintance, and walked over to the President's palace. Middle-aged Afro-American tourists were photo-graphing the guards and the pair of cranes walking behind the gate. A man in a blue boiler suit was sweeping the pavement. Policemen strolled past. Nothing out of the ordinary ruffled the dull landscape of cement and iron.

He learned nothing from his stroll.

He jumped into a taxi, sitting in front next to the driver. They struck up a conversation, about religion, about the cost of living.

'What's going on with the policemen?'

'It's not normal, boss,' began the taxi-driver, after overcoming his initial wariness. 'It's not normal! They're saying Mignane is senile; that there's a Cabinet reshuffle. Daouda is too young to be a leader. The ministers are all at each other's throats. The cops are bleeding us dry. My cousin from the village told me soldiers are doing the customs officers' job. They're searching everywhere. It's not normal, boss. I was in the army once myself.'

'You're right, brother. It's not normal,' agreed Kad, to keep up the flow.

'For instance,' the man continued confidingly, 'at my petrol-shop* this morning, my petrol-man† refused to fill my jerry-can; and on the radio, they're going on about that government driver who was killed by some thugs. Instead of arresting criminals, the cops are after us.

*Petrol-shop *(essencerie):* service station
†Petrol-man *(essencier):* service-station attendant

Nothing's right, boss.'

'I agree with you.'

'It's not normal,' repeated the driver, stopping at a red light.

Men with walkie-talkies were patrolling the area.

When Kad paid off the taxi, he had heard a broadcast from Radio Street-Corner. His doubts had become presumptions. Something fishy was going on at the top echelon of the ruling class. But what? . . .

'What is it?' asked Bádou, the younger son of Doyen Cheikh Tidiane Sall, who was just leaving the *lycée* where he taught. He didn't much like impromptu visits from journalists.

'I've been trying to reach your father on the 'phone, but there's nothing doing.'

'My father's a grown man,' objected Badou, opening the door of his Renault 4L. Once inside, he opened the door on the other side.

Kad leapt into the car.

The car started off after a few hiccups of the engine, avoiding the groups of boys and girls from the *lycée*. The air was hot and sticky.

'Don't you find it odd that there are so many armed men about?'

Badou was manoeuvring to get out from between a bus and a big Chevrolet.

He said abruptly:

'Come to the point, Kad.'

'I've always thought you'd make a good psychologist. It's true, I want to meet your father. I'll be frank with you. I have a feeling something nasty's going on. But I'm still in the dark.'

Badou was manoeuvring to move out from between a bus and a big Chevrolet.

'What's going on, then?'

'I have a hunch. You may say that's not scientific,' began Kad, turning towards him. Badou looked just like his father, except for the beard. He cut short the comparison, and returned to the topic at hand: 'In my travels I've witnessed many a putsch, failed or successful. I've the same sort of hunch today. Furthermore, I'm certain something really ugly's brewing. They say Léon Mignane is ill. There's no lack of heirs about.'

Kad told him about the press conference, and the way people's attention was being drawn to the attack on the driver. He ended by asking:

'Have you seen your dad these days?'

'We had dinner at his place last night.'

'The Sall clan?'

'Yes.'

Kad grunted several times, before remarking:

'If only I could have been there, as a fly on the wall! Do you have the text of the speech he made on the occasion of the President's birthday?'

'No.'

'Pity! He resigned yesterday. And it was yesterday the newsflash came out. Coincidence! Did he tell you about things?'

'He's finished with politics . . .'

'Not the government?'

'Do you think that being a journalist gives you the right to invade people's privacy,' Badou asked in scathing tones.

'The best thing in my job is to be as honest as possible. The trouble with us Africans, especially the politicos, is that we make an open secret into a towering mystery. As soon as a European journalist turns up, we rush to tell him all. The Europeans already know everything that goes on at the top.'

'They're our rulers' advisers,' admitted Badou in spite of himself.

'So I'm obliged to pick up news where I can. I'd like to meet your father. You can help me . . .'

Badou was thinking of something else as he drove. He had listened to the morning news. Yesterday evening, *Joom Galle* had privately asked him: 'Can you see a man of caste as President of the Republic?'

'What's a man of caste? We aren't against men because of their birth or their religion . . . We look at the social implications of their political views,' Badou had replied, without connecting his father's question with anything in particular.

'I've got to stop by the agency before going home . . . If you're in a hurry, you can drop me off now.'

Badou swerved to the right, narrowly missing two pedestrians. The 4–L stopped in front of an elderly building, painted green; a former shop with three metal-shuttered doors. The middle door was open, and Kad went in.

By the time Badou had smoked another cigarette, Kad was back, looking meditative above his bow-tie. Driving off, they exchanged impressions about the course of modern history.

'So you're sure something's afoot,' said Badou, returning to their former topic.

'My third eye keeps flashing. As a freelance* . . .'

'Temporary worker,' rectified the teacher, concerned for the purity of the French language.

*In English in the original (Translator's note).

114

'Temporary worker,' repeated Kad, 'I want to write a good article' — he had thought scoop.

'Writing isn't enough to change things. You have to go farther. Do you remember these lines of Sembène:

J'ai mon élan et mon envergure
A la dimension du continent
Mon souffle est à la mesure
Des vents unifiés soufflant
Des aubes aux crépuscules
Des sables nus du Sahara
Des forêts denses et velues
Des rives accidentées
De mon étreinte de ce jour . . .
Surgira demain aurore
D'une Afrique . . . Une . . .'*

'With him at least, you knew what side of the barricade he was on,' concluded Badou. He had his students recite the poem.

'That was a stainless-steel generation; a good vintage, I agree. But we must forge new ways of fighting. Here we are; it's over there, behind the barrel. Coming in for a drink?'

'Some other time. I'll ask my father for an appointment, then ring you.'

'Thanks,' said Kad.

A dog, Lawbe, wriggling with joy, leapt up to greet him at the open gate. He stroked its flanks and muzzle before going into the sitting-room.

Angéle, the maid, appeared. She had heard Lawbe leaping at the door.

'Hullo, angel!'

The name he had given her made her smile.

'Madame isn't back yet,' she said before leaving the room.

Kad took off his jacket, and unfastened his bow-tie; sitting on the imitation leather couch, he slipped off his shoes, one foot helping the other. He opened his case and took out a writing-pad. He let his mind roam, reconstituting fragments of information: the President's illness, the Minister of Justice's resignation, the press conference, the reinforced security measures, and the unexplained death . . . The

*My strength and stride/Span the continent/My breath can match/The winds that blow/From dawn to dusk/From Sahara's naked sands/From dense matted forests/From jagged coasts/From my embrace today . . ./Will spring tomorrow dawn/Of one Africa . . . One . . .'

different pieces didn't fit together. He wanted to discover the thread that connected them all. He was practically certain there must be a connection. He took up his notes again, examining each episode. He couldn't make anything of it. He leaned over to turn on the radio, and moved the dial to Radio-France International's wavelength. He found it. Mouloudji was singing low, '*Comme un coquelicot*'.

CHAPTER 18

Daouda had listened to the direct retransmission of the Minister of Information's press conference in the President's office. His thoughts were wandering. The Venerable One had been gone for two days now. Two important days. The people will have to be told the truth! But what truth? Failure of a social policy? Premeditated flight? At the thought of the statement he would have to make, the blood ran cold in his veins. The ache of weariness weighed upon his shoulders. He had less and less room for manoeuvre. Who would legitimize him? Who would make him a licit acting Head of State? Already both Mam Lat Soukabé and Attorney Ndaw had shown disrespect towards him as Prime Minister. All the humiliations and affronts he had endured, surfaced in his memory.

Six months before this Saturday, an English journalist had asked him: 'Prime Minister, people are talking about the post-Mignane era. What do you think about it, as his future successor?' After a moment's pause, he had replied: 'A team of men would be needed to replace the Venerable One. No single man can have the stature, the culture which characterize him. We of the Second Generation are no more than his disciples. We hope to have him among us for as long as possible.'

Daouda remembered that answer as if he had just uttered it. But in the light of today, he wondered if he had been sincere at the time. He had never nurtured presidential ambitions. He had no support, no electoral clientele. He gauged how much his reputation as a faithful second would be worth. If he were to give up now, who would benefit? Why that one and not him?

Soutapha came back stealthily and informed him that Professor Djibril Saar was waiting, as was Corréa.

'Show Corréa in first.'

Corréa shut the door and stated:

'Mapathé handled his press conference very well.' (He had listened to it thanks to the recording made by Diatta, who had concealed in his pocket a miniature tape-recorder, the microphone fastened to his lapel. It was his second visit to the palace since morning.)

'. . . Here is Djibril Saar's file. He's a devoted follower of the Venerable One. He broke up a law students' strike. What about Attorney Ndaw?'

'He turned down the offer.'

'So much the better. You should have about you only people you can control. I've brought a file with me: Mam Lat Soukabé's.'

Corréa placed before Daouda a file bearing in red the inscription: 'M L S CONFIDENTIAL'. Daouda scanned the pages, flicking them over with his tapered fingers. From time to time he looked up at Corréa, then resumed his reading. What he read caused him great satisfaction.

'Are you certain of what's written here?'

'Yes.'

'For how long has this file been in existence?'

The Prime Minister's question was naïve. Each of them had a file. The Minister of the Interior felt a passing willingness to oblige, which vanished as quickly as it had come.

'The Venerable One asked me to do it. With this,' continued Corréa, pointing, 'you'll be able to shut his trap. It's certain that Mam Lat has contacted conservative elements, the right-wing party and certain members of our own party as well. With this file, you can bury him politically. We'll need a journalist who's highly thought of in Africa and in Europe. Kad, for instance . . .'

To convince him, Corréa looked him straight in the face. He was aware that the Head of State was vulnerable.

Daouda toyed unthinkingly with the arms of his glasses. A vengeful sneer twisted a corner of his mouth.

'I'll see Saar now. Then we can meet . . . with Haïdara, Adolphe and young Soutapha.'

Saying this, Daouda pressed a button, and carefully put his glasses back on.

Corréa left to carry out instructions.

Djibril Saar was about forty years old. He was wearing his best suit, the one he saved for important occasions. The Prime Minister intimidated him. His glasses paralyzed his faculties.

Daouda broached the matter directly:

'Are you aware that the Minister of Justice has resigned?'

'Yes, I read your statement in the *National Daily*.'

'Fine,' boomed Daouda boldly. 'Ever since completing your secondary school studies, you've been a model party worker. In view of your merits, the party and government are offering you the justice portfolio, now vacant.'

Whether out of shyness or an excess of joy, Djibril Saar lowered his gaze.

'What do you say to that,' asked Daouda curtly.

'I accept,' replied Saar in a timorous voice.

'Very good.'

'There will be certain matters to deal with, Sir.'

'Such as?' asked Daouda quickly.

Saar noticed his sharp tone of voice.

'You will have to inform the Minister of Higher Education, and the Rector,' explained Saar in a crushed tone.

Daouda's bad temper was immediately dispelled. He had feared accusations.

'There will be no problem in that quarter. Everything will be taken care of. Allow me to be the first to congratulate you.'

Djibril Saar was overcome. He stammered courtesies, while gratefully shaking the Prime Minister's hand.

In less than two hours he would officially be named Minister of Justice, replacing Doyen Cheikh Tidiane Sall who had reached retirement age.

At 11.24 a.m. Daouda strode resolutely into the Cabinet's conference room, Mam Lat Soukabé's file under his arm.

Corréa, Haïdara, Adolphe and young Soutapha turned towards him as he came in. Corréa was struck by the sudden change in his manner, and wondered what had occasioned it.

'Let's sit at the other end,' ordered the Prime Minister. His concealed gaze had rested on each of them in turn, before searching the room.

He sat down defiantly in Talla's chair, as if challenging the empty throne. The Ministers of the Interior and of Foreign Affairs sat on his right, Soutapha on his left. Adolphe, disconcerted by this change from the usual pattern, wondered where he should sit. With the others, or behind the Prime Minister?

'Adolphe, sit next to Soutapha,' ordered Daouda.

The European obeyed.

An empty place had been filled. 'Djibril Saar has accepted,' explained Daouda, his face slightly turned towards Soutapha. 'How do matters stand as of now?' He had pronounced his question clearly, in a tone of voice he tried to keep natural and firm, but which betrayed his inner turmoil. Corréa was alarmed at the Prime Minister's abruptness; he felt constrained to speak:

'I can't answer that! It's lucky that his illness is credible; but for how long? ... Constitutionally, you're the supreme authority,' he added, observing Daouda who had stiffened alarmingly.

118

'Adolphe, what do you think?'

The European would have preferred to be a mere witness. It wasn't his business to put forward hypotheses. He had submitted a long report to his ambassador. Annoyed at being made to speak, he said:

'This temporary state of affairs must be brought to an end. Excuse me for saying so . . .'

'Please do,' invited Daouda, glancing at the empty throne without a twinge of fear.

'Thank you! You should bring this transitional stage to a close, as quickly as possible . . .'

'Do you mean . . . that I should take the place of the Venerable One?'

The European and Corréa gazed at each other.

'I realize the serious implications of what I'm saying. But the longer this provisional state of things drags on, without being clearly designated as such, the more likelihood there seems to me of a coup.'

'Why should the army carry out a coup?' murmured Haïdara. 'Wade, the Minister of State in charge of Defence, is a party man. The military respect him,' he concluded.

They all weighed the possibility of a sudden reversal of the situation. The names of heads of state, of ministers who had fallen victim to pronunciamentos, filed through their heads. Daouda clenched his jaws tight as if someone had clubbed him behind the ears.

Soutapha raised his hand and began:

'I think that . . .'

'Since this morning, you've been "thinking",' interrupted Daouda, without any ulterior motive.

Soutapha lowered his gaze, because of the glasses, and continued:

'I think it would be best to set up a crisis committee, including the top military and police. That would isolate Mam Lat Soukabé . . .'

'Especially as Mam Lat Soukabé is wasting no time,' added Corréa.

Soutapha expounded his ideas with such pertinence and eloquence that the others present could only agree. Daouda considered him with amazement. He began to think of him for Foreign Affairs.

'Yes, Adolphe.'

'Couldn't you meet with Doyen Cheikh Tidiane Sall?'

'Why?' asked Daouda, irritated, like a child who's not allowed to behave like a responsible adult.

Adolphe, his expression contrite, looked about for support. Corréa avoided his gaze.

'Cheikh Tidiane is an elder . . . He can give advice.'

Ever since Adolphe had begun travelling throughout the continent, dealing with Africans, his thoughts had been attuned to

119

mediaeval Africa, which he loved. He loathed the masterful tone of these new technocrats.

'So you're sure the doyen had nothing to do with the Venerable One's disappearance?' asked Daouda, vexed.

The European's cheeks flushed. They had all noted the Prime Minister's irritable tone of voice. Behind the transparent shield that protected him, he had taken on the bold authority of a leader. He added, more for himself than for the others:

'Why didn't the doyen change his mind? He's always dreamed of being Head of State. He wants me to go after him . . . No! Never.'

'Quite right!' approved Soutapha, to ingratiate himself.

'Best draft a speech.'

Adolphe could not make out the nature of this sentence. Was it a statement? An order? As he grew older, Adolphe was as emotional as an elderly spinster faced with a group of exuberant adolescents.

'Adolphe, draft me a statement.'

The Prime Minister's order wounded his feelings. A black man's nigger, he was being dismissed to the kitchen. Nursing his anger, he left.

Once alone, the four men drew up their battle plan.

CHAPTER 19

Saturday, 12.28 p.m.

'You're just lost in a dream, man.'

Madjiguène had arrived. She was wearing a long loose flower-printed green and purple gown, that flowed down to her ankles. She tossed her handbag on to the sideboard.

'Yeah,' admitted Kad, surfacing from his plunge into the sea of current affairs.

'How was your press conference?' she asked.

'Mapathé trotted out the same old bag of tricks. Léon Mignane's still unwell.'

'That's what Radio Street-Corner says too. This afternoon they're burying the murdered driver. The imams have urged all Muslims to protest against juvenile delinquency. The parents are at a loss, so they turn them against the kids. Are you thirsty?'

'Yes! It's all pretty obvious . . .'

'Angèle! Angèle!'

'Madame.'

'Hullo ... Bring me some ice and the Scotch ...'

Madjiguène Ndoye worked as a private secretary in a mixed-economy company. She was thirty-two years, old, and looked her age. She had divorced her first husband, a cadre named Attoumane Diop. She knew the members of the ruling class well, having spent her seven years of married life among them. She was openly living with Kad. He repaid her social courage by being faithful to her.

The signature tune of 'Twenty-four hours in Africa' rang out. The voices of the two announcers, after reading through the African news headlines, started with Senegal.

At a press conference held this morning, the Minister of Information, in his capacity as government spokesman, formally denied yesterday's rumours ...

The government spokesman stated, quote: 'According to his personal physician, His Excellency Léon Mignane, President of the Republic, is suffering from a chill and has been advised to rest.' End of quote. This official statement also counters the mendacious insinuations of certain opposition groups. Replying to journalists' questions, the spokesman added: 'The resignation of Doyen Cheikh Tidiane Sall has not in any way disrupted the Cabinet team led by Prime Minister Daouda, the Venerable One's right-hand man. The former Minister of Justice has opted for a well-deserved retirement. His successor will be announced within the next few hours, Monday evening at the latest.' End of quote. The Minister of Information declared that nothing untoward has happened throughout the national territory. Monsieur Mapathé, Minister of Information, added the following: 'The Minister of Finance and his team are at the moment reviewing the procedures by which European companies based in Dakar transfer profits out of the country. On Monday, or Tuesday morning at the latest, funds will be permitted to circulate freely once more, and the present restrictions will be lifted.'

A burst of *kora* music interrupted the announcer. The voice continued:

We've just heard that the new Minister of Justice has been named. He is Djibril Saar, Professor of Law at the University of Dakar. This will be his first government post. He will attend next Tuesday's Cabinet meeting.

Now some news from the Horn of Africa ...

'The President's ill,' said Madjiguène, sitting down on the couch She had changed, and was now wearing a thin kaftan. 'I hear the old man's dying. Who's going to replace him?'

121

Angèle brought the bottle of whisky, ice and two glasses. Madjiguène poured the drinks, and handed him his.

'Who do you expect? Daouda, the PM!'

'What!' she exclaimed, looking at him inquiringly with a sly half-smile.

'Why are you looking at me like that?'

'Surely you know about Daouda's caste origins . . .'

Like a giant cottonwood tree split by lightning, Kad stared open-mouthed.

'It's true!' she insisted, surprised at Kad's amazement.

'What are you on about?'

'It's the truth. Everyone knows it,' she said with an indulgent smile for his ignorance.

'We're not living in kola-nut and millet-beer Africa . . . More like potato-crisp and Johnnie Walker Africa. People of our generation have got over those ideas,' he declared.

'You're too logical by half. Do you think I would be living with you if you were of casted birth?'

'We would have screwed, at any rate.'

'Too logical! Only a man would think screwing commits you to anything. Screwing and living together are poles apart. Have you thought of what the people think, and the top cadres? I know that Mam Lat Soukabé and his gang, as well as my ex-husband, are opposed to Daouda because of his origins.'

Kad remained silent. He muttered his private thoughts out loud.

'And Doyen Cheikh Tidiane resigned, in order not to serve under a man of caste. No!'

'No . . . A man like him . . . I can't believe it.'

'It's precisely men like him who are the most conservative.'

'Let's drink your health. I must see the doyen.'

They drank.

'Do you realize you've just given me the key to the problem! The President is ill; his companion, one of the survivors of the old days, leaves in a huff. Why? The illegitimate adopted son, named as political heir by his dying father-protector . . . will be denied his inheritance . . . Madjiguène, can you imagine what's going on in the country . . . and what will happen later. An explosive situation, created by the whims of two old men. What a scoop!'

While talking, he had drawn the woman close to him. She liked Kad's unpredictable behaviour. She cuddled up to him, compliantly. He slipped his hand beneath her clothing. She was naked underneath. The man's fingers voluptuously traced the curve of her buttocks . . .

CHAPTER 20

The funeral of Siin, the driver, had an even greater impact than the psychological action team had expected. All available channels had been used to focus the public's attention: radio, television, word of mouth via public transport. In less than seven hours' time, the man's murder had become common knowledge, discussed in government offices, private offices and the market-place.

The radio broadcasts on the subject of this brutal, savage, unspeakable murder aroused widespread indignation. The first broadcast lasted thirty minutes, with subsequent repeats every fifteen minutes. The theme was taken up again and again, and embroidered with the testimonial of various people: the head of the presidential car fleet; colleagues, friends, relatives; his grown-up children. They spoke of his religious faith, his assiduity at prayer. A model of piety. He was evoked in his role as husband and father; his generosity was mentioned, and his fairness towards his three wives and twenty-five children.

Anonymous in life, illustrious in death, the driver Siin had become a martyr, a victim of modern times.

People denounced the young people: lazy, parasitical, debauched, perverse, immoral youth.

A vast heaving crowd stretched from the water-tower to the hospital gates. The dead man's former colleagues, dressed in white suits — their official ceremonial dress — escorted the hearse. They chanted verses of the Koran, taken up by the crowd following them. Groups of clerics, wearing white skull-caps and holding prayer-beads, walked between the hearse and the procession. Behind them walked the Prime Minister, representing the Head of State; three of the dead man's sons; Haïdara, Mapathé, Wade and other ministers. In the next row walked side by side the Governor of the region, Corréa, the new Minister of Justice Djibril Saar ... and various imams ... The eddying throng moved forward slowly.

People were watching from windows and balconies. Flowers were thrown, caught and passed forward until they reached the hearse. Passers-by stopped, doffed their headgear, crossed themselves or recited verses of the Koran.

From time to time a powerful voice boomed out: *'Allahu Akbar'*. Then came the murmur of thousands of throats, and the shuffle of thousands of feet along the pavement was drowned out by the echoing chants.

Traffic had come to a halt ...

Mam Lat Soukabé, escorted by a squad of confederates, all in African dress, joined the funeral procession as it passed the cathedral. Their arrival perturbed the peace of the procession, and did not pass unnoticed. 'Sartorial demagoguery,' thought Corréa cynically. He and Daouda exchanged glances. Mam Lat Soukabé had known the Prime Minister would be there, and had not wanted to miss the occasion.

The vultures that soar over a conflagration are in quest of their daily pittance.

The body, covered with costly cloths, was laid down on the concrete esplanade in front of the mosque. The assembly lined up to say the prayer for the dead.

When prayers were over, Mam Lat Soukabé and three others lifted the coffin and placed it in the hearse. This calculated gesture of the Finance Minister's would be interpreted as a sign of social conscience.

The representatives of temporal power withdrew ... A fleet of buses moved off towards the cemetery at Yoff, some fifteen kilometres away.

That Saturday evening, a panel composed of a commissioner of police, a representative of the constabulary, a jurist, a sociologist, a lawyer and two Imams was to conduct a debate on the current crime wave ...

The attack on Siin would provide a starting-point for the discussion ...

CHAPTER 21

Saturday, 3.21 p.m.

Kad couldn't get over it. 'Doyen Cheikh Tidiane resigned in order not to serve under Daouda. Then why did he remain as Minister of Justice in a Cabinet headed by this same Daouda? Did he hope to be ...' He suddenly dismissed all his deductions. Not having heard from Badou, he decided to try and see the doyen anyway, excited at the thought of writing an in-depth scoop on African democracy.

Madjiguène stopped her metallic-finish BMW at the corner. The neighbourhood was quiet, its inhabitants just awakening from their long weekend nap.

'Where shall we meet,' asked Madjiguène once more, ill concealing her desire to accompany him.

'At the *patisserie*! In an hour and a half.'

She drove off as he vanished behind the curve of the bougainvillea hedge.

Kad rang at the little garden gate and waited, his heart pounding.

Mamadou appeared.

'Good afternoon! I should like to see Monsieur or Madame,' he said in French, his manner self-confident, straightening his bow-tie. He added authoritatively: 'Go and see! I'll wait here.'

Mamadou eyed him warily. But he hesitated to shut the door in his face, as required by the orders he had been given. Subjugated, he said to himself: 'This one's a chief.' He withdrew, then came back and opened the door. Kad rewarded him with a 'thank you'. Ushered into the sitting-room, Kad inspected the lay of the land and chose his position: facing the door, the sun behind him.

'Good afternoon, Monsieur.'

The voice of old Djia Umrel, coming from the back of the room, made him turn round. Her face was exposed, without make-up, her white hair combed back.

Kad held out his hand, forcing the woman to take it. He bowed deeply. (That was a performance of his that often succeeded.) Djia Umrel Ba was struck by the antiquated, Japanese-style ceremonial. She was also deeply shocked by the pink bow-tie with blue polka dots. His suit, of the newly fashionable old-fashioned style, was well cut. 'This is a peculiar man,' she thought. 'The next thing is for him to kiss my hand.' But Kad refrained.

'Good afternoon, Madame. Excuse me for disturbing you. I am a journalist,' he said, proffering his professional card.

She shivered, looking the intruder up and down before glancing at the card.

'Didn't Badou let you know?' she asked somewhat abruptly.

'No, Madame. At least I hadn't had a call from him before leaving home.'

Djia Umrel refused to believe him. She had clearly told her son that she would not receive him. Did this interloper want her to believe that Badou hadn't dared tell him his mother was opposed to his visit? Better yet, he had forced himself into her home.

'Perhaps Badou rang after I had left,' said Kad, determined to impose himself. So near the goal ... He wasn't going to give in easily.

'Where do you live?'

'Sicap. I left home nearly an hour ago.'

'Ah,' she said, comparing the time since her son's call with 'nearly an hour ago'. She looked for a polite way to get rid of him: 'You're Kad, are you ...'

'That's my pen name. I'm an old acquaintance of your children,' he said, seeking every possible advantage.

'You were students together in Paris.'

'It was well before university. We were friends at school.'

Stimulated by the vague feeling that he was scoring points, Kad persisted.

'Don't you recognize me, Madame?'

Djia Umrel looked at him closely, between narrowed eyelids. She thought hard. So many boys came to see her two sons! Besides, that was a long time ago. She admitted that she couldn't place him.

'A sad memory! Someone once accidentally broke the arm of your daughter, Nene Mariam. At the time, you were living in the villa that bore her name.'

The old woman was moved by this painful memory, and reacted with an instinctive gesture, raising her hand to her mouth.

'Oh! . . .' she sighed, trying to overcome the sorrow this stranger had revived in her, weakening her resolve to dismiss him. 'So it's you,' she continued. 'I remember you now. You're a grown man. Sit down! Sit down, my son.'

Kad sat down, keeping his eyes on the old woman's face.

She was reliving the incident.

The children were playing, climbing the guava tree, when a shrill scream rent the air: the voice of Nene Mariam Sall. She had fallen; when they picked her up, she was found to have a fractured arm. Young Kabirou Amadou Diop – KAD – was arrested and taken to the police station. For his parents, it meant ruin. They saw themselves being stripped of their house in order to pay damages. In the 1940s, the Sall represented the élite, the *tubabs bu/nuls*. Nene Mariam declared that she'd been pushed.

Prominent local people intervened to have the boy released. The palaver lasted two days and a night before Djia Umrel yielded to the pleas of the community. During all the time the little girl wore a cast, every week Kad's father or mother brought a chicken or some eggs – never less than a dozen – which the Sall never turned down. In retaliation, the house was henceforth out of bounds for black children.

'My father gave me such a hiding the next day, that I've still got the scars,' said Kad to absolve himself.

'You must know that she's dead! She died years ago,' said Djia Umrel, deploring the way she had behaved then. She raised her face, and the frame of her spectacles cast a horizontal shadow across her wrinkled eyelids.

'Yes.'

She looked away over the euphorbia. For months after her daughter's death she had taken refuge in silence. Emotionally hypersensi-

126

tive, she had reacted so violently to the sound of words, of doors and windows shutting, that the whole household lived in fear of provoking an outburst. For her sake more than for the dead girl, an oppressive silence filled the house. Wearing the halo of bereavement, her features set in a mask of grief, the mother had made martyrs of her two sons and her husband because of her inconsolable maternal grief.

Death exists only for the living.

For years she had longed to have another daughter. But unfortunately, as they say, 'God did not grant her wish.' The subsequent years had buried the brief existence of Nene Mariam Sall ever deeper in oblivion. Only cold ashes remained of her past grief.

'You've reminded me of painful things,' she said, as if to dispel the last shreds of the past. She continued: 'Have you a family?'

'Yes and no,' answered Kad, glad to change the subject.

'What does that mean?'

'I'm living with a woman, in parentheses you might say.'

Still attached to the morality of her girlhood, this admission of immorality struck her like a blow. Nevertheless, she asked: 'Any children?'

'Not me . . . She has two from her first marriage.'

'And you don't want children.'

'Mother . . . May I . . .'

'Yes.'

'Mother, the question of children also concerns the woman who shares my life. Madjiguène and I haven't reached that point yet. It's simple, I live at her place.'

'Don't you feel diminished as a man?'

'No. I haven't the soul of a paterfamilias. And I'm very fond of Madjiguène.'

'What do your parents say?'

'Well, my parents don't hesitate to criticize.'

'But you do just as you like.'

'My parents lived in their Africa. We too are living in our time.'

'Are there many couples living in parentheses, as you put it?'

'It's hard to say! But their number is increasing steadily.'

'What will become of Africa if marriage no longer exists? The institution of marriage is a guarantee for society as a whole.'

'People will continue to contract marriages for the sake of religious or community morality. That tradition will always exist, it's like religion. But . . . people will live on the fringe of these institutions, especially in our cities. That doesn't mean they're asocial or immoral.'

Listening to Kad, she realized the extent of the changes taking place among young people. She had been guided by the norms of her

127

time: total obedience to a strict father, respect of the principles of an unyielding community. There had been only one man in her life: Cheikh Tidiane Sall.

To bring to an end this exposure of his private life, Kad returned to the subject that concerned him.

'I would like to have a talk with the doyen . . . I asked Badou to help me.'

'You must know he's left the government.'

'Yes.'

'What more do you want to know?' she asked, looking at him gloomily. Was she so disappointed with his way of life? She added: 'I don't trust journalists.'

Kad laughed, and answered:

'I want to see the doyen for a piece on aspects of modern democracy in Africa.'

'For what paper?'

'At the moment, I've no idea. I earn my living as a freelance.'

'Good afternoon, young man,' said the doyen, standing in the doorway. He was wearing trousers and a casual jacket. A crest of white hair showed at the neck of his vest. He sat at the opposite side of the table, in order to have room to stretch his legs.

'Guess who this is?' asked the old woman, inviting Kad's complicity with a glance.

Doyen Cheikh Tidiane frowned.

'I confess ignorance.'

'Try again,' she insisted.

He adjusted his bifocals.

'No . . . I don't recognize him.'

'He's the son of . . . what was your father's name again?' she asked Kad with the greatest of ease.

'Gornarou Diop.'

'Gornarou Diop,' repeated Cheikh Tidiane, and asked: 'What did he do in the Ministry?'

'You've lost! This is the boy who broke Nene Mariam's arm. Do you remember him now?'

Cheikh Tidiane leaned back and scrutinized Kad.

'Well! You at least can claim to be a landmark in our family history. Weren't you a friend of Badou's?'

'Yes. In fact, I saw him this morning. He was going to introduce me . . .'

The old man had asked his wife: 'Who was that on the 'phone?' She had answered: 'Badou; nothing special.'

'You don't need an introduction. What do you do for a living?'

'I'm a pen-pusher.'

'But it's Kad . . .' interrupted the woman, 'that's his pen name.'

'So you're the famous Kad ... The tree that casts no shadow for kings.* Twice awarded the prize for best journalist! You can boast of having rattled more than one Head of State, upsetting whole ministries and earning department heads the sack. Did you know that?'

'No!' he answered, embarrassed by so much praise.

'We must have a drink, to celebrate,' said the old man. 'I'll have some lemonade, if you've any left. What about you, Kad, a whisky?'

'I'll have lemonade as well.'

The old woman left the room, (in spite of herself) under the visitor's spell.

Left alone, the two men talked about current affairs in Africa and the world.

She came back with Mamadou, carrying the drinks; Mamadou glanced at the strange man his mistress herself was waiting on. He was pleased at his flair.

'Your health, young man,' said the old man once she had filled their glasses.

All three drank together.

'Very refreshing,' approved the old man. 'Now, Kad! What can I do for you. You must be the sort who doesn't beat about the bush.'

'It's not an interview I want, strictly speaking. I have a feeling that things are going on that have to do with democracy, authority, and men who hold power or aspire to do so. Do you follow me?'

'Yes, yes!'

'The President, Léon Mignane, is slightly unwell. At least ... that's what we've been told. I attended the press conference held by Mapathé, the Minister of Information. And you've left the government — to enjoy a well-earned retirement, as the radio put it. Is Daouda, the PM, already in trouble? There are too many things taking place at once; each may seem unimportant, but together the combination may be explosive ...'

Kad fell silent. With his hand, he brushed away a fly that was persistently buzzing near his cheek. He continued:

'For my article, I need to make some sense out of this muddle.'

Cheikh Tidiane thought to himself: 'Lucky he doesn't know that Léon's vanished and his driver's been murdered.'

'Are you asking me to reveal state secrets?'

'I don't think so. An agency release has just named your successor: Djibril Saar.'

'I don't know him.'

'He's young. A party member.'

---

*The *kad* is a tree that is leafless during the rainy season; so chiefs cannot sit in its shade to watch others work.

'I see,' said the old man. He was pleased at the news. So Attorney Ndaw had turned down the offer.

'You've resigned from the government. Why?'

'Personal convenience.'

'A good answer,' complimented Kad. 'Why are there so many men from security, the special intervention squad and the political police watching over government buildings?'

'When I was in the Cabinet, I was Minister of Justice. Only the Minister of the Interior can answer that question.'

A smile lit up the journalist's face. He was dealing with a man accustomed to this game of question-and-answer; the other's evident wariness stimulated him. He was resolved to make him talk. He changed his approach, became deferential.

'If the occasion were specifically to arise, do you think the people would accept a man of caste as President?'

Kad had articulated clearly, to emphasize what his question implied. Djia Umrel frowned, and glanced from one to the other; her gaze met Kad's, who was keeping an eye on her.

'Why do you ask that?' replied the doyen. A moving dark spot — the shadow of a leaf outside — momentarily concealed his eyes. His fixed gaze betrayed inner turmoil.

'I would like to know if we're ready for modern democracy. Would you be prepared to serve under a casted President?'

'I served for years under Daouda, the PM. I condemn such negative, racist ideas, whenever I encounter them. Yesterday evening, my son brought up the same problem.'

'Which?' asked the woman, breaking her silence.

'Diouldé.'

Husband and wife looked at each other.

'Why wouldn't your son accept a casted president?' asked Kad, remembering that the Sall were descended from a ruling family. Provocatively, he continued:

'To what do you attribute this superiority complex of your son's?'

'We didn't bring him up to be arrogant. His mother and I have always lived on a footing of equality with everyone else. You think this an important point, do you?'

The old woman felt that her husband was evading the issue. She gazed at Kad, who was explaining himself.

'It's a point that still has an impact on our society, even on many of our European-educated cadres. Ancient traditions still hold sway, out of habit — even when, as now, the tradition no longer fits contemporary reality. When I came to see you, I believed this point had been a determining factor in your retirement.'

'Thank you for being so frank,' replied Doyen Cheikh Tidiané, smiling. He violently repressed the urge to reveal Léon's disappearance, and said: 'Your article is very dangerous. It could start quarrels, disrupt families. Young people ... Aggressiveness ... No ... No ...'

Refusing to pursue his thoughts about the present, he took refuge in the past.

'In my political youth, we didn't think about those problems.'

'As "Father" of our Independence, could you give me a few indications?'

Cheikh Tidiane shifted his feet. He remained silent for a moment.

Kad took two sips of his drink, one after the other.

'We who had obtained our Independence without an armed struggle, belonged to all the strata of the society of that time. We were members of liberal professions, schoolmasters and schoolmistresses, trade-unionists, small and middle traders, workers, peasants, housewives, etc. We had faith in the future, and believed that once we had Independence, things would proceed smoothly. We believed that rice, sugar, water, electricity, schools, hospitals, would all be within the reach of everyone.'

He stopped speaking, and glanced at his wife before continuing.

'Independence is – will be – complete only when we control our economy. At the time, aware of our weak points and of our lack of professional training, we, the "fathers" of Independence, channelled the Independence generation: academics, economists, engineers, agronomists, teachers, judges, former soldiers of the ex-colonial army, into state employment, so that they might manage community affairs for the good of the population. These young people soon bared their hyena fangs, greedy for pleasure. They came to power with empty hands, but privileged through their education. They soon constituted a gentry that rapidly grew rich on public funds, making populist speeches to conceal their embezzlements. Having at their disposal the entire machinery of administration, finance and justice, this stratum behaved like those who formerly occupied the country, whose licensed agents they had become. This younger generation is more corrupt, and ten thousand times wealthier, than the small pre-Independence political groups.'

They fell silent. Indistinct sounds reached them from outside. The doyen emptied his glass, and added:

' ... and since then, we have witnessed the renewed cult of a dying tradition ... Lavish expenditure on all occasions. The rise of religious mystiques. The unlimited influence of certain religious leaders, whose theocratic power sometimes takes precedence over the Constitution.'

Taking advantage of the doyen's talkative mood, Kad returned to his former topic.

'In your opinion, why did the President choose a man of caste?'

An avalanche of answers rushed through his mind. He leaned back to avoid a ray of sunlight; his bald head gleamed, but the rest of his face was in shadow.

'I never asked myself that question,' answered the old man, thinking about it. As if speaking to himself, he continued: 'Yes, why was Léon so stubborn?'

'*Was* so stubborn, you say?' Kad leapt on the phrase, and asked: 'Why the past tense?'

Cheikh Tidiane instantaneously broke off his monologue, and stiffened. Wrinkles like birds' wings reappeared on his forehead. He remembered a phrase he had noted somewhere: 'When a leader who cannot be removed from his post enacts his own rigid rules and regulations, if this leader goes mad, the only course left is to cheat him, and to cheat at everything else.'

Djia Umrel had been struck by *Joom Galle's* lack of self-control. She was gripping the arms of her chair, the veins on the back of her hands prominent. Anxiety filmed her gaze like a storm at sunset, and her breathing quickened. Kad interpreted this as a pre-ordained sign, a signal of alarm addressed to her husband. Perhaps we must accept that a couple who have lived together for many years, sharing everything, are eventually able to communicate by sounds, or silent signals.

Kad thought to himself: 'Doyen, you've talked too much.' Recording every gesture in his memory, and with the perfidy of innocence, he declared in order to stay with the subject:

'Perhaps the President wants to lead us towards the New Democracy. To impose it from within the pyramid?'

'That's a point of view that could be defended, in an evolutionary process,' said Cheikh Tidiane.

'Would he himself have accepted it, if he weren't at the top?' added Kad, placing his banderillas.

Clucking sounds escaped the old woman's lips. Although they were involuntary, and almost imperceptible, they attracted the attention of the two men. Whether she was nervous of what she wanted to say (which is doubtful) or wished to avoid contradicting her man in front of a third person, thus conforming to the three pillars of her upbringing – submissiveness, docility and modesty – she said apologetically:

'Please excuse me.'

In spite of her age, she humbly lowered her gaze.

Kad would have liked to hear more. He had noticed the old woman's mouth quivering. He would have liked to know the opinion of this woman, who for years and years, since well before Independence, had been living in intimacy with this highly respected man

'What did he think of his son Dioulde?' he wondered. He said out loud:

'I know Catholic girls who've refused to marry men of caste. Yet their religion takes no account of this aspect of custom.'

Cheikh Tidiane crossed his legs before speaking.

'Religions are only superstructures. They are the summit, not the source of our culture. The Catholic minority is influenced by our common culture. They belong to the same tradition as the Muslim majority. There have been Catholic girls who've turned down highly qualified men, because of their lineage ... They didn't turn them down for religious reasons, but for fear of what people would say. It is difficult to deny the permanence and power of tradition.'

'If I may, I'd like to ask Mother a question ... If you had to choose between a head of state whose wife is a non-African, and a couple in which the husband, the country's leader, is of casted birth, which of these couples would you prefer?'

The old woman remained silent for a moment, looking at her hands.

The clock struck the half-hour.

'The First Lady of a country should have been born in that country. To be precise, I would be in favour of denying all men and women married to foreigners access to highly political positions.'

She had spoken without haste or excitement.

Kad glanced at the doyen. After a moment's silence, the old man said:

'I wouldn't be as extreme as my wife. However, I must acknowledge that for the sake of national pride, the presidential couple should be of native birth. Casted or not.'

'Aren't you afraid people might accuse you of racism,' objected Kad, to keep the discussion going.

Cheikh Tidiane folded his arms.

'Why should that be considered racism? And who are "people"?' asked the old woman. Receiving no answer, she continued:

'Would people in Washington accept a Negro as First Lady? A woman from an African country? Or in Moscow, Peking, London, Tokyo, Rome, Paris ... The problem of castes is a live issue in Europe. Take the case of the Prince of Wales — Edward the ... I forget which — who had a choice to make: a commoner, or the throne of England. The woman was of his race, but not of his aristocratic caste. He chose the woman. For a woman, the Prince's attitude is very flattering. More recently, take the case of President Bourguiba. No one can doubt his nationalism, nor the loyalty of the woman who was with him during his years of struggle. But the time came when for the sake of his fellow-countrymen and their pride, he

133

had to choose a wife from his own country, or resign. He chose to remain Tunisia's Head of State, and married a Tunisian woman. Even in France, a black West Indian could through a historical accident have become President temporarily. What happened? He simply vanished. Our Independence is of very recent date. And you men are very sensitive to "people". In view of the powerful influence a wife can have over her husband's actions, it seems to me that there's no doubt at all on this point.'

She paused. Djia Umrel Ba was merely voicing opinions she had long meditated. *Joom Galle*, startled, was gazing at his wife. She raised her head and continued without vehemence:

'Consider the question from another angle! We all know heads of state, men and women, who claim royal descent – great-grandchildren of a king, an emperor, a great warrior. These glorious names from the past cement our unity today. These links with legend lend present fame a lustre that extends to the clan, the tribe as a whole. There are still praise-singers to single out deeds and facts to feed our pride. A people needs these labels, these stamps of approval.'

'Maybe! Maybe, Umrel. But what you are saying is very dangerous,' interrupted *Joom Galle*.

'I am a narrow-minded woman, and set in my views ... Fear of what "people" will say is a sign of weakness on the part of the élite, and of governments. We live like pebbles in a creek, tossed from one bank to the other. When the African side suits our needs of the moment, we cling to it. But as soon as it hinders us, we fling ourselves in the stream to cross to the modernity imported from Europe. We are forever fleeing our African realities. In the case of Senegal, this two-sidedness dates from a long way back, before you were born ...'

'How's that?' asked Kad eagerly.

'How's that?' The old man became agitated. Behind the crystal clearness of his glasses, his old eyes, rimmed with silver, glanced at each of them in turn. 'How's that? Look at the inhabitants of the towns, Saint-Louis, Dakar, Rufisque, Gorée ... Because of their long period of contact with Europeans, they thought themselves more "civilized" than the other bush Africans living in forest or savanna. This arrogance grew when they alone were given the vote and considered French citizens. People from these four *communes*, and their descendants, were proud of being the equals of Europeans. They began to parody them, and acquired a pretentious mentality ... How many times have we heard a man from Dakar, Gorée, Rufisque or Ndar (Saint-Louis) say contemptuously to his country cousin: "I was civilized before you were." These alienated, rootless people, enslaved from within – of whom I was and still am one –

134

were unconsciously the most faithful and devoted servants of the then prevailing system of occupation . . .'

The doyen paused to catch his breath. Behind his distant deep gaze, his thoughts were gathering momentum. He continued:

'In the years 1945–50, Léon Mignane would say during his election campaigns: "I will free you from the serfdom of 'native' status . . . I will make you . . . French citizens." That was why the peasants supported him. Twenty years after our Independence, our thinking still bears the marks of serfdom. When we talk of foreign goods . . . we never mean French cars or goods. The foreigners in our country are English, American, Japanese, Chinese, Russian.'

'Similarly, I've known Africans who were highly critical of certain régimes or ideologies, without realizing that their opinion was based on the European system, their gold standard,' concluded Kad.

'Exactly,' exclaimed Djia Umrel. 'What model of society are we offered through the media? We're made to swallow outdated values, no longer accepted in their countries of origin. Our television and radio programmes are stupid. And our leaders, instead of foreseeing and planning for the future, evade their duty. Russia, America, Europe and Asia are no longer examples or models for us.'

'It would be a dangerous step backwards, to revert to our traditions . . .'

'That's not what I'm saying, *Joom Galle*,' she interrupted. 'We must achieve a synthesis . . . Yes, a synthesis . . . I don't mean a step backwards . . . A new type of society,' she ended, blinking.

There followed a brief silence.

Kad was observing them. This elderly couple amazed him. He was full of admiration for them.

'You've a most interesting theme there, Kad, you must work it out well,' said the old man, his masculine vanity slightly wounded by his wife's forceful points.

'Don't you agree that *Joom Galle* ought to write his memoirs,' suggested Djia Umrel.

'A very good idea,' Kad replied. 'You must enlighten us on many aspects of the past. Those of my generation and the next know nothing about the conflicts between French citizens and French subjects – at that time.'

'I improvise my speeches. I don't know how to write. After a couple of pages my thoughts run dry, as if the blank page had the power to frighten them off. I can only express myself instinctively.'

'Writing imposes a certain discipline upon thought. Whereas speech flows spontaneously from those who have an instinctive gift . . . You could easily record what you have to say. It can be typed out afterwards.'

'Who would do that?'

'I could ask Madjiguène. She types better than I do. We can help you.'

'I can help you too. I have all your letters, and press cuttings,' she added, to force his hand. With a book to write, *Joom Galle* would be kept busy.

'It would be like drawing up our final statement of accounts: the accounts of an era! That's not a bad title,' he said, with a questioning glance at his wife.

'It has a fine commercial ring to it! But it's not literary,' she replied.

'Ah!' exclaimed *Joom Galle*.

'When do you think you could start, Kad?'

'We could set aside two evenings a week for recording. As for transcribing the tapes, I'll ask Madjiguène what she can fit in.'

'Let's start next Tuesday.'

'Umrel, that's a bit much. You're disposing of our time, just like that.'

'*Joom Galle,* if you don't agree, you can always say so!'

The old man fell silent. His lips quivered in a submissive smile. This plunge into his past life worried him. Had enough time elapsed for him to be impartial? To talk about his father? Pascal Wellé? Léon Mignane . . . and himself?

'That's fine,' said Kad to break the silence, 'Tuesday at nine o'clock.'

'Why don't you and your woman come to dinner . . .'

'Thank you, Mother. We'll be there. Doyen, thank you for talking to me. I'll find my own way out.'

CHAPTER 22

Kad congratulated himself on his daring. He wasn't disappointed with his call on Doyen Cheikh Tidiane. What did 'personal convenience' mean, and why 'he was so stubborn'? He ought to go and see Diouldé . . . Strike while the iron is hot.

Repeated hooting drew his attention to Madjiguène's BMW.

'Didn't you do your shopping?' he asked her, getting in.

'There are people keeping an eye on you . . .'

From the car, he saw two men in suits, in a black Peugeot.

' . . . They have a walkie-talkie,' remarked Madjiguène, starting off. 'Now can I have my ice-cream?'

136

'First I'd like to go by Dioulde's ... The doyen's son. Do you know his wife?'

'Eugénie? Is it her you're interested in?' she asked, glancing back.

The black car was following them.

'Her man, actually.'

'Should I stay behind to cover you?'

'No! Let them follow us.'

She drove towards the Western Corniche. Kad told her of the doyen's plans, and the promise he had made on her behalf.

Behind the Ile aux Serpents, clouds rose like foothills in an empty sky. Clusters of vultures wheeled above the cliffs, veered towards the old Muslim cemetery and the Medina market, then returned to float over the sea.

The traffic-free road stretched like a black ribbon before her.

At an intersection, a red light forced her to stop.

'Don't pay any attention to them,' advised Kad.

'Easy for you to say,' she replied, swiftly moving off again. She slowed down, her gaze fixed on the outside rear-view mirror, watching the car following them.

The road became narrower between the Soumbedioune artisans' village and the Total petrol station: cars were parked on both sides. The fishermen's boats had come in, and the fish market was thronged with people.

Madjiguène was playing games with the Peugeot ... Behind it were two other cars, a Renault and a Honda. She pulled over to the right, then moved out to the left, braked to let a man cross carrying a huge basket from which protruded fish heads and tails. She signalled a left turn, accelerated, then braked sharply ... and accelerated again. The Renault collided with the rear of the Peugeot, with a crash.

A triumphant laugh burst from her.

'That's really clever,' remarked Kad, turning round to see a crowd begin to gather.

'Yes, isn't it?'

'Do you imagine you've got rid of them?'

'That lot? Yes. The Léon Mignane style socialism trick always pays.'

'What kind of socialism is that?'

'You signal left and turn right.'

'Not bad!'

'No, it isn't, is it?'

After the university, the BMW turned down a side street. It wound past villas with names like castles, their neo-Sahelian façades vying with each other from behind bougainvillea hedges, their doors all closed, their windows guarded with iron bars. After the fourth inter-

137

section, Madjiguène parked in front of a black painted gate bearing in large white letters: *'Beware of the Dog'*. She rang the bell twice. A plump steward let them in.

'I've come to see Madame,' she felt required to say as they followed him towards the sitting-room.

When they had been shown in, Kad looked about him. Daylight filtered through smoked-glass windows in aluminium frames. High-fidelity speakers and swivelling spotlights were positioned in the corners of the room. The curtains, and the doilies on the stark Scandinavian furniture, matched the off-white walls. Kad thought to himself: 'Symbols of success and an art of living.' Completing the inspection, his gaze met Madjiguène's. They admired the setting. Kad stretched out his arm to pick up an old copy of *L'Express*. Madjiguène was content with *Elle*.

Eugénie, perched on high heels, wearing filmy Turkish trousers gathered at the ankle and a hip-length smock, exclaimed:

'Madjiguène . . . Ndoye.'

The two women kissed. Eugénie offered her right cheek, then the left, then the right again, for Kad's lips to touch soundlessly. The whole room was fragrant with her *Miss Dior*.

'What have you been doing with yourself, Ma [short for Madjiguène]? Only last week we were talking about you. It was at Béa's remarriage. You surely remember her at least.'

'I certainly do . . . I hope she's not part of a . . . matrimonial mixed bag.'

'In third position, my dear . . . A third wife,' said Eugénie, flashing a broad smile. 'We're all on the brink of old age. And what about you, Ma . . .?'

Smiling, Eugénie patted her visitor. The gentle murmur of their voices was broken by occasional exclamations and expressive onomatopoeia. Through her first marriage to Attoumane, Madjiguène had belonged to high society. By living with the journalist, she had broken free. The women chatted, evoking common memories.

'Where's your man?' asked Madjiguène.

'Hm!' sighed Eugénie glumly. 'He's just back from the funeral of that driver who was murdered by some thugs. He's changing to go out again,' she added, with unspoken implications. 'I really am pleased to see you again.'

She effusively seized hold of Madjiguène's hands, and addressed Kad:

'Don't make my girl miserable, now!'

'Never! Quite the opposite, in fact.'

'Do you think so? That's what they all say,' Madjiguène flashed back, laughing.

'What can I give you to drink?' asked Eugénie, moving towards the bar at the other end of the sitting-room.

'What a pleasure to see you young lovers . . .'

Diouldé held out his hand to Kad, and kissed Madjiguène, one arm round her waist, adding:

'You're more beautiful then ever.'

'And you're still a flatterer.'

'Eugénie, isn't Ma . . . more beautiful than before?'

'Of course! She did well to dare . . .'

'Dare, ladies! Dare everything,' proclaimed Diouldé jovially, turning aside from the storm he saw gathering on his wife's face. 'And you, Kad, still scribbling?'

'I don't know how to do anything else. What about you, *Monsieur le Député?*'

'I'm defending the Republic.'

'You haven't named your poison. What'll it be?'

'I'll take care of that, Eugénie.'

Diouldé took her place behind the mahogany bar. She came back to sit with Madjiguène, who said:

'Something non-alcoholic.'

'That's what this bar lacks,' said Eugénie, then suggested: 'Orangeade, or lemonade?'

'Lemonade! They say it helps you lose weight. I'm keeping an eye on my figure . . . With a new generation of girls arriving on the market, we'd best learn how to freshen ourselves up.'

Eugénie giggled, leaning against her. They both burst out laughing.

Kad joined Diouldé at the bar, and sat on a stool.

'Whisky?'

'Just an inch, with water.'

'You'll ruin it that way. Chivas should be drunk "on the rocks".'

'Very well, "on the rocks" then,' repeated Kad, imitating his host's accent.

'It's the real thing. I brought it back from a parliamentary trip to Scotland.'

Diouldé set two straw-clad glasses down on the counter. The ice-cubes tinkled under the flow of grain-coloured liquid.

'Your health, my boy.'

'Same to you, *gran-bi.*'

The conversation turned upon memories of student days . . . Friends, fellow-students now in responsible positions, leaders, figures in international organisations, UN, FAO, UNESCO. Girls they had known, now married, mothers, divorced, widowed.

'We're a lost generation,' declared Diouldé in a melancholy tone.

Kad said to himself: 'I've heard that before.' In his opinion

Diouldé was obsessed with his own future, with success. He wasn't of the stuff that makes leaders, nor did he have the moral courage of his father or his younger brother. Behind the semblance of a broad-minded, free-spirited man, lurked a docile creature who needed to be led.

'All generations say the same thing: "We've been sacrificed." I don't see in what sense we, the élite, can say that.'

'I'm going to show Ma ... the house,' said Eugénie, rising, followed by the other woman.

'Yes, do,' said Diouldé. His gaze followed Madjiguène. Turning back to Kad, he remarked: 'Her husband's terribly unhappy, you know. Ever since their divorce, he changes women as readily as changing socks. You're a cool customer ... Well ... As I was saying ... Don't judge by all this (his arm swept the sitting-room.) We're still struggling, economically speaking; a covert struggle, without weapons. We higher-echelon people feel frustrated; we feel we've been robbed ... We've had something taken from us ...Don't you agree?' he asked, concluding.

Kad did not reply. He knew how such self-pitying complaints ended. He thought otherwise. What Diouldé called 'frustration', was only the crumbs they were given by the multinationals.

'You wanted to see me?'

'Yes, *gran-bi*.'

Diouldé deftly tapped his hands, to interrupt him. The tips of his fingers were icy cold.

'Frankly, *boy-bi*, I'm broke. I've had to ask my bank for another six months' overdraft. My deputy's pay is just enough to keep things ticking over. You're a younger brother, like Badou, and I feel I must tell you the truth, straight off.'

'I haven't come to ask you for money, *gran-bi*.'

Relieved, Diouldé resumed his bantering tone, and excused himself:

'It's no picnic being a deputy in this country. Everyone thinks you're loaded.'

'That's no reason to think everyone's after your money.'

'Easy for you to say. Very few people come and see us for any other reason than to strip us naked. You don't know what a burden it is to be an elected representative. I have colleagues who flee — actually flee — their homes at dawn, and return there late at night ... Very late. Every voter thinks he can cash in his vote.'

He sipped his drink, and glanced at his watch, a large Timex.

'Are you a friend of Mam Lat Soukabé, *gran-bi?*'

'The Finance Minister?'

'Yes.'

'You want to meet him? You should have asked me sooner. Do

you want to negotiate a loan?'

'I want to meet him, talk with him. Not borrow money from him.'

'I must say, you're a true idealist.'

By exercising his profession in his own way, Kad had acquired a certain amount of knowledge of the people he spoke to. He worked as a psychologist rather than a journalist. He had met only six leaders who had impressed him by their maturity, their ease of manner and the precision of their replies: Frantz Fanon, Nkrumah, Mondlane, Julius Nyerere, Neto and Amilcar Cabral.

'No, I'm not an idealist,' he replied, pushing his glass aside: '*gran-bi,* why did your father resign?'

'I've really no idea,' replied Diouldé warily.

'I thought you would be one of "those in the know". Well, never mind! I liked the speech you made in the assembly in favour of sending troops to Shaba.'

'I was inspired that day. There are days like that,' he said with an expansive gesture.

A playboy, he knew how to turn radio and television coverage of parliamentary debates to his advantage. All viewers knew his face. He was not displeased at being recognized in the street and in shops.

'Are you still convinced that the soldiers we sent there fought to defend freedom?'

He threw out his chest; his open shirt collar showed two gold chains round his neck. Kad did not want to interrupt him, in spite of his peremptory tone.

'That country was being invaded! All we did was show our solidarity as Africans.'

'The others were Africans too.'

'Communist-inspired. Besides, we weren't the only ones to rush to the rescue.'

'That's true! Now that Zaïre and Angola are good neighbours again . . . what do you think of it?'

'That's all politics, my boy. As representatives of the people, we aren't meant to know anything about Léon Mignane's personal relations with third parties.'

'Could be. At the time, they said that your father didn't go along with that display of solidarity. Isn't that one of the many personal reasons which have led to his retirement? His resignation comes at a critical time. Léon Mignane is ill. The PM, Daouda, will inherit the presidency, *gran-bi.*'

Kad slipped in the *'gran-bi'* to lull suspicion.

Diouldé left the bar, and returned with a box of Davidoffs which he offered Kad.

'Cigars! Too strong for me.'

'You surprise me, *boy-bi*! You don't smoke, you drink in moderation. Maybe you're a . . .'

'I'm not a queer yet. I drink in moderation, I smoke, and you've seen my woman, Madjiguène! A real animal! I've got to keep her satisfied.'

Having said that, Kad took out his packet of Gauloises, took one and lit it himself. Diouldé rolled his cigar delicately between his palms. He cut off the end, before striking a match. The roar of a Concorde overhead compelled them to silence. The noise slowly diminished. Diouldé waited, then said:

'*Joom Galle's* resignation wasn't a surprise for anyone. He should have done it a long time ago. Out of friendship for the Venerable One, he stayed on beyond the age limit.'

'Age limit! Léon Mignane's as old as he is, isn't he?'

Kad's statement startled the son of Doyen Cheikh Tidiane. He hadn't made the connection between the age of the two men.

'So the two veterans are leaving the ship,' remarked Kad.

It was a quip. It worked.

Fish get caught by fishermen because they open their mouths.

'True! Léon Mignane is in his dotage. His fits of absentmindedness are getting longer, and more frequent. He keeps talking about giving up power.'

'Your father would have been a great president,' said Kad, to stimulate the other's imagination.

'My father!' said Diouldé, sucking his cigar, his gaze remote. 'My father could have been president . . . It's too late. Did you know, my boy, that it was through my father than Léon Mignane came to power.'

'No, *gran-bi.*'

'It's history!' declared Diouldé, who for a second dreamed of seeing his father as Head of State. The dream quickly vanished in the smoke of his cigar.

'How are relations between the PM and Mam Lat Soukabé? Radio Street-Corner keeps broadcasting . . . If Daouda comes to power . . .'

'Do you really think that Daouda will be the country's second President?'

Diouldé looked closely at the journalist, who shrugged, his face non-committal. He breathed deeply, then added:

'Daouda's a nonentity: you should have seen him this afternoon, at Siin's funeral. I felt sorry for him. Really! He's strictly small-time. He's got no popular appeal, no voting strength. He can only hang on under Léon Mignane's umbrella . . . No . . . Daouda's not the man we need.'

'He's in line for the succession! . . . And he's already in place.'

'Really, you disappoint me, my boy! I thought you were smarter

142

than that,' objected Dioulde. 'Daouda? He's of casted birth.'

'Now we have it,' said Kad to himself.

'You, I, your father all obey the government headed by Daouda. As a deputy, you voted for the bill that makes him Léon Mignane's successor. Was Daouda a man of caste then, according to your party?'

While speaking, Kad deliberately paused from time to time.

'I wasn't in the assembly that day.'

'But you didn't raise any objections before the bill was tabled.'

'Easy to say, my boy . . . Everything is easy for you journalists. At the time there was only one party in the assembly. There's party discipline . . .'

'Whose idea was it?'

'My father's.'

'Really.'

'While Léon Mignane still had all his faculties, everyone pretended to accept that clause. Léon Mignane acted dishonestly. If Daouda insists on staying in power, he'll be swept away by the people. He represents nothing . . . The man we need is Mam Lat. You should . . .'

Dioulde set his cigar down in the ashtray. He had turned to gaze in the same direction as Kad.

'What do you have in your whatsit?'

'My case . . .' exclaimed Kad. His features froze with astonishment.

He slipped off his stool, brought his case to the bar and emptied its contents on to the counter.

'That's all right then. I don't trust journalists. You might have had a tape-recorder.'

'*Gran-bi*,' began Kad, startled by this lack of trust, 'I've never written anything against your group. You're bourgeois nationalists. Something's going on just now. It's no secret any more.'

'It's not that I don't trust you, but it's always best to be sure . . . As I was saying, as Finance Minister Mam Lat has done a great deal for our country's economic operators. He's encouraged nationals to set up businesses: chemists' shops, private clinics, car showrooms, insurance, public works, commerce. Such a staunch nationalist is the right man to succeed Léon Mignane.'

'It's true that some Senegalese nationals have come into their own.'

'I'm glad you acknowledge it . . . For us economic operators . . .'

'Economic operators?'

'Ever since Sembène's film *Xala*, we businessmen have started calling ourselves economic operators.'

'Good old Sembène . . .'

'An idiot, you mean. To return to Mam Lat, he's the man we need, the right man in the right place.'

'*Gran-bi*, if Daouda weren't of casted birth, would you think as highly of him as you do of Mam Lat?'

'Daouda is a real nonentity. I've said so already. He's a cipher, with nothing behind him. Furthermore, the country isn't a family property, to be handed down to him. Our country is attached to the values of Authenegraficanitus. It's dangerous to arouse the anger of the people.'

'Did you know that your father thinks differently on the subject?' asked Kad, refraining from revealing his mother's opinion.

'*Joom Galle* is a man of the past. For months, we in the BP have been talking about repealing that clause.'

'Will Léon Mignane, as Secretary-General of the party, go along with that?'

'The Venerable One is very tired. He ought to step down before it's too late.'

'Threats again,' thought Kad to himself. He would remember the phrase, and the reaction it evoked in him, making logical connections in his mind.

'By eliminating Daouda because of his origins, you're behaving like monarchists.'

'No . . . It's not because I'm descended from a ruling family, like Mam Lat who's also a *Guelewar*, that we want to get rid of Daouda. There's . . . European democracy, and there's our own African democracy as well . . .'

'Mystification,' thought Kad, stubbing out his cigarette.

'With Mam Lat the country will make a great leap forward. We'll vary our economic partners. We'll open our country to Japanese and German investors. And we'll suppress our preferential agreements with certain countries. As far as you're concerned, have you seen our *National Daily*? Pure shit! Excuse me, but it's true. Once you've found out what films are on, there's nothing left to read. You could take it over in the near future, give it new scope. Give me your 'phone number. I'll arrange for you to meet Mam Lat. For you, it's the right time to act.'

Kad scribbled down Madjiguène's number.

'You can call anytime, day or night.'

'What about the President's illness?'

He pressed the cigar between his lips and took a draw. It had gone out. Kad handed him his box of matches. He lit up, and breathed out a plume of smoke. The dark glasses moved away from Kad's face, then moved closer again.

'*Boy-bi*, let me tell you something in confidence! We're bankrupt

144

... Down to nothing, economically speaking. Léon Mignane is a thing of the past. You understand ...'

'I don't catch your meaning, *gran-bi.*'

'I can't tell you any more. But ...'

'Hey, you men, haven't you finished trading secrets yet?' called out Madjiguène, returning with Eugénie. 'Diouldé, you have a beautiful home. I congratulate you both.'

'Thanks. We do what we can.'

'Could we go now, Monsieur Kad?'

'I was waiting for you,' he replied, picking up his case and shaking hands with Diouldé.

The two women kissed once more.

Outside, Madjiguène looked about her before starting the car.

'Do you still want your ice-cream?'

'More than ever,' she answered, changing gears.

'Everybody loves Saturday night ...' is a popular song, sung in every language.

Saturday erases from the mind the week's fatigue; it is a day full of plans, of intense recreation, of ecstatic pleasure-seeking.

On Saturday afternoon, the Plateau holds its breath. The deafening flow of traffic of the previous days dwindles to a trickle. The streets are deserted — the noisy weekday throng vanishes within a few hours. A commercial and administrative centre, a ghetto, it closes in upon itself and takes on the appearance of a provincial suburb in France.

Those free-flight virtuosos, the vultures, who move from place to place in the city, inscribe arabesques in the sky over the tall buildings.

The Plateau is a setting for a tropical Father Christmas; its shops, boutiques, restaurants, cinemas display European taste, European fashions ...

At night, the Plateau is like a window open on to Europe, by the ocean; like something thrusting into the body of Senegal, its lights glowing ... A vivid, glittering landscape.

It's good to roam the Plateau on Saturday night, amidst the African throng come from the humid bush, from the arid savanna, from the parched and starving Sahel. Pedestrians, strollers, whores, homosexuals, lesbians, the unemployed, government employees, workers and clusters of women shepherding their offspring pass by every shop window. From one halt to the next, from one shop to another, they admire and covet: name-brand shirts, shoes for men, women and children, the latest style in suits, evening and cocktail

145

dresses, perfume, a toilet kit, toys etc. . . . In their dreams, they carry off the coveted article. They dream of a happy life, a model existence.

At night people rush to the cinemas, to escape . . . far, far away, to America, to France, to Italy, to England . . .

Saturday night. A night of pleasure for the eyes and the senses. A night of feasting and carousing. Laden with hope, fortune amidst wretchedness, Saturday night is sacred. It is a cult; a religion without fear of hell, where life is the only priestess. Young people, dancing, live with their bodies, rejoice in their bodies.

'Everybody loves Saturday night . . .'

CHAPTER 23

Kad was puzzled at receiving an invitation from Alassane – Director and Editor-in-Chief of the *National Daily*. Especially for Saturday night. He had had a drink with the man only this morning. Alassane wasn't just anyone. He belonged to Daouda's clan, and his connection with Corréa and Diatta – the police – was no longer a secret to the press. He was suspected of working for the CIA. Alassane had telephoned twice — according to Angèle. He had sent a hastily scrawled note, an invitation to dinner: 'Just us men, at the '*3 Filaos*'.'

Badou had left a message as well: his father would not talk to a journalist. Kad was no longer concerned with the doyen's son. It was out of the question to turn down a meeting with Alassane. 'Who knows, he might cast some light on zones still dark, thus enabling to carry still further his exploration of New Democracy, African-style?' His interview with Dioulde had enabled him to form an opinion about one of the clans. He still had to encounter the other side.

As for Madjiguène, she was worried about the appointment with Alassane. This afternoon, she had enjoyed shaking off the people tailing them. Now she was afraid. Anything can happen at night. With Kad, she had found herself as a companion, a human being, not a sex object. He showed that he needed her. She would go to the cinema, and join him later at the '*3 Filaos*'.

The night-club was known by all those who moved in high society. Built on two levels, it was set within luxuriant gardens, on the beach. On Saturday nights it was a private club, for members only. They could invite friends. The members, carefully selected, were men in positions of power: directors, presidents, top officials, company chairmen, etc. ... The atmosphere, reminiscent of the 1950s and 1960s, evoked their student youth. Each had his own key, and his own bottle in a private pigeon-hole.

At the foot of the stairs a silhouette blocked the way. Accustomed to fending off gatecrashers, the man eyed him with disdain.

'I'm here as a guest of Alassane,' stated Kad, standing on the bottom step, in order to justify his presence. He felt it necessary to add: 'Director and Editor-in-Chief of the *National Daily*.'

'*Wossa nyme,*' mouthed the doorman, with a self-satisfied air of one complying with orders. The light shone on his puffy face. He looked every inch an ex-serviceman.

'Kad – K A D.'

The man took out a flat red electric torch, and moved its white beam up and down the guest list. Watching him spell out the names, Kad was certain the doorman hadn't made it through primary school. He saw the name at the foot of the fourth page. He put his finger on it, and switched off the torch.

'*Vi ... messeu.*'

'And my wife.'

The man scowled. He ungraciously looked at the list once more, and stated:

'*Messeu ... no Madame.*'

'How's that?' Kad exclaimed. 'Kindly add her name, please.'

His arrogant tone, dress and self-confident manner made the man comply, against his will.

'*Wosser nyme?*'

'Madjiguène Ndoye,' pronounced Kad, stepping on to the landing.

Defeated by the spelling, the doorman sheepishly opened his mouth. His teeth, eroded by cheap red wine and kola-nut, were a dental ruin.

Kad spelled it for him: 'Madjiguène Ndoye.'

For the doorman, Kad was a faker. An unpredictable race of people. They come with their mistress and say she's their wife. Any woman who doesn't bear her husband's name is nothing but a 'spare tyre'. He glared with hate until Kad vanished into the dark night-club.

On the floor, closely intertwined couples were moving in slow motion to the rhythm of an old tune. People seated at tables could be seen only by the glow of their cigarettes. A few spotlights filtered dim rays of light on to the tiled floor. Kad moved carefully through a maze of tables. People stretched out hands to help him on his way.

Kad walked along a passage-way. Behind him, the singer's voice was fading away.

Alassane was dining with the dancer they had seen that morning after the press conference. A table-lamp with a yellow shade cast a mask-like glow on his face. His companion had her back to the door. The back of her black satin dress was a very low-cut V.

'Evening, all,' said Kad upon reaching their table.

'At last! At last!' exclaimed Alassane, looking up. He had loosened his tie, unbuttoned his jacket and laid a napkin over his pot-belly. 'At last ... Natou ... you now have before you the famous Kad. The famous tree! This is Natou,' he added offhand, as if pointing out a new purchase. 'We've eaten already. The mutton is good ... Grilled chops.'

'I've already eaten.'

'And I was waiting for you!'

'I hope I'm not disturbing you, at least?' asked Kad without responding to Alassane's remark. He had thought the two of them would be meeting alone.

'Not at all! I asked you to come. One should always mix business with pleasure.'

'I've always wanted to meet you,' began Natou.

She moved her handbag from the chair next to hers. The lighting, and her outrageously bleached skin, made her look pumpkin-coloured. Sitting down, Kad smiled and thanked her.

Alassane moved the pail containing the bottle of wine, and suggested:

'Shall we stay with Médoc, or would you prefer a *digestif*?'

'*Digestif*,' piped Natou, moving a shoulder forward with a winning smile. Her low-cut dress displayed her small breasts, with which she was very pleased. Two gold chains trickled down between the two globes.

Alassane raised his arm and snapped his fingers.

'Three double Napoleon brandies,' he told the waiter. 'Unless you prefer something else?'

'Napoleon will do fine,' answered Kad.

'So you're Kad! I've read all your articles. My brothers recite them,' said Natou. 'I was saying to Alassane that we performing artists should be written up, to make us better known to the people.'

'A great idea,' added Alassane, seizing on the topic to draw Kad into the conversation. 'If he writes it, I'll publish it.'

'Will you really, darling,' she cooed, pouting. She acted out her life, especially with men. She could already see herself handing out autographs.

'At the moment, Mademoiselle, I've got some urgent work to do. But Alassane's the boss; he can designate another journalist for the job, if he can't do it himself.'

Alassane smiled calmly. Kad had turned the tables on him.

148

Natou's anticipatory delight melted away, like a lump of shea-butter in a heated pot. Her slanted eyes fastened on Alassane.

'I'll put a journalist on the job. You'll have your picture in the *Daily*,' said Alassane to soothe her, not wanting to lose his prey.

The waiter set down three glasses and served their drinks. He took away the remains of the cheese course.

'Let's drink the health of women.'

'Yes, yes,' applauded Natou.

'To one woman,' replied Kad.

An Epicurian, Alassane smacked his tongue. Sudden bursts of laughter coming from the beach made him turn his head in that direction.

'There are people who live, who take advantage of life.'

'Do you want to go for a swim?' asked Natou.

'Later,' answered Alassane, in a detached proprietary tone. After a sip of brandy, he addressed Kad: 'I've seen your boss! He's not keen to give you a week's leave, even without pay. I may be able to help there.'

'So long as it's not with a doctor like Prof. Fall,' quipped Kad, startled at the mention of his request for leave. This morning he had asked his employer for a week off — in private. he returned to the topic: 'You saw my boss today?'

'Yes, we talked about you. You know that the *Tubabs* are getting complexes, now that we're asserting our own personality. It seems you're putting the finishing touches to a special piece ... That interests me.'

'I'll leave you two alone for a moment. Take advantage of it! I came here to have a good time,' announced Natou as she rose. She had belted her tight-fitting dress with a triple strand of beads.

'It's getting harder and harder to find a real black woman. The African woman is losing her personality with all those bleaching creams,' remarked Alassane, his gaze following Natou's skinny rear.

Kad lit a cigarette.

'I intend to create a forum for open debate, give intellectuals and cadres free access to the paper. I've even found a title: *"GEEW"*. Yours would be the opening article. Three quarter-columns on the front page, the rest on page two. You can be in charge. Believe it or not, your boss thought I wanted to lure you away from him ... But let's talk business. You've hit on a great topic: "Democracy and its problems in Africa". I really like it.'

'I doubt if you'll publish the article.'

'Why?'

'Because it won't suit your rag's political line.'

'I intend to make the *National Daily* the best paper in our part of the continent.'

'Your subscribers must have cancelled their subscriptions,' remarked Kad sarcastically.

His tone hurt the director's tender feelings. He concealed this, however, and said:

'I'm tired of cinema programmes and stories about stray dogs.'

'Now that really is something! You're going to break new ground, Alassane!'

'I'm going to change the paper's profile.'

He was interrupted by a sudden uproar. At the next table, two couples had burst out laughing. A bottle of Johnnie Walker had broken, and its scent was filling the air. One of the men bent down and dipped his forefinger into the liquid on the floor, then touched each of their foreheads in turn. 'It's your fault, you wouldn't pour a drink for the ancestors,' joked the other man. 'In that case, the shades of the ancestors have had their ration for the year,' replied the first man in his role as fetishist.

Alassane sententiously murmured: 'They ought to keep an eye on club members. Things are getting out of hand.'

'Is it true that the President is ill?'

'We were both at the press conference this morning. You don't believe anyone.'

'I know that Mapathé and Prof. Fall are lying. Why?'

'Yes, why?' asked Alassane.

'I was hoping to find out from you.'

'Why don't you believe them?'

'Because of what I hear from Radio Street-Corner! And I've found out a lot since this morning. Besides, I'm not a woman, nor a piece of capital; why are you so interested in me?'

'It's up to me to find out whether I can make capital out of you. Intellectual honesty requires that one check all facts thoroughly before writing anything.'

'Oh?' said Kad, startled at this lesson in professional ethics. 'What's going on, Alassane?'

Alassane refrained from replying. Skirmishes between the two clans were becoming more and more frequent. Tactical withdrawals and alliances were being made.

'You seem to forget that I'm a member of the PB and in charge of the government press.'

'What are things like in your PB at the moment? Daouda, the heir apparent, is being challenged by Mam Lat. What is the patriarch, Léon Mignane, doing about it?'

'He's legitimate. In democratic terms, he's legitimate.'

'Who?'

'Daouda! Is there any other PM?' asked Alassane. At the next table, they had started on another bottle of Johnnie Walker.

150

'What do people have against Daouda? His loyalty to the Father of the Nation?' Alassane inquired.

'What else?'

'What do you mean?' snapped Alassane, his mouth twisted into a scowl that flattened his chin.

'Why do his colleagues want to get rid of him?'

Alassane downed his brandy in one gulp, and licked his lips greedily.

'Jealousy! Jealousy *rek;* just jealousy. We must adapt to modern times. Mam Lat is a feudalist. A megalomaniac.'

'It's an explosive situation.'

'Now you understand,' said Alassane in a friendly tone. 'Democracy is in retreat. Anything could happen.'

That last remark made Kad think of his article. He began to ask himself questions. 'Why did Léon Mignane persist in his choice of Daouda, against all advice? Was he, Léon Mignane, paving the way for . . .?'

'Talking to yourself, are you? What are you thinking about?'

The question was accompanied by a slap on the back.

Kad looked closely at Alassane before answering.

'Nothing.'

'Forget about your article . . . Don't be a bloody fool. Put your money on a winner. I've a tip for you; it's worth a fortune.'

'I don't understand what you mean.'

Alassane leaned closer. By the light of the table-lamp, his eyes were gleaming slits between his lashes. His voice became confidential:

'You and I know the power of words. We know how much influence a leading article, favourable or unfavourable, can have on our government and the political class as a whole. You're not just anybody. You have a name, a reputation, a readership. You're a maker of opinion. So I suggest you forget about your . . . personal choice, and write about how Mam Lat Soukabé's mismanagement of the economy is leading the country to bankruptcy. That's what's important at the moment.'

'Why don't you write it?'

Alassane leaned back. The two columns of fat at the back of his neck relaxed into their usual folds. He glanced at a waiter carrying a drink-laden tray.

'The thing is, the article would have more effect coming from you, over your signature. In our profession, you work for whoever pays. My suggestion is perfectly straightforward.'

'Frankly, there's nothing much to choose between Daouda and Mam Lat. Mam Lat may be a nasty piece of goods, but Daouda's not much better.'

151

'So who do you attack first? Whoever is not with me, is against me; that's a well-known saying. What difference is one article more or less going to make to you? Just a name at the foot of the page. And twelve hours later that page will be wrapping food in the market-place . . . unless it serves as toilet-paper for the troops.'

Alassane continued, in the condescending tone of a man in the know:

'Our continent's evolution is a very delicate thing. It has its ups and downs. Let's say we're in a down phase at the moment. Don't make yourself enemies. Unfortunately, our government has to use force to maintain its authority.'

'So when things aren't going well, you suppress criticism. That's passive fascism . . . African-style.'

'Straight away, you use the jargon of the European Left. Why should preserving democracy in our own way be considered passive fascism?' asked Alassane, drinking out of Natou's glass.

'I'm not for sale. Not for Daouda, not for Mam Lat Soukabé; they're both the same. A dead fish rots from the head down; that's what's happening now.'

'Very well! Very well!' said Alassane. 'I suspected you were a communist, and you've just given me a fine display of your convictions.'

'Whenever you want to destroy someone in public opinion, you brandish the spectre of communism. People who stay in power that way are potential killers. There's no real difference between the champions of *apartheid,* and many of our independent states. Tell Corréa and Diatta to stop having me tailed. I've nothing to hide. You'll be reading my article.'

'All the editors of publications based outside our borders know that we have . . . the best customers. For a business manager, it's the market that counts. What's an article . . . to a businessman who risks losing customers. Natou's coming back,' he warned. 'You're being a bloody fool.'

Natou's dress clung to her body like a second skin. As she crossed the brightly lit floor, she knew men were eyeing her covetously.

'Here I am again,' she said.

'Let's dance,' said Alassane, proffering his arm.

Natou bounced away beside him. Alassane was twice her size.

Kad was furious. They were trying to intimidate him. The threat levelled at him was the threat that hung over the entire country. Which group would win out? And what would it do to the country? He turned and gazed at the diners. They were all members of high society; all in charge of the nation's affairs, working for a government on the brink of collapse. He swallowed his brandy and walked down to the beach.

The sky was studded with stars. The lights of boats further out pushed the cloud-heavy horizon into the background. The sinuous curve of the coastline was marked by lamps, their light reflected on the dark water. Laughing swimmers gambolled, draped in night. Gentle waves spread their tongues of damp phosphorescent foam, murmuring in monotonous repetition.

'Their present attitude is a foretaste of the way they'll behave when the article comes out,' said Kad to himself. He smoked cigarette upon cigarette, pacing along the beach. Then he went back to the restaurant.

'You haven't been waiting too long?' he asked Madjiguène.

'I'm here,' was her only answer.

'It's good to see you again.'

'What did you do to the doorman?'

'I pulled the Léon Mignane-socialism trick.'

'Is that so!'

They burst out laughing as they strolled hand in hand into the night-club. On the dance-floor, they fitted together to the rhythm of a bolero . . . a very, very slow rhythm.

Kad and Madjiguène left the '3 Filaos' at about four in the morning, without having seen Alassane or his partner again.

Opening the door of the BMW on the driver's side, Kad noticed a folded sheet of paper slipped between the windscreen-wiper and the windscreen. He lit the overhead light, glanced at it and said: 'Let's go.'

'What is it?'

'Round one,' he said, handing her the paper.

He drove up the steep slope by the Hotel Téranga, then round Place de l'Indépendence.

There were police cars parked at every intersection.

Kad bought a loaf of fresh bread at the Médina bakery, and they went home.

Lawbe – the dog – barked with pleasure at seeing his mistress again. He tried to come into the sitting-room, but Madjiguène ordered him to stay outside. Lawbe took his orders in Wolof.

'The process of disintegration is under way,' said Kad, rereading the denunciatory leaflet for the third time.

'Who wrote it?' asked Madjiguène.

'I suspect Mam Lat and Dioulé's clan.'

'But they don't say anything about Léon Mignane.'

'Léon must be really ill. Unless he's keeping something under wraps. This leaflet is really very revealing.' He leaned back on the couch.

'Do you think people will do anything?'

'There's one item of information I'd need before saying anything: on what side is – or will be – Léon Mignane ... Well ... Do you want some coffee?'

'No, hot chocolate.'

'Chocolate's fattening.'

'You'll give me a massage,' she said, removing her high-heeled shoes.

'I will, will I?'

'Yes.'

CHAPTER 24

Sunday

The inhabitants of Dakar-Plateau woke with a shock. Sunday morning was usually as peaceful and lazy as still water. The leaflet entitled 'How to rob the nation legally' was discussed everywhere. Its content, revealing corruption, nepotism, embezzlement and squandering of public funds, was greeted with indignation. The information given was so precise that no reader could remain indifferent. The names of the beneficiaries were quoted: top officials, ministers, deputies, departmental heads, directors of parastatal companies and companies where the state was a major shareholder ...

Courtyards, streets, squares, shops and markets were forums for debate on the subject.

The afternoon's soccer match between two top teams was relegated to the background.

Crushed by taxes; crushed by housing levies on wretched salaries, while living in crowded unhealthy slums; crushed by the special development tax, when monthly wages were no longer enough to provide for the individual's basic needs, and he had five, seven, nine, eleven, up to twenty-five mouths to feed as well; crushed by the insolence of technocrats and executives riding past in luxury cars with their wives, while their children, maids or stewards were driven to school or market in official cars; crushed by want ... by lack of schools, hospitals, dispensaries, maternity clinics, while luxurious villas were being built for the ruling class; crushed by unemployment; crushed by the need to educate their children, the people were ready to heed such a leaflet.

Elderly people were content to evoke reassuring ideas, and hope that God would provide the solution.

Such was not the case with the young (both girls and boys). They had known neither the colonial era, nor the Africa of old and its religious practices. Old Africa and its morality, that of the grandparents and parents of today, no longer satisfied them. The relative freedom of speeches made at celebrations, inaugurations, festivals of culture, honouring the culture of the past, praising African solidarity and African democracy, did not flatter them; it meant nothing to them.

They were born at the time when the now defunct system was passing from the scene, having corrupted and eroded their society. Disappointed in those who were running the country, they had no way of expressing themselves other than violence. For the resignation of older people, moderate and timorous, had been replaced by a new ideal: the cult of bravery, of daring, of economic and political nationalism. Their times were rich in people's heroes who had died fighting, exemplars of the same struggle being fought in many places: their names were Nkrumah, Sékou Touré, Frantz Fanon, Amilcar Cabral, Steve Biko, Che Guevara, Patrice Lumumba, Neto, Uncle Ho.

Their spiritual capitals were in turn Hanoi, Havana, Accra, Conakry, Alger, Maputo, Luanda, Soweto, Dar-es-Salaam. They expressed themselves freely, and found themselves writers and thinkers near to hand, on African soil: Fanon, Cabral, Nkrumah, Pathé Diagne, Mongo Beti, Amedy Dieng, Nyerere, Cheikh Anta Diop.

Trusting in their instinct, aware of their parents' unspoken discontent, they roamed streets and avenues, smashing everything in their path: traffic-lights, police cars, buses.

During this violent Sunday, youths and girls still at school, well-informed about new methods, used a new urban guerilla tactic, borrowed from the young *fedayeen* in Zionist-occupied territory. The system consisted of burning in the streets heaps of tyres on which petrol or paraffin had been poured. Thick clouds of smoke rose, giving off stifling heat and a nauseating smell. The intense heat emanating from the heaps detonated the police's ammunition and tear-gas canisters.

Neither the fire brigade nor the police dared venture into this sea of flame.

Violence had taken over the streets. Confrontations between young people and the police were reported everywhere.

By two o'clock in the afternoon, the city had taken on a new aspect. The soccer match was postponed.

CHAPTER 25

Monday morning

Buses and vans carried throngs of workers towards the city centre, the harbour, the industrial areas. Anonymous, the passengers observed the coercive presence of the Legion of Intervention. Their unhappy glances, their gestures, their voluntary silence betrayed suppressed anger.

The five main streets into the Plateau area were cordoned off. Annoyed drivers waited at check-points.

Trouble was sparked off again at the *lycée,* where a platoon of *gardes mobiles* had forced their way in. In less than half an hour the establishment had become a fortress where *gardes* and teenagers fought. Pupils spread through the city, taking over other private and public establishments, even the university.

Conflicts multiplied all over the Cap-Vert area. Pupils, students and the people plundered and destroyed everything ... The police could no longer control the situation.

As the morning wore on the Plateau, the heart of the capital city, was dying from inactivity. The silent streets, without the flower and vegetable sellers, peanut vendors, lepers, beggars, pedlars and cripples, who usually thronged outside chemists' shops, banks, stores and grocers', sank into melancholy depression.

Expatriates drove their offspring home, and contacted their consular services.

Lebano-Syrians long established in the country, new arrivals escaped from the hell of Lebanon, and their sons, usually much in evidence showing off their motorcycles, all stayed home in the family apartment buildings.

Outside the Plateau area, pitched battles were being fought.

CHAPTER 26

Corréa had woken that Monday with a dreadful headache. The pouches under his eyes were swollen. His face had taken on the baked-earth colour of the Niayes sand-dunes. Like a sudden epidemic, his hair was falling out by the combful, while thick tufts were sprouting in his ears. His electric razor scraped his flabby cheeks. He stretched the skin, to let the blade shave closely. When he passed his fingers over the shaven area, it felt rough. He used all kinds of lotions to soften his skin , but in vain. He examined his face in the mirror. His complexion was blotched with blackish broken veins, spreading over his cheeks and the bridge of his nose. 'I must have some tests done,' he said to himself.

Yesterday, Sunday, he had spent working with the various security services.

In the afternoon he had gone to the stadium with his staff, to support the police team. For Corréa, a police win would be his own. His ambition was to overcome prejudice, to erase from public consciousness the idea that the forces of order are by definition repressive. In keeping with this aim, the city's security forces took part in all sporting and cultural events.

Although the sky was overcast, the stadium was filled to overflowing with a brightly coloured throng. Vendors circulated, hawking fruit and refreshments. A dull roar rose.

At a distance, over near the east side, myriad leaflets were fluttering about, landing on the heads of people who occasionally scuffled to retrieve them.

The same thing started over on the west side, causing an uproar. The shouting grew louder.

From his seat – in the official stand – Corréa thought it was an advertising campaign. But as as mass agitation spread to other parts of the stadium, he asked Bounama: 'What are those papers?' Bounama ordered a policeman to bring him one. At that precise moment, leaflets landed near them. Corréa read the text. Raising his head, he glanced about him, and saw only pairs of eyes gazing hungrily at him. He was the only government representative there.

Some over-zealous policemen tried to collect the leaflets. Shrill whistles blew from one end of the stadium to the other.

The crowd reacted with aggressive gestures, brandishing the leaflets. One part of the stadium after the other took up the hostile shouts: 'Down with the police, Down with Corréa,' 'Government of thieves.' Projectiles were thrown at the forces of order standing at the foot of the stands, a position from where they could not defend themselves ... Seeing that they were a minority, the security forces decamped.

Corréa escaped, under escort.

The match was postponed.

In the 'Coffin House', the news coming in from the different areas of the city was highly alarming. Unrest, like a malarial fever, was spreading all over the capital.

Corréa rang Daouda at the Little Palace (even on Sundays Daouda always had work to catch up with). They decided to meet at the President's office, along with Wade.

After reading the leaflet and briefly analyzing its contents, they agreed that only Mam Lat Soukabé could be responsible for such calumny. The names cited, the bank account numbers revealed, the descriptions of villas could only have been supplied by him.

'We must have him arrested for incitement to rebellion, spreading false news, slander, etc. . . .' Wade suggested angrily . . .

Corréa's telephone call had interrupted him while he was making love to his third wife.

'We must first restore public order. The whole police force is on the alert. The Legion of Intervention has been called out. I must acknowledge, however, that the young people are a bit of a handful for them . . .' admitted Corréa.

'The army must take part in maintaining order,' said Daouda, looking at Wade.

'I will order General Ousmane Mbaye, Chief of Staff, to occupy public buildings.'

The three of them decided to carry out the emergency plan. Neither yesterday, Sunday, nor this Monday morning, had there been any indication of social peace.

This Monday, Corréa's morale was sub-zero. He was beginning to worry, and to ask himself questions: 'Will the operation be a success?' The radios of neighbouring countries, as well as European stations, were broadcasting news about *the tragic situation in Dakar*'. Commentators kept busy suggesting hypotheses and drawing their own conclusions.

Daouda ordered him to set up a crisis committee as soon as possible, and chair it himself.

He set up a crisis committee with a judicious choice of men, including Baïdy, the Commander of the Legion of Intervention, who had been to Coëtquidan. Ten years earlier Baïdy had led an attack on trade-unionists that resulted in two dead and many wounded. A slip-up. For years he had been eager for promotion. Now there was an opportunity to distinguish himself.

Then there was Médoune, Governor of the Cap-Vert Region and District Administrator: a politician.

Diatta, who viewed the course of events scientifically, was on the committee. His task was to discern trends.

Also Wade, the Minister of Defence, was included. He was surly, nursing his bad temper.

Since yesterday, the behaviour of the Armed Forces had been equivocal. They had maintained a benevolent neutrality towards the demonstrators. Officers had retorted to legion men: 'We've not received orders to fire.'

At 9.15 a.m., the members of the crisis committee met. Adolphe was chatting with Diatta and Corréa. The President's adviser kept blowing his nose. He was sniffling, and said over and over: 'Today's weather is worse than the *simoon* in Ténéré.' Few of them knew that corner of the Sahara.

Diatta was giving details on the rout of the forces of order. He expanded: 'The present disturbances against the Establishment aren't based on a true ideology. That is to say, they don't stem from the fringe of the legal opposition ... nor from the small clandestine opposition groups. If you look at the leaflets carefully, you'll see that there's no call for workers' rights there, nor any political slogan. It's politicians' politics.'

'What about the legal opposition?' asked Corréa.

Diatta glanced at him with bloodshot eyes.

'They've been taken by surprise by the scale of unrest. If the leaders don't come out in support of the young people, they'll be taxed with being a collaborationist opposition ... On the other hand, the legal opposition can't risk the government accusing them of causing unrest, which might mean being declared illegal.'

'So who's manipulating the people?'

Diatta looked sideways at the governor.

'Is there someone? A foreign country? An imported ideology?' rattled off Médoune.

'Mam Lat Soukabé,' said Diatta with offhand insolence.

Corréa, who knew what was really going on, chose to look elsewhere. Adolphe snatched another Kleenex from his box, and emitted three incongruous sounds. Wade was tense. Baïdy lit a cigarette. He was furious: 'What are we waiting for? Just order an attack!' The name of Mam Lat Soukabé had cast a pall over the gathering.

Diatta waited until Adolphe had finished titillating his nostrils before proceeding.

'Mam Lat has had talks with right-wing elements: the Muslim religious leaders, community leaders, a fraction of the Arabic language and Francophone intelligentsia, the mollahs and ayatollahs, and dissidents within Léon Mignane's party.'

'Léon Mignane's party is the ruling party,' interrupted Wade.

'Please continue, Diatta,' said Corréa, exchanging a glance with Adolphe.

'This evening there will be a gathering at Mam Lat's house. Dioulde Sall, Doyen Cheikh Tidiane's elder son, is his right-hand man. Their aim is to topple Daouda . . .'

'What is their political line?'

After this question, Adolphe sneezed, and dabbed at his nostrils before wiping his eyes.

Diatta was conscious of the impact his answer would have. His tawny left eye followed the sinuous trail, now dry, left by dew on the window-pane. He stated in an impersonal tone of voice:

'It seems possible that this dissident fringe of the majority party now in power, might carry out the same policies as Léon Mignane . . .'

'As the President of the Republic! Show some respect for supreme authority,' objected Wade, seeking to assert himself over this young whippersnapper.

'Minister, I have shown no disrespect for persons or for their office. My job is to present the facts . . .'

'All right! All right! Nothing else?' asked Corréa.

'Kad, the journalist, is up to something. He's preparing an article . . . He's met with the communists, Doyen Cheikh Tidiane, Mam Lat's clique. On Saturday evening he had dinner with Alassane, of the *National Daily*.'

Corréa and Adolphe gazed at each other. The former shook his head, to indicate: 'He didn't accept.' The latter bit his lower lip.

'Kad is a very good journalist,' remarked Médoune, for whom moral qualities were enough to safeguard people.

'He can be neutralized, as can Mam Lat Soukabé. We know where to find them. True, Mam Lat is a minister. But in these troubled times, no minister can be guaranteed parliamentary immunity.'

Baïdy saw the two ministers glance at him sharply. He realized his mistake, and looked away fidgeting with his beret, stroking the badge with his index finger.

'We could arrest the leaders of the students and pupils, and enlist them by force in the army. The others could be kept in prison,' suggested Wade, for whom this was an ideal solution.

The sudden dislike Diatta felt towards the Minister of Defence, confirmed his deductions. This older generation daren't call a cat by its proper name. Unable to control himself, he burst out:

'Arrest! Arrest! Then what . . . ward off the storm? That won't get rid of the root of the trouble.'

'Are you by some chance on their side?' asked Wade. That generalization was too rationalistic for his taste.

Diatta laughed briefly, creasing his owl-like face.

'Everyone's entitled to an opinion.'

'I'm going to see the doctor,' said Adolphe, holding his hand to his forehead.

'Perhaps you have flu?'

'That must be it . . .' he said, moving towards the door.

Early this Monday, he had had a talk with the local agents of the SDEC. Léon Mignane's succession was now assured.

CHAPTER 27

Blood attracts sharks. The young people rushed towards strategic intersections. Running wild, they attacked police stations, armed with pepper and . . . Molotov cocktails.

In the streets, teenagers checked cars, stopping all vehicles marked SO (*Service Officiel*). The drivers, and passengers if any, had to abandon the vehicle and proceed on foot.

'Get out, old man.'

'Why?'

'Why are you driving a SO car?'

'I'm the wife of . . . the father of . . . the uncle of . . . the mother of . . . the son of . . . the daughter of . . .'

'What about us, who are we?'

'Yes, are we the bastards of Independence?' thundered a voice.

The others took up the question in chorus.

'Get out, old man,' the first youth repeated firmly.

The driver reluctantly complied, objecting:

'It's not my car; it belongs to the state.'

'We are the state,' announced the youth, who seemed of the stuff that makes leaders.

'Children, I live far from here,' whimpered the woman passenger, extricating herself from the car.

'Our mothers, fathers, aunts, sisters and brothers walk miles and miles every day . . . And petrol is very dear . . .'

The leader banged the door shut.

'You'll end your days in prison,' shouted the driver angrily.

'If that's so, Pa, before leaving you can dance for us.'

Straight away, the car became a drum. The rhythm was accompanied with clapping and clicking tongues. A beat was established. A circle formed about the old man. The boldest youth, his face hard, pushed him into the *geew*.

With tears in her eyes, the woman begged for mercy.

'Lift your feet, old man! One . . . two . . . One . . . two . . . three . . .

That's it, Pa ... One ... two ... three ... Once more ... lift your feet ... Pa.'

The atmosphere was one of laughter and merriment. Their childlike gaiety spread; the woman wiped her tears and laughed with them.

'Let him go ... on foot,' ordered the youth.

The *geew* opened.

The driver and his companion moved off resentfully. But the man had kept the car keys.

Such scenes were repeated in many places.

CHAPTER 28

Since Saturday, Mam Lat Soukabé hadn't been wasting his time. A master of ambiguity, he had had talks with many people, while remaining within the bounds of the ruling party.

Saturday night and Sunday morning, he had hired unemployed men to distribute the leaflets, thus spreading them throughout the Cap-Vert area. He was not displeased at having caused the soccer match to be postponed.

He was busy recruiting allies and companions. But there was one man still missing from his list.

That Monday morning at 9.30 a.m., he stopped the black Peugeot 604 belonging to the Speaker of the National Assembly, by hooting loudly. 'That Mam Lat really lacks breeding,' said Magatte Kane to himself, instructing his driver to stop.

Mam Lat had (almost) leapt from his car, to stride briskly towards the 604. Gripping the handle firmly, he opened the door, while saying:

'Speaker, I rang you up at home ... yesterday and this morning.'

'Didn't they tell you? I left a message,' replied Magatte Kane. Slightly stooped, he emerged from his vehicle.

Magatte Kane, in his sixties, dressed with discreet elegance. Sober and courteous in manner, he had the ready smile and enduring patience that went with his position as Speaker of the National Assembly. During parliamentary sessions, from his seat at the rostrum, his gaze (his spectacles had a magnifying effect, and made his eyes look huge) swept the hemicycle. He would notice if a deputy were dozing, or talking with a colleague, or behaving in a manner inappropriate to the time and place. And before introducing the next orator, he would make remarks such as: *'Monsieur le député* So-and-so, our House is not a dormitory . . . please show some respect for your voters, at least.' Or: *'Monsieur le député,* the election campaign is over and done with,' when the man was over-talkative.

Magatte Kane's driver brought him his Eden hat. He put it on, tilting it slightly towards his right ear. 'Thank you, Abdou,' he said.

'What is it?'

'The situation is serious,' said Mam Lat Soukabé in an offhand manner. 'It's about the Venerable One.'

'Dead?'

Magatte Kane's face grew sombre. Ominous spots flitted before his eyes. These past few days, alarming news had been reaching him. The Venerable One's illness had taken on an unusual dimension. The deputies had plagued him with questions. 'I've spoken to the Prime Minister on the telephone. He assured me that the President's condition is improving.' He gave the same answer to each of the hundred deputies.

'Worse than that,' said Mam Lat, and when he saw the Speaker's rabbit eyes grow smaller, he quickly broke the suspense: 'It's Daouda. He wants to seize power.'

'How's that?'

He broke off to reply to the greeting of two deputies walking past.

'Until the Judiciary recognizes that the position is vacant, the Prime Minister cannot succeed the President,' he pursued, answering his own question.

Mam Lat Soukabé glanced about him. He then took a step nearer Magatte Kane, and confided in his ear:

'Léon Mignane disappeared on Thursday night or early Friday morning. Everything that's being said on the radio or written in the *National Daily* is untrue.'

Magatte Kane took off his hat to wipe his forehead. His gaze swept over the façade of the building, which bore in golden letters the inscription: *Assemblée Nationale.* Its windows reflected the country's flag, indistinct, fluttering in a light breeze.

Magatte Kane was a figure fairly typical of the period from the 1940s to the 1960s: a schoolteacher who had graduated from the Ecole Normale William Ponty, which prided itself on having been the seed-bed for most of the first Heads of State of Francophone Africa. (A good many of them were toppled by soldiers of the former Colonial Army.) He had participated fully in the anti-colonial struggle; had known harassment, intimidation, being shunted from one school to another and one region to another. A moderate, he espoused Léon Mignane's theory of Authenegraficanitus, and became one of his companions.

As a member of parliament, then Deputy Speaker of the National Assembly, he was the most virulent of those who attacked the former Head of Cabinet, Ahmet Ndour. He was a witness for the prosecution at the latter's trial for attempting a coup. Léon Mignane appointed him Speaker of the National Assembly, and sent him to the Palais-Bourbon in Paris to learn the ropes. For months he was the number two man in the country, until Mam Lat took his place. As the years passed, he had lost his former fighting spirit, corroded by his obsessive desire to be someone. He had finally resigned himself to the inevitable.

'Who knows about it?' he asked, repressing his private thoughts. He wanted to know if the people knew.

'The Secretaries of State.'

'Once the judiciary has done its duty, there's no question of it, Daouda will become the second President of the Republic,' he argued, out of scrupulous respect for the rule of law.

'The deputies who voted for that law were merely obeying orders,' asserted Mam Lat.

'You seem to forget that that law was the object of a referendum. The people voted for it, and the National Assembly ratified it.'

'Magatte, that law is iniquitous. No President has the right to will the Republic to another. We're neither a kingdom nor an empire. Léon Mignane perpetrated a moral confidence trick. You must consider your responsibilities.'

'Who? . . . Me . . . Why?' asked Magatte Kane, shifting his stance.

'Because the people won't let it happen. Daouda could use that clause to impose his son, or anyone else he chose, as President . . . You must consider your responsibilities and take a stand . . . now.'

Magatte Kane was displeased at this injunction. He turned his head to look at an armed policeman standing on the other side of the Etoile roundabout.

'I too had brought up the subject with Léon Mignane,' he reluctantly confided, turning back towards him.

'It's not a personal attack. All men are born free and equal,' said Mam Lat Soukabé, not wishing to offend the other man's susceptibilities on so delicate a topic as caste. He pursued, in an affable tone: 'Why not bring back the procedure formerly adopted by the First Republic? After the Presidency has been officially declared vacant, the Speaker of the National Assembly, that is to say you, acts as interim President while preparing for elections. We belong to the same party . . . Simple, no?'

'Our Constitution was patterned on the American model . . . If the President is unable to carry out his duties, the Prime Minister automatically replaces him. Furthermore, you've served under Daouda, if I'm not mistaken,' said Magatte Kane, seeking to disconcert him.

'I was the only one to object to that clause within the central com-

164

mittee. I spoke to you about it at the time. Let's be frank. When you refer to the American system, you seem to forget that over there, the Vice-President is elected. That's not the case here. We must set that right before it's too late. With Léon Mignane gone, there's going to be open struggle for power.'

'All this is ... very delicate,' said Magatte Kane, noting the Finance Minister's angry tone of voice. He glanced at his wrist-watch. 'I'm late.'

'Very well,' said Mam Lat, 'come and see me at home, this evening at nine.' Sensing the other man's reluctance, he added: 'This is a momentous time.'

The tone was peremptory.

'I'll see if I can free myself,' said the Speaker of the National Assembly. Mam Lat made him nervous; he didn't want his name to feature in a leaflet. He owed the public treasury substantial sums. To be toppled by the people's anger would be a dishonourable end for him in his old age, and would ruin his family.

'At nine o'clock,' Mam Lat said once more, looking him up and down.

They parted.

The Speaker of the National Assembly returned to his 604, a prey to contradictory feelings.

From before Independence to the present, he had thirty-five years in politics under his belt. Proud of his glorious – anti-colonial – past, he was always ready to advise young deputies, and proud to evoke key moments of the struggle.

Abdou, his driver, drove off slowly.

CHAPTER 29

At ten o'clock, Bounama came to announce that the military men had arrived. There were four, in paratroopers' dress with Bigeard-style caps. Each wore pinned over his left breast-pocket a badge engraved with his name and rank.

Brigadier-General Ousmane Mbaye, Chief of Staff, was accompanied by two colonels and by the Lieutenant-Colonel in command of Dakar-based units. General Ousmane, his paunch ballooning out like a goodsized water-jar, was wearing all his medals: those won in Indo-China, Morocco and Algeria, as well as his French military medals and those, more recent, received since Independence.

'General,' said Corréa, inviting him to take the seat opposite him.

'Thank you,' he said, and motioned the others to be seated.

The two Colonels, who looked very young, sat down on his right. One took out a packet of cigarettes, which he laid on the table.

Corréa introduced what he called 'the object of concertation'. He stated: 'The President has strongly recommended that a crisis committee be set up quickly, and he himself has appointed us to do so.' He then evoked the current situation. Disintegration of the social fabric. Insecurity. Lowered productivity. Subversive activities of agents in the pay of a foreign power. He concluded: 'The army must give up its attitude of passive neutrality.'

The Brigadier-General glanced right and left before saying:

'Thank you Minister, for your statement, and also for your sense of duty. I know all about what's going on, and has been going on since Saturday. I twice asked to speak to the President . . . In vain! Why? Now, suddenly, everyone seems to have remembered our existence . . . The Armed Forces will remain neutral until such time as they have met with the President.'

'As you know, General, the President is slightly unwell. I saw the PM this morning, and he confirmed that the Venerable One will receive you within a few days.'

'General, the capital is being asphyxiated.'

'Please express yourself more clearly, Defence Minister.'

'Impose order, General. That's what you're armed for . . . Act! . . .' said Wade. Since yesterday, he had been repeating rules and regulations that the General Staff rejected.

'Do you mean to say . . .'

'I'm telling you to shoot, General,' snapped Wade. His tone was unmistakeable.

'General, social peace must be restored. If the workers go on strike, there'll be total paralysis,' added Médoune, Governor of the region.

'You're suggesting, gentlemen, that the soldiers should fire on people?'

A corner of Corréa's mouth tightened in a grimace of pain. He didn't care for the General's brutal way of putting things, and said:

'Not fire, General . . . But enforce respect for order and authority.'

'How?'

'By intimidating them, General,' repeated Corréa.

Lieutenant-Colonel Gor Dia, a man of ascetic countenance, looked Corréa full in the face.

'It's an order, General! An order from the President of the Republic, Commander-in-Chief of the Armed Forces.'

Wade felt Diatta's gaze upon him.

The General took out a packet of Dunhills from his right-hand

166

pocket. Colonel Gomis lit his cigarette for him. Replacing the packet, he said 'Thank you, Colonel' from between clenched teeth, and inhaled deeply several times.

'I want to see the President,' he demanded.

'General, I am your minister. You must bring anarchy to a halt. We are confronted with a plot hatched by enemies of the nation. You can't deny this . . .'

Wade pushed the pile of leaflets towards the General.

'We too have read the leaflets.'

'Then what's stopping you from giving orders?'

Colonel Mané was fuming. He didn't like the minister's tone. He said to himself; 'There's nothing sour about the General. He's as sweet as honey.'

It wasn't the General's temperament that had earned him the nickname 'Sour'. He owned orchards, and needed to sell their sour fruit: oranges, mangoes, tangerines. He had contrived to force the Military Commissariat to purchase them for the troops' dessert.

'Minister, are you asking us, as soldiers, to fire on the population?' asked Colonel Mané once more, gazing remotely at Wade.

'To each his function, Colonel.'

'Where do you live, minister? . . .' asked Colonel Mané mockingly.

'I see no connection between your question and the present situation.'

'You haven't answered my question.'

'Your duty as a soldier, Colonel, is to obey the government chosen by the people of the country,' replied Wade, offended to see officers declining to take orders from him.

'That same people is also free to withdraw its support from that government. There can be no question of us soldiers forcing the people to accept a government or a set of men it rejects . . . Is that clear?'

Breaking off sharply, Colonel Mané fixed his angry gaze upon the Minister of Defence.

Diatta leaned towards Médoune, and whispered:

'Mané seems to have a sound training.'

'Are you in favour of khaki power, then?'

'All power wears an uniform: whether it consists of palm-fronds, bark, feathers, a tunic, a frock-coat, a boiler suit, a Mao outfit, a cassock or a djellabah . . .'

The Governor of the Cap-Vert Region resolved to have Diatta put under surveillance. He turned away from him to listen to the others.

'. . . it's the government that employs you,' Wade exclaimed angrily.

'Excuse me, General,' began Corréa, adopting a gentle tone of voice in the hope of defusing the tension. 'All of us, General, hold

167

high responsibilities. And these responsibilities imply duties ... I acknowledge that some tasks are more difficult than others. Unpleasant tasks of social prophylaxis are entrusted to the police, and sometimes to the army. That said, let us consider the present situation. In less than three days, our capital has become a ghost town. They're trying to destabilize the country ... To do away with the central authority. That cannot be allowed to continue.'

Corréa avoided certain words which might offend the military men's susceptibilities.

'Mr Corréa, as Minister of the Interior you have a fair number of men at your disposal. They should suffice to maintain order ... Don't you think so?' Colonel Mané spoke once more.

Corréa swallowed. He tried to forget the Colonel's accusations, and repeated:

'General, we must act.'

'Until I've seen the President, the army will maintain the status quo.'

'You're refusing to obey an order, General.'

The officers exchanged glances. Diatta noted their complicity. Corréa took advantage of the pause to add:

'General, we are only spokesmen of the President, Commander-in-Chief of the Armed Forces. It was he who suggested the creation of this crisis committee. For there is a crisis.'

'Maybe!' interrupted the General. 'Since Friday, contradictory rumours have been circulating ... What's the truth? Is the President dead? Abroad? Ill?'

All eyes focused on Corréa.

'General, the Venerable One has been advised to stay in bed by his personal physician, Professor Fall ... Do you know him?'

'By name! Well ... In order not to waste your time, could you inform the President that the highest ranks of the three Armed Forces have decided to remain neutral. We won't reconsider until we've seen the President.'

'That's an abuse of authority! You've no right to take such decisions in ... very serious circumstances.'

Colonel Mané stiffened.

'General, while we wait, things may take a turn for the worse. I appeal to your civic spirit,' said Médoune, irritated by the officers' pretensions.

'I shall have to make a report to the President and Commander-in-Chief of the Armed Forces,' said Wade.

'You're mad ... minister,' exclaimed Colonel Mané. 'You dare to threaten us!'

'Please do, minister! Please do,' pronounced the General. 'Gentlemen!'

They all rose at the same time as the General. A well-executed manoeuvre.

'General, there's been a misunderstanding . . .'

'Commander Baïdy! Commander Baïdy!' thundered the General.

The Commander of the Legion of Intervention stood to attention.

Brigadier-General Ousmane Mbaye disdainfully cast his eyes over the frightened civilians. Médoune, governor of the region, could see himself being arrested. In his mind, he already began devising his defence. He had merely being carrying out the orders of the Venerable One. A purple colour spread over Corréa's rough-skinned cheeks. He blamed everything, everything on Daouda and Mam Lat Soukabé. Diatta made ready to provide information, telling himself: 'Whatever the political régime, it will always need intelligence agents.'

'It will never be said that General Ousmane Mbaye gave orders to fire on the population. Is that clear, Commander?'

'Quite clear, General.'

'Goodbye, gentlemen. We know the way.'

Colonel Gomis, alert, opened the door.

Colonel Mané, a fine figure in his battledress, was the last to leave.

Corréa was thinking. He kept his impressions to himself. What did this exit mean? If they wanted to be rid of Wade, that was easy enough.

Baïdy had turned to Médoune.

'What does the army want?'

'I've no idea. None whatsoever. The Venerable One must take steps quickly,' answered the latter.

'My men are demoralized. You can't make an omelette without breaking eggs. I could try tear-gas,' suggested Baïdy, just as Corréa, lost in thought, moved towards them.

Diatta's face clouded. He knew the chemical make-up of his grenades: the same as the Americans used against the Vietnamese; the French expeditionary force against Algerian nationalists, and the French police against the May 1968 demonstrators in Paris; the Israelis against the Arabs and Palestinians; Ian Smith's Rhodesia against the freedom fighters; South Africa at Soweto and in Namibia; Portugal against the nationalists.

'Do it carefully,' suggested Corréa, adding ironically: 'Half a loaf is better than no bread.'

Commander Baïdy proudly put his beret back on before leaving.

'Gentlemen, you'll soon be called to another meeting.'

That first meeting of the crisis committee was also its last.

CHAPTER 30

Clashes with the Legion of Intervention were becoming more and more frequent. Pupils and students held damp rags over their nostrils to face Commander Baïdy's men. Swamped by numbers, cut off by the piles of burning tyres, the legion's men fell back behind the soldiers.

The air stank of tear-gas and the strong smell of burnt rubber.

The wide boulevard had been cleared. Pedestrians walked hastily. Further down, near the mosque, tear-gas canisters were exploding. Shouts and screams rose on all sides.

While this battle was taking place, some enterprising people took advantage of it to plunder shops.

Coming from further up the boulevard, an ash-grey van mounted the pavement, backing towards a shoe shop. 'Good shoes sold cheap,' said the sign, in black letters on white.

A stroke of an iron bar smashed the shop-window. The hefty man who struck the blow, operating with single-minded calm, struck once more to widen the opening. He entered the shop through the gaping hole. Two similarly built accomplices, in shirt-sleeves, their biceps showing, got out of the van and joined him inside.

They made several journeys back and forth, loading cartons into the van, then rifled the till and left as quickly as they had come.

Passers-by, intrigued (or pretending to be) glanced at each other. One bold man snatched a pair of shoes on display in the window.

That started off the looting.

People who lived on the boulevard, men, women and children, rushed down from their flats and into the shop. The noise attracted other looters. People fought, tearing shoes from each other's grasp. They would emerge victorious from the throng, clothing torn, bareheaded, their arms full of cartons, clutching a pair of shoes in one hand.

Apart from the uproar, two middle-aged men were bargaining.

'I have the left foot! I'll buy your right,' said the man in a khaki suit. The cut of his clothing gave him the look of an embassy or company driver. He had two cardboard shoe-boxes wedged under his arm.

'In the name of God, brother, give me that foot. You've got two pairs already,' replied the other man.

He had a bony face, hollow temples, a mouth like a muzzle. He was wearing a torn and threadbare pink kaftan. A small boy, barefoot, his skin greyish, clutched in his hand the right foot of a pair. He stared at the other shoe with great hungry eyes.

'What do you need it for? I'll buy it from you,' repeated the man in khaki.

'You're a Muslim the same as me. This child has never owned a proper pair of shoes . . . Look . . . They make a pair . . .'

He held one shoe against the other. He looked at them both closely.

A loud female voice rang out, bellowing insults against all the males on earth. People turned round to look. She was half-naked, with pendulous rolls of flesh hanging down to her hips. Two little girls were helping her carry shoes in her blouse, doing duty as a bag. The woman shouted: 'Me too . . . I'm entitled . . . We pay taxes just like everyone.'

This interlude cooled the discussion between the two men.

'Give me 1,000 francs,' said the father of the boy, seeing the other man move away.

'A thousand francs for that . . . when you didn't even pay for it? . . . You mean 150 francs.'

'One hundred and fifty francs . . .'

'Yes. What can you do with it . . . With 150 francs, you can buy a kilo and half of rice . . . Or buy him a pair of plastic shoes,' said the man in khaki decisively.

'Did you hear that, Baye?' the father asked his son, looking down. 'Only 150 francs . . . Well . . . Five hundred. It's leather . . . You work for the big bosses . . .'

Just then, the two men were jostled. Someone had snatched the two cartons from behind, and was running away. The man in khaki shouted 'Stop, thief,' chasing after a fleet-footed teenager. As he ran after the thief, he called for help. Behind him, the thief's accomplice tried to slow him down by calling: 'Listen, Dad . . . Listen, Dad.'

The youth with the cartons sprinted well away. He twice veered sharply, then disappeared from sight.

Bereft, the man in khaki stood breathing deeply. That short run had worn him out. He glanced right and left.

A wailing ambulance was driving fast down the boulevard. At the intersection, thin columns of smoke rose from the remains of tyres. A man wearing a Legion of Intervention helmet was picking up various objects abandoned by fleeing demonstrators.

The man in khaki walked on alone; cursing to himself this depraved and disrespectful younger generation. As he walked, he glanced at his one child's shoe. Over a kilometre further, he finally threw it away.

The father and son, who had been following him from afar, rushed to pick it up.

Baye pulled on the shoes without undoing the laces.

'The're not too tight, are they, Baye?'

'No, father,' said Baye, taking a few steps.

'*Alhamdulillahi!* Let's go home.'

The boy proudly glanced at his feet while trotting along beside his father.

The shoes were made of imitation leather.

CHAPTER 31

Monday, 11.07 a.m.

Daouda glanced through the document that Corréa, accompanied by Wade, had just handed him.

'The General insists on seeing the Venerable One. The higher ranking officers have formed a committee, with members from all three forces,' Corréa informed him.

Daouda turned a flat gaze upon each in turn.

'I wasn't informed that they were setting up this committee,' began Wade, who felt himself to be at fault. The military were taking advantage of the situation.

Feeling a need to justify himself, Wade avoided Daouda's dark glasses.

'At the moment, it's difficult to tell what they have in mind. You'd best summon Brigadier-General Ousmane Mbaye, straight away.'

Daouda pressed a button. Soutapha entered.

'Tell General Ousmane Mbaye I want to see him.'

'Yes, Sir.'

'Wade, go back to your ministry.'

Thus dismissed, the latter followed Soutapha out of the room.

Now that he was alone with Daouda, Corréa criticized Wade. He reminded Daouda of the importance of sacking him, along with Mam Lat Soukabé. 'We should consider making use of our military assistance agreement with France . . . as of tonight.'

'Make use of . . .' repeated Daouda to himself, without finishing the sentence. His blood suddenly ran cold, and he shivered. The silence deepened. He rose from his seat and walked towards the window.

'Call on France for help,' he said, watching two members of the Legion of Intervention going the rounds, each armed with a machine-gun . . . 'Neither our army nor the security forces have lost control of the situation. Nor have our borders been attacked.'

'The forces of order have not been able to restore peace,' argued Corréa, lifting his trouser-leg to scratch his right calf.

'What will the officers say?'

'Whether you make use of the agreement with France will depend on your conversation with the Chief of Staff.'

'Such a major decision can only be taken by the Venerable One.'

'Where is he?' asked Corréa, letting his trouser-leg slide back down.

'I'll ask you the same question. You're the Minister of the Interior. Where is the President?'

Daouda walked back towards the table, took out a bottle of mineral water, and swallowed two pills before drinking.

'What if you just took over,' suggested Corréa, knowing that the Prime Minister was the type of man that can act only when impelled from outside.

Acknowledged by all — on paper — as the official heir, he had never felt the need to rush things. Léon Mignane, over seventy, had only two or three years left in office. Then Daouda would officially ascend the throne, and everything would go smoothly: a legal take-over. Now the situation compelled him to oust his absent mentor!

'If you don't act, Mam Lat will. To get at the honey, you have to deal with the bees.'

'What about the Judiciary, the party ...'

'The party is just the guarantee of electoral support. All the people falling over themselves to join, do it for money ... Nothing more. Whoever controls the purse-strings, holds the key to people's tongues, and can make them do what he wants. The government appoints the judiciary.'

Daouda couldn't believe that the Venerable One's oldest companion was saying all this. He would have been dumbfounded at such language coming from anyone else, in different circumstances. Was Corréa trying to test him? ... To do him down? ... Why should he betray a friendship of so many years' standing? For what purpose? He remembered the day when the Venerable One had decided to sink Ahmet Ndour, Head of Cabinet during the First Republic. Ahmet had been a sincere and faithful ally. He had seen how the Venerable One had made use of Ahmet's sincerity to push him towards the brink.

'I'm not joking,' continued Corréa. 'If within twelve hours — the next twelve hours — you don't get a move on, all will be lost. Someone else will take your place. There's no question of letting the communists take over. Your potential opponent is Mam Lat Soukabé. He'll win the West's support from under your very nose. I admit that if I weren't a half-caste, born in France, I'd take power today ... this very evening.'

This last phrase, spoken with a ring of sincerity, startled Daouda. He had never thought about the colour of Corréa's skin, or his mixed blood.

'Is the Venerable One alive?' asked Daouda with considerable political tact, repressing the other questions rising to his lips.

'Yes,' answered Corréa, looking up at him.

'But . . .' began Daouda, seized with sudden anger and unable to add another word. He was frustrated. He wanted to speak.

Corréa gazed deep into his eyes and said:

'For the moment, we have to settle the army problem. I've given the legion orders to fire. The agreement with France is the only solution available. You'll have to decide.'

In his mind, Daouda was retracing the winding path that led to supreme power. He pressed the button once more.

Soutapha entered and announced:

'I've sent the message to the General.'

'Fine! Ask Haïdara to come. On the way, tell Adolphe that I want to see him.'

'Yes, Sir.'

'Give me a few hours, until ten or eleven tonight, to reorganize the legion . . . That's in case the Chief of Staff has lost control of the officers.'

They discussed the constitutional implications of the case.

They agreed that they were the legal authorities.

Daouda thought of his family.

CHAPTER 32

As of Sunday evening, Daouda thought of sending his family to safety. He thought about it at length, with apprehension. In bed, he revealed the state secret to Guylène.

'I have no one in France. Where would I go?'

'To our house. You'll be safe there, with the children.'

'Safe from what? You're my husband. I'm staying with you.'

'What about the children?'

'Is that the solution you suggest?'

'Is there any other, Guylène?'

'Have you tried to find one?'

Her voice was harsh. She had raised herself on one elbow, blinking. Daouda, lying on his side, turned over on his back. He had started, and would have to go on to the end.

174

'I'm glad you want to stay. But let's be realistic. Anything can happen, at any moment. The absence of the Venerable One complicates everything.'

'Are you afraid of being arrested?'

'Not for myself, no . . . But for my family. I know what people of my class are like. When you're down, no one helps you.'

Guylène got out of bed to look for a cigarette and ashtray. Leaning against a pillow, she lit one . . .

She knew by hearsay of the social handicap others attributed to her husband. By reading, she had learned about the intricate web of caste in Wolof, Manding and Pulaar society. She didn't want to trouble her husband with insidious questions. Their acquaintances were all members of the élite, preoccupied with present-day problems. So they feigned indifference, reduced the topic to a mere question of changing mentalities.

When they came to live in Dakar – it was the first time she had ever been in Africa – she wanted to be accepted by her in-laws. She gave financial help to her sisters-in-law, aunts, uncles, nephews, nieces and cousins.

It was Coumba – Daouda's elder sister – who reopened the hidden wound. At a child's name-day ceremony, Coumba tried to instruct Guylène in the role played by her in-laws. She took offence; losing her temper, she angrily rebuked Coumba, before witnesses. Men and women intervened to restore peace, and explain to Guylène 'their function as a collective memory'.

She was descended from victims of the slave trade. On her island, she had dreamed of Africa . . . Land of her ancestors! Land of freedom! She could not tolerate, even as a matter of form, being deemed of inferior birth. She had picked up a few Wolof words, jokes, stupid remarks: *'Bambara geec! Jam u geec!'* Those prejudiced expressions made her furious.

A few months after that incident, Coumba had come to spend a few days in Dakar, with a child she wanted to give her brother to raise. At that time, Daouda and his two children – one from Guylène's first marriage — were living in a flat. The presence of Coumba and her child created an oppressive atmosphere. Daouda wanted to consult his wife. Coumba saw matters differently. She attacked Guylène. When Guylène came near her, Coumba would glance at her with contempt.

This enmity made Guylène feel as if her whole body were on fire. This climate of tension, of insecurity for herself and her children, was very painful to her. She tried not to lose her temper . . .

'David-Daouda, do you think that if I were white, your sister would behave like that to me? We aren't going to keep that child,' she said in a hard voice.

Daouda knew what she meant. He found it difficult to defend his sister against the charge of racism.

'Try and understand.'

'What? Tell me what I can't understand. Coumba turns up and decides everything. I'm not prepared to accept everything . . . neither from you, nor from her.'

Daouda repressed the short speech he had ready on tradition, culture and civilization.

'I'm listening, David,' she continued angrily. Her heavy jaws tightened. 'I wasn't brought up in this humiliating mentality. And I don't want my children to inherit her inferiority complex; not for all the world.'

Her words wounded Daouda deeply. His present pain reminded him of the humiliating incident with Madeleine, during his student years. He could understand his wife, but he couldn't sever his roots.

During the following days, he took steps to elude his sister's influence. He refused to take on responsibility for a child not his. He kept his family at a distance. He painstakingly smoothed out the tensions in his marriage, eased Guylène's long-stifled resentment. And when the President had co-opted Daouda as Head of Cabinet, Guylène saw this appointment as a revolutionary act, overthrowing the dead hand of tradition.

'What are you thinking about?' asked Daouda, breaking into Guylène's silence. He looked at her.

A cloud of smoke half-concealed her face. In the lamplight her skin was a warm glowing calabash-colour.

'Won't this situation revive old quarrels?'

'It's all connected,' answered Daouda, having understood what she meant.

Guylène knew about the skirmishes between the Prime Minister and the Finance Minister. Mam Lat Soukabé annoyed her with his pseudo-baronial manner, his exaggerated courtesy . . . She suspected him of having illicit relations with the President's wife. 'What won't you think of next,' Daouda had said at the time.

'I'm a woman. We notice these things. The Venerable One is far too obliging towards Mam Lat.'

'Don't trust in appearances. There's nothing between Madame and that idiot Mam Lat.'

She stubbed out her cigarette in the ashtray, and set the ashtray on the floor.

'David, I won't leave you. I'm staying with you . . . and the children are staying too.'

Having said that, she slipped under the sheets and into her husband's arms. She thought to herself: 'What has happened to the wives of the heads of state, prime ministers, deputies, top officials, whose husbands are slowly dying in prisons throughout the continent?'

CHAPTER 33

Daouda was toying with his glasses, his thoughts elsewhere, looking at Corréa without seeing him. He wondered if he hadn't been weak in yielding to his wife?

'Guylène still has French nationality. There's nothing to worry about. We'll take care of your family.'

'Just as you took care of the Venerable One!' thought Daouda, before saying:

'I never held dual nationality.'

'No matter.'

Adolphe came in. His nose was as red as a ripe pepper.

'Excuse me, Sir. I was at the doctor's.'

He blew his nose and wiped his eyes.

'Any better?' inquired Corréa.

'I've some prescriptions. The chemists are all shut. But I have what I need,' explained Adolphe, as if to say: 'I won't leave you in the lurch.'

'Look up our military assistance agreements with France.'

Adolphe nodded acquiescence, after glancing at Corréa. Leaving, he bumped into Soutapha, who announced:

'The Brigadier-General is here.'

'Show him into the conference room.'

'Yes, Sir.'

Soutapha ushered in General Ousmane Mbaye, accompanied by Colonel Mané.

'Please be so good as to wait for a moment, General. The President is engaged. May I offer you something?'

'Like what?' asked the General, startled. Was he suddenly in an officers' mess?

'Whatever you like, General.'

'A Pernod . . . What about you, Colonel Mané?'

'For me? Nothing, General,' answered Mané.

'Very well,' said Soutapha obsequiously.

He went over to the built-in cupboards, and served the drink.

'Two fingers,' advised the Chief of Staff, supervising the operation.

Soutapha held up the glass, and asked: 'Is that all right?' The scent of anisette teased his nostrils.

'More water! I'm very thirsty.'

'Sorry, General.'

'Carry on, my boy . . .'

Holding the glass in his left hand, he paced up and down the room. He knew the place. Every New Year's Eve, the Brigadier-General, as army Chief of Staff, came to present good wishes for the coming year to the President, in the presence of the high-ranking officers. On that occasion, he would renew in the name of all the military men his oath of allegiance to the Commander-in-Chief of the Army. The pronunciamentos causing upheavals in one African country after another inspired in them no wish to do the same. To discourage officers from any impulse in that direction, the army's structures were modified. No military man could take part in elections, nor belong to a political party, nor voice his opinions in the press. A journalist had once asked him: 'Would the military not be tempted to seize power, should it fall vacant?' The General had replied: 'I can't see why we should ever do anything so foolish. We enjoy all the privileges of elected officials, without any of their disadvantages. We don't meddle in politics.'

He remembered past moments of pride and satisfaction. He had twice had the honour of taking part in the July 14th parade in Paris, marching from the Place de la Concorde to the Arc de Triomphe with his black troops. He recalled the great moments experienced during the years he had spent in the Colonial Army — all his youth. He had risen through the ranks, aided by his servile mentality . . . At the start of African Independence, he suddenly experienced nationalistic feelings. He returned to his country to set up the first National Army.

Today, his loyalties were divided. What was he to do?

'How do you do, General! How do you do, Colonel!'

'Ah . . .' he started, his thoughts interrupted. His lowered eyelids betrayed disappointment. 'How do you do, Prime Minister,' he said, shaking his hand. He hadn't expected to meet him; especially here, and with dark glasses. 'Maybe he's been crying! The President was like a father to him,' he said to himself.

'I see you've helped yourself.'

'No, the young man served me.'

Daouda led them over to the small table. They sat down, Colonel Mané at a slight distance. He declined Daouda's offer of a drink, invoking as an excuse the stifling weather. This led to conversation about the illnesses caused by a torrid climate. Daouda took advantage of this, to compare the state of anarchy prevailing since Sunday with unhealthy weather. He tried to convince them, and concluded:

'The present state of affairs, General, could ruin years of effort and sacrifice.'

General Ousmane had crossed his legs, and listened attentively. His sideways glance rested on Colonel Mané's face.

'We came to see the President.'

A respecter of rank, the General did not call people by name, but always by rank. His reply emerged from considerable inner turmoil.

'The President,' repeated Daouda.

'Yes.'

Daouda clasped his hands, hunched his shoulders forward. In spite of his dark glasses, he could not bring himself to look the officers in the face. For days, he had been lying to everyone. He could only keep on doing so. In his view, the monstrous fact of the President's disappearance could not be explained. Such was his blind, boundless faith in the Venerable One, that he could not consider he might be to blame. Also, he distrusted everyone. Corréa was suggesting that he take power.

'Tell the truth, Prime Minister,' demanded the General, lighting a cigarette.

'What truth, General?'

'There's only one! We want to see the President.'

The request struck him like a blow.

'I don't know.'

The atmosphere was laden with electric effluvia, growing more and more tense as silence thickened.

The General drew on his cigarette.

His military adviser (a European) had let him into the secret: 'The President's done a bunk.' He had eyed the European suspiciously, before replying: 'I hope he's not gone off with the till.' Although he did not admit it, his national pride was wounded. The adviser had added: 'The position is vacant. Now is the time to occupy it ... General.' This hint had disorientated him. A large landowner, he was about to retire and look after his property.

On his return from the crisis committee meeting, he had found the young officers ready to take immediate action. He advised them to be cautious ... not wanting to place his trust in remarks by expatriates. When the message from Léon Mignane arrived, he was relieved of his worries about, in particular, Colonel Mané.

Now, once again, his gaze met Colonel Mané's dry look. He studied the tip of his cigarette, and asked:

'Who asked me to come here, then?'

'I did, General.'

'You!' he thundered.

'Yes, General, in my capacity as Prime Minister.'

'The hell you say!' he exclaimed with an old soldier's roughness.

'What about the signature at the foot of the page?'

'It was me,' answered Daouda persuasively, persevering in untruth. 'General, it's time you knew the truth.'

'What truth?'

'About the President.'

'What about the President?'

'He's disappeared. He can't be found.'

A sepulchral silence descended upon them.

The General lit another Dunhill and poured himself another drink. The same amount. The water changed colour.

'Since when?'

'Thursday night or Friday morning, General,' replied Daouda with a feeling of relief. No more beating about the bush.

'Why did you wait until today to tell me . . .'

'In the interest of the state, General.'

'In the interest of the state!' he gibed. 'And who is the state? We General Staff officers are just trash! When I rang you in person to inquire about the President's health, you lied to me. It took Europeans, yes Europeans, to tell me the truth. I twice asked to be received by the President. No answer. And that stupid bugger [that was the word he used] Wade . . .'

This tirade was delivered in ringing tones. The General's indignation was genuine.

'If you don't want Wade any more, General, suggest someone else . . . Even a military man. But law and order must be maintained.'

Some years earlier, as a young personal assistant, Daouda had been the unwilling witness of a painful scene between the Venerable One and Doyen Cheikh Tidiane Sall. The latter threatened to leave the government, and applied derogatory epithets to the Head of State. The Venerable One smiled tamely, evoking their past, their long friendship. He spoke eloquently, and the full range of expressions of a neophyte actor flashed across his black face. He was humble, played the flatterer to hold Cheikh Tidiane. Daouda was mortified to see his idol lower himself thus. Two days later, the Venerable One gave him this advice:

'David, there is one thing you must understand. Politics is a profession these days . . . Power is strength. It's important to remember that. When the person you're talking to is stronger than you are, because he's in a position to hinder what you want to achieve, don't be ashamed to lower yourself. You'll touch his feelings. The black man is a creature of sentiment . . . of instant pride. He yields to humility. The moral of the story is: it is better to shame yourself before two eyes, than to be dishonoured in public. When your time comes, remember my words.'

Now was the time to heed that advice.

'General, I am your son [in African terms]. I was frightened. I'm not really a politician. I found myself in this position without having sought it. The Venerable One is a father to me. I was ashamed of my father . . . and for myself, his son. I acknowledge that I concealed the truth from you. I was disorientated by the Venerable One's disappearance. I need you, and your advice.'

Brigadier-General Ousmane Mbaye deflected his gaze. He was touched. His anger began to fade. He swelled his cheeks with cigarette smoke, and drew another puff without exhaling.

Colonel Mané coughed discreetly.

'The police and the legion should suffice to maintain order.'

'Yes, General,' said Daouda humbly.

'Did you receive the Armed Forces memo?'

'Yes.'

'I too must tell you the truth. We can't fire on the people. The army will remain in barracks.'

'General!'

'You must understand, son, that . . . *Caaf da Xëm*. The President has decamped . . . He's abandoned his post . . . So . . .'

'General, in the absence of the Commander-in-Chief, I enjoy the same prerogatives.'

'We're not disputing your rank, Prime Minister.'

'In that case, General, I shall have to take other steps,' interrupted Daouda haughtily.

'But my boy: *Caaf da Xëm,*' repeated the General, looking Daouda deep in the eyes.

Carried away, the Prime Minister did not heed this Wolof phrase . . . nor its meaning.

'General, I'm going to make use of our military assistance agreements . . .'

The remaining words tumbled from the Prime Minister's lips. Colonel Mané's cold gaze pierced his dark glasses. Feeling guilty, Daouda tried to justify himself.

'I'm obliged to! Obliged!'

'One piece of advice! Why not call in the Vietnamese army; they got rid of both the French and the Americans. This isn't Zaïre here, nor Bangui, nor N'Djamena.'

'You misunderstand me, General,' said Daouda, retreating. He had brandished this threat without really believing in it.

'We've understood! If we don't carry out your orders, you'll call in a foreign army. I tell you once more: *Caaf da Xëm . . .*'

'Why, General?'

'As surrogate President, you've told too many lies . . . Too many. You'll sign your first and last decree . . . Goodbye, Prime Minister.'

The General left the room with military stride, with Colonel Mané close behind him, like a shadow.

What dizzying fluctuations! What did the army's refusal portend? One more opponent to fight. Had he not been a devoted disciple of the Venerable One? An unconditional supporter? Scenes from the successive stages of his life as a subordinate, a collaborator, floated past him. They were painful memories. Why had the Venerable One chosen him? He had never been politically active, whether on the Left or the Right: he became convinced that he was being used for some purpose . . . The Venerable One was using him as a tool.

After having rebelled (mentally), he removed his glasses. The room seemed larger. At the end of the long table, the raised and isolated throne seemed to taunt him. Instinctively, with the tread of a lion, he moved towards it. Two steps away, his impulse weakened. His heart beat faster. He hesitated. The whole throne frozen, motionless, challenged him.

Daouda put his glasses back on. The throne seemed bare. The carved details were no longer visible. He laid his hand on it. The smooth polished wood invited him to sit down. He listened to his heart . . . Not a cry, not a howl. He recited the *Fatiha-al-kitab* and other incantations. His Koranic training had returned to his memory. He sat down. From the Venerable One's raised seat, his veiled gaze (because of the glasses) swept the two sides of the table. There was nothing there, just emptiness. Now calm, he felt a new sensation flooding gently through his veins. To be so close to power, and lose it? To be Number One. A man of caste, was he? Good . . . I'll play it close . . . He leaned back on the panther.

Soutapha and Haïdara burst into the room.

Without leaving the presidential seat, Daouda let them draw near under his hidden gaze. Intimidated, the two new arrivals walked along the carpet, their eyes lowered.

'Sit down here,' ordered Daouda in a relaxed tone of voice.

They obeyed. Haïdara seemed to have made himself inconspicuous. He wrinkled his nose to push his spectacles back up, a tic of his.

'I've drawn up the request,' announced Soutapha, laying down the file. He opened it in front of Daouda, then remained standing two paces behind him.

Daouda read the text, then turned to Haïdara.

'You've read it.'

'Yes.'

'You'll append your signature, and Wade's . . . It's important that the Minister of Defence accompany you.'

'All right.'

'I thought of ringing the ambassador.'

'You thought of it, or you've already done so?'

'I've rung him, Sir,' admitted Soutapha, looking at the back of Daouda's neck; for once, he hadn't turned round to look at him.

'The ambassador will be at the Ministry of Foreign Affairs in less than half an hour,' added Haïdara, a willing accomplice.

'You mustn't keep him waiting. Pick up Wade on the way. That's all, Haïdara.'

The words 'that's all', pronounced in an inaudible tone, were heard nevertheless. Haïdara, a man of the forest and permeated with the herd instinct, had seen in this occupation of the throne, the Father's place, a sacred continuity. He left quickly. He was eager to show the new leader how active he was in his service.

'The Minister of Information and the technicians are here for your recording,' said Soutapha once they were alone.

'Soutapha, who signed the summons to the Brigadier-General?'

'I did.'

Daouda turned sharply towards him.

'You forged the Venerable One's signature?'

'Me?' asked Soutapha, startled. 'Me . . . ? No . . . I always have a supply of blank sheets signed by the Venerable One . . . for emergencies.'

'You'll give me all the sheets bearing his signature. You know that he's alive.'

Soutapha nodded.

'You seem to know more than I do, Soutapha.'

'Yes, sir.'

'That's all, Soutapha.'

Daouda leaned on one elbow, to think. What kind of government would he set up? . . .

CHAPTER 34

For the past three days Doyen Cheikh Tidiane Sall had led a solitary life, alone with his wife.

On Saturday afternoon, after Kad's departure, the old couple began to look over their past.

The journalist's unexpected visit had brought a breath of fresh air. They eagerly engaged in lively controversy over dates, names and nicknames. The old woman would counter his arguments by retorting: 'Don't tell me that was before our marriage.' The corner of her eyes sparkled, like crystals bleached by the sea air. 'Before our marriage! You're a funny one, like all old ladies,' claimed the old man, intent on defending his assertions.

They spent Sunday morning looking through old letters in chests, old trunks, cupboards, files tied up with string. Hosts of cockroaches fled over the lawn. Two servants (those on Sunday duty) killed them with broom and stick. 'Must I reread all this?' asked *Joom Galle*. 'You'll have to re-create the atmosphere of each period! Remember a thousand and one details. It's very important,' *Debbo* encouraged him.

'Moving house?' asked Badou from the door, coming towards them.

'I'm planning the best seller of the century,' his father replied enthusiastically. He talked about Kad's visit. He was still under the influence of the visitor's charm.

Mother and son exchanged inquiring glances. She winked at him, and drawing nearer, confided: 'Kad forced his way in. But I'm not sorry he did.'

He kissed his mother on both cheeks, and handed her a jar full of *gongo*.

'You should disinfect your house,' he said, shaking his father's hand.

'Oh! What fragrance!' exclaimed his mother, tossing her head to shift a corner of her headscarf that was tickling her neck. *'Joom Galle,* just smell that.'

She tilted the jar in front of her husband's nose, and awaited his response.

'That's superb . . . Pre-war quality . . .'

'Thank Fatimata for me,' said the mother, closing the jar. She walked towards the porch.

'Can I be of use?'

'We're sorting out all the publications. Just put them in chronological order. You know that on Tuesday I'm starting to write my memoirs, with the help of your friend Kad. You're invited.'

'I'd rather read the book.'

'As you like.'

Cheikh Tidiane unfolded magazines, then folded them again before setting them aside. Piles of crumpled paper were forming by his feet.

Sunday passed in an atmosphere of relaxation. From time to time a yellowed photograph dating from colonial times, a view of old Dakar, of Saint-Louis, of former fellow-students, or a press cutting would pass from hand to hand.

They interpreted, commented, lingered over the picture of a long-lost friend, a family photograph, a colonial minister touring Africa

184

... That's Paris ... The Eiffel Tower ... There we're at the Etoile. A trip to Rome ... Our first sea voyage.

'A man's life is made up of a hoard of futile things,' stated *Joom Galle*.

'Not for a writer. It's a pity that only Doctor Birago Diop has left us something, with his *Plume raboutée* ... but ...'

'Badou, President Lamine Guèye wrote *Itinéraire africain*.'

'True! I'd forgotten about that. But neither of those two authors gave a satisfactory account of their times. The people play no part in their books.'

'Spoken like a true communist: the people. Already criticizing.'

'I agree with Badou there. Those two great men talked only about the place of Africa in the French-speaking world.'

'There's room for me, then!' commented *Joom Galle*.

They discussed literature. Each had his own idea on how to write a deathless masterpiece.

The old man quietly left them to it.

In his mind, he sketched out chapters. His parents. His childhood. His tutors. Arabic school. French school. His further studies. Pascal Wellé. The heyday of assimilationism. The Second World War. De Gaulle. Independence. Léon Mignane.

Badou left hurriedly at about one.

After their nap, they continued their work of sorting papers. They didn't go for their usual Sunday walk by the ocean.

At about seven in the evening, Mamadou, who had been off duty since the previous evening, returned bringing news of local events: 'The young people are fighting with the police. Buses have been overturned.' The radio stated:

Unsporting, chauvinistic elements disrupted the match which was to have counted for the quarter-finals of the National Cup.

Joom Galle flung himself on the set, hunting foreign stations in quest of information. All the broadcasts were focused on a meeting to be held somewhere. In Dakar, the International Network was relaying a French programme. 'They're all out of their minds,' he exclaimed to his wife.

'If the match has really been postponed, that means Corréa was out of his depth. That game meant a lot to him.'

On the eight o'clock news, the broadcaster said:

Deprived of an important high-level match by the fault of troublemakers, soccer fans have complained to the Ministry of Youth and Sports. Such incidents are to be deplored .

The rest of the news lapsed into complete banality. The doyen put on a record, and forgot all about it.

Early on Monday morning, the radio stations of neighbouring countries confirmed the worsening social situation. They all said the same sort of thing:

The capital of Senegal is paralyzed. Yesterday, a soccer match between the police and government employees' teams sparked off disturbances. The match has been postponed. During this same match, leaflets were distributed denouncing misappropriation of public funds and acts of corruption by certain high-placed government figures. Well-informed observers fear that the struggle between two factions within Léon Mignane's party may degenerate into rioting. The President, an elderly man, is bedridden and unable to participate in current decision-making, which causes his friends considerable anxiety.

'I've not seen those leaflets,' said *Joom Galle,* his face preoccupied.

Old Djia Umrel looked at him with the peaceful authority of wives whose gentle tyranny bends husbands to their will.

'What about ringing up the children,' he suggested, without venturing to impose his wishes.

'That's a good idea,' she replied, aware of her power.

She first spoke to Eugénie over the telephone. She complained bitterly about Diouldé, who was spending his nights elsewhere. She was just about ready to wish for the end of the world . . . 'I see, I see . . . I'll speak to him. You must have patience, my daughter. We're well . . . Have a good day,' she ended, to get rid of her. Then she spoke to Fatimata. She had the leaflets . . . Mimeographed sheets of paper. She was alone with her youngest child. Badou had gone out . . . on business. She would send the leaflets over. 'Mother, don't let *Joom Galle* go out.'

'So you think as I do.'

'Yes, mother! The worm is in the fruit. *Cëb lëkë bënë na ngi-cibir.* If you like, I'll come and keep you company.'

'Thank you, daughter. Come as soon as you can.'

'What are you saying,' shouted the old man, feeling useless.

'Joom Galle's complaining . . . I'll see you later,' she said to her daughter-in-law, before hanging up.

She went over to him and confirmed that leaflets had been distributed. She sat back in the cane armchair. She was determined to keep him home . . . like a mother with an over-active child.

'Here I am, doing nothing,' he muttered under his breath, but loudly enough to be overheard.

She did not answer, and tightened her lips severely.

The morning passed thus. The old man talked, listened to the

186

radio, went in and out of the sitting-room. She gazed at him word-lessly, as if mute. Old Cheikh Tidiane was bored to death with being isolated. He was suffering from inactivity, from the endless hours of boredom active men experience when forced to stay home. He went out into the garden. The old woman followed him.

'Why are you following me about like that?'

'I'm allowed to stretch my legs too, am I not?'

The gate creaked behind them.

'Hullo, *Joom Galle,*' called Fatimata gaily.

They kissed, before settling down under the flame-tree.

'I've brought you the leaflets.'

Fatimata opened her shopping-basket and deposited the pile of paper in front of the old man.

Joom Galle began to read the leaflets avidly.

'I'm going to get dressed,' apologized the mother-in-law, winking towards her husband.

'I've two chapters of Aoua Keita's book left to read.'

Joom Galle was thunderstruck. He had just come across a full transcript of his speech.

'Who dared associate me with this business?'

'*Joom Galle,* it's being distributed around town. You can see it's not signed.'

'That's not true ... They quote me here ... Listen ... Speech delivered by Doyen Cheikh Tidiane Sall. They've no right to use my name like that. It's dishonest.'

Fatimata remained silent.

Djia Umrel returned with refreshments. 'Look,' demanded her husband. She read. That text now took on a prophetic dimension. It increased her anxiety.

'Did you know about this?'

'Don't be silly! How could I know about it? I hadn't written any of it down at the time,' he objected, with the virulence of a man con-fronted with something he cannot change.

'True, I'd forgotten that,' said his wife, out of courtesy more than ignorance.

'Do you realize! Do you realize what a lack of political honesty. Using my name for their rubbish ...'

'At least you have a text for your book,' said Fatimata cautiously.

'Especially as Kad and his woman are coming tomorrow.'

'People will think I'm plotting with these ... these ...'

'Trouble-makers,' supplied Djia Umrel.

' ... trouble-makers ... No, boors. I'd like to go and tell them a thing or two.'

The two women occupied themselves as best they could, while

waiting for the storm to blow over. They cast sidelong glances at him. Fatimata's presence helped time to pass. But she could not stay to lunch.

After her departure, the abyss yawned once more. Now that they were alone, the demon of politics awoke in the doyen. He announced that he wanted to go out.

'After lunch, *Joom Galle.*'

He agreed. They went in to lunch. After the meal of *Cëbu Jën* the old woman brought him his coffee. He drank it, while making plans. He had some harsh things to say to ... He did not finish his sentence. He fell asleep right at the table. With Mamadou's help, the old woman carried him to bed.

As the servant was looking at her with alarm, she explained: 'I've put him to sleep. He wanted to go out.' Mamadou remained perplexed. She dared keep her husband from going out! That old woman was a she-devil.

The telephone rang. She hurried out of the bedroom; it was Fatimata. 'I've put him to sleep ... No risk. Do you think? His heart, at his age? Oh! don't frighten me, girl! Wait, hold on a minute, I'll go and see.' She went back into the bedroom. The old man was snoring, lying on his back, his mouth open. She held the back of her hand near his nostrils, and felt his breath. 'He's sleeping like an old child.' Luckily! They're fighting in town.

The hours dragged on, as did her anxiety.

At eight in the evening, she set the table and listened to the radio, walking back and forth from the bedroom to the sitting-room ... She wasn't hungry. On this day of all days, there were no calls or visits. Just Mamadou coming to say: 'He's still sleeping.'

She passed a sleepless night, starting at every noise heard or imagined. Finally, she lay down ... at his side, fully dressed.

CHAPTER 35

Monday night

Magatte Kane — Speaker of the National Assembly — was astonished to find so many people at Mam Lat Soukabé's. He cast a wary glance over the gathering: the President of the Economic Operators' Association, with the members of the board; trade-union leaders, directors of mixed-economy companies and of nationalized companies; doctors, professors, deputies led by Diouldé; members of the Political Bureau and the Central Committee; a sizeable group of women, standing to one side with the Minister for Women's Affairs; ministers and party dissidents. Leaning back in well-padded leather-covered armchairs, these people filled the sitting-room with their murmurs, drowning out the hissing of the air-conditioners. Rising cigarette smoke formed a halo round the lights. Highlights gleamed on people's faces.

Magatte Kane recognized nearly everyone. He was still at the door when he saw Elimane Baba Gaye coming towards him. There was no way of avoiding him.

'Well, Mr. Speaker, so we are orphans,' said Elimane Baba Gaye, taking him by the hand.

Magatte Kane forced himself to smile. He didn't know what meaning to attribute to those words.

'I knew it . . . I knew that no-good so-and-so would leave us in the lurch. He's left us in a proper mess . . . Do you know which African head of state visits Senegal most often? . . .'

Magatte Kane looked away . . . towards a man who was twisting his left ear lobe . . . Prudently, he widened his eyes as if to say: I've no idea.

'It's Léon Mignane!' concluded Elimane Baba Gaye, pleased with his joke.

The Speaker of the National Assembly looked at this man, whom he disliked. Elimane Baba Gaye represented tactlessness and lack of moderation. An old hand at politics, he had worked alongside him in the party. Elected as a deputy in Léon Mignane's group during the early years of Independence, he had then been excluded from the party for indiscipline and fractionalism [their word, not mine]. Tenacious and persevering, he never tired of condemning 'Léon Mignane's personal power.' A man of faith, a mosque orator, he castigated the degenerate mores of today. He was in favour of reinstating the old morality.

Elimane Baba Gaye added in a severe tone:

'You can say all you want about the liberal policies of a Houphouët-Boigny. But you must recognize things have changed in the Ivory Coast. And there's no doubt about his nationalistic feelings. He's convinced his people that the country's future is in his hands. Another Head of State who'll leave something for his people is Ahmed Sékou Touré. You can criticize his tyrannical love of Africa. But he's given his fellow-citizens a strong feeling of dignity and pride. He's made them love Guinea and Africa, by renewing the national culture. What about us? Us . . . What's the Venerable One left us? His Authenegraficanitus? Shit . . . What we'll remember is that he was the best product of the *métropole* since Faidherbe, the best proconsul sent by Paris to Black Africa.'

He had uttered these harsh criticisms with contempt. His eyes cast sparks under jutting eyebrows.

Magatte Kane, moulded by his role as Speaker, knew how to repress his own opinions.

'There's Diouldé over there. Do excuse me . . . We'll continue this interesting discussion later.'

He slipped away to join the group of deputies. On the way, Kad approached him.

'Mr Speaker.'

'There's no Speaker here.'

The Minister of Higher Education, Talla, joined them and revealed:

'The new Minister of Justice already has a file in hand: Mam Lat Soukabé's . . . Tomorrow there'll be a general strike, throughout the country.'

'Why a strike?' inquired Kad.

'You'll find out tomorrow . . .'

Magatte Kane looked around once more. His large eyes rested on people's animated faces: 'Is this movement too strong to be countered?' he wondered, panic-stricken. He remembered the time, long ago, when he took part in clandestine meetings, street fights, bill-posting at night. He felt a slight twinge of the heart.

Relaxed, dressed in a sober suit, Mam Lat Soukabé was moving between groups. He greeted newcomers, led them to a place or left them free to choose according to affinities. He came over and rested a hand on Magatte Kane's shoulder.

'Well, Speaker! I'm pleased to see you.'

'I'd promised . . .'

They glanced about them, and moved off towards the garden.

At Diouldé's invitation, they all gathered in the drawing-room. After the usual compliments and introductions of prominent people present, he began: 'This evening's meeting is an informal gathering of people who share the same concern . . . for our future and that of our country.' He went on to describe the precarious present situation 'resulting from the selfishness of a sick old man preoccupied only with his own ephemeral personal fame'. He painted a bleak picture. Daring (in words), he launched into criticism of the parliamentary group, himself included, who had voted for the clause that made the Prime Minister the direct heir of the Head of State.

He was a handsome man, and his hand-sewn suit enhanced his every gesture. To add spice to his speech and show off his reading, he quoted the writings of Mao-Tse-Tung: 'When the leaders of a people make a mistake, they drag all the people into error.' He dwelt on the reasons for his father's resignation. He asked those who had been at the National Assembly on the morning of Léon Mignane's birthday, to remember his father's speech . . .

At this point, leaflets were handed out . . .

Magatte Kane was astonished. He knew that the speech had been recorded. He had kept it in his secret archives. Only Corréa, the Minister of the Interior, had a copy.

Kad was pleased. He appropriated four copies. He had been invited to attend this meeting as an observer.

Various people spoke. They all used the same language, the same key words kept recurring. Democracy. Freedom. Respect for the people. Economic independence. They were all in favour of changing the famous clause that enabled the Prime Minister automatically to become Head of State.

Nafissatou spoke in a piping voice. She drew parallels with the deaths of President Boumedienne (Algeria) and Jomo Kenyatta (Kenya). She instanced the Republic of Haiti, where a fascist father was succeeded by his son. She concluded: 'We don't want the Government of Senegal to be handed down from father to son.' Applause greeted the end of her speech.

Elimane Baba Gaye stood up. He began to recite the *Fatiha,* his eyes closed. He evoked his personal struggle against colonialism, against Léon Mignane; his fiery gaze swept the room. He spoke in a harsh, gravelly voice, using his limbs and his whole body. 'It's time for us to tell each other the truth. We can't let Daouda inherit office. A state isn't a piece of family property. We've seen what happened in Iran. When a people is determined . . . nothing can stop them.' He ended by suggesting that only the great religious leaders could find a way out of the present confusion, to avoid a fratricidal struggle that would divide the nation. He was loudly applauded.

Mam Lat Soukabé waited until the applause had died down. As a potential leader, he spoke with condescension: 'We must avoid subjectivism. Let us be quite clear! We're not speaking of Daouda as an individual. But of a certain clause . . .'

Magatte Kane craned his neck a bit, in order to hear better.

'. . . If Daouda comes to power this way, we'll have the start of a dynasty. This could establish a statutory precedent. In the long run, the result might be the break-up of our national unity. Our Republic is made up of very diverse ethnic groups.'

Mam Lat Soukabé, jurist, diplomat, politician, explained the ins and outs of the clause in question. His tone was that of an inspired fishmonger. He displayed a thoughtful face, such as would disarm all suspicion. He suggested a goal: 'A return to the norms of modern democracy. The Speaker of the National Assembly, here with us this evening, will act as interim president pending new elections.'

The debate was launched. He acted as moderator of the palaver. Everyone felt constrained to give his opinion. Two people, however, remained silent: Kad was excluded from the discussion, and Magatte Kane refrained from speaking.

'We haven't heard from the Speaker of the National Assembly,' pointed out Elimane Baba Gaye.

All eyes converged upon him. He was not intimidated.

'Mr Speaker, the floor is yours,' announced Mam Lat Soukabé.

He rose, unwillingly. He didn't agree with them. Most of them had access to administrative channels, and could make themselves heard ... He declared firmly:

'If the people want to change the Constitution, they need only make their wishes known.'

'How?' interrupted Elimane.

'How!' repeated Magatte Kane ... 'By informing their elected representatives.'

'Don't take us for a pack of school-kids. Aren't we part of the people? Have your deputies never heard the voice of the people? Then why has Léon Mignane run away?'

'What?' exclaimed a man's voice.

'Léon Mignane is nowhere to be found. At the moment, the people are without a President. Have the people been informed?'

The collective monologue drowned out all comments.

Kad tugged Magatte Kane's jacket. The latter sat down again, eyeing the assembled throng. Kad lit a cigarette, saying to himself: 'Mam Lat's a real Jesuit. He's learned a thing or two from Léon Mignane.'

'Gentlemen,' declared a Captain in lieu of greeting, on entering the room. 'Ladies,' he added, noticing the small group of women.

The heated atmosphere suddenly sank to freezing. They all stood up, huddled together. A wind of terror blew upon their faces.

The officer was followed by two other soldiers of lesser rank. The Captain, a fine figure of a man, advanced to the middle of the room. He unfolded a sheet of paper:

'The persons whose names are on this list will come with us. The others will be free to go home.'

'What's going on?' inquired Mam Lat Soukabé.

'Yes, tell us what's going on,' echoed Diouldé.

'I don't owe you any explanations.'

'Why not? You have no right to enter people's homes like this. It's a breach of private property.'

The Captain turned on his heels and ordered the Lieutenant: 'Tell them to come in.' Immediately, a platoon of men each armed with submachine guns deployed in extended order throughout the room.

People turned round to watch them take up position, legs spread, guns at the ready.

All faces betrayed bleak fear.

'I am the Speaker of the National Assembly,' said Magatte Kane, who had pushed his way up to the Captain.

'You're to come with us,' said the Captain, after consulting his list.

'I was here inadvertently. I didn't know what they were plotting.'

'Traitor!' exclaimed Elimane Baba Gaye, aiming a blow at the back of his neck.

In less than a moment Elimane Baba Gaye was prone on the carpet, with a paratrooper prodding his belly with his weapon.

'Bring the two of them along.'

'Captain, this isn't legal,' exclaimed Mam Lat.

'Please be quiet,' interrupted the Captain. 'I'm going to read out the list of names. Those who hear their names called will please go outside ... Don't tax my patience ... Mr Mam Lat Soukabé ... Minister of Finance.'

'That's me' ...

A soldier moved up to him. They eyed each other with hostility.

'Monsieur Talla ... Minister of Higher Education. Madame Nafissatou ... Minister for Women's Affairs ...'

As the officer called their names, they filed towards the exit — between two rows of paratroopers. The others, powerless, witnessed the scene in silence.

CHAPTER 36

Before noon, in strictest secrecy, a small group of officers had held a clandestine meeting, after hearing the report by Brigadier-General Ousmane Mbaye, Chief of Staff. They considered that the decision to call in foreign troops was a humiliation for them, and decided to take the offensive.

'Have you thought this over seriously?'

'Yes, General. Forgive me, but you'd best retire from the Forces. Please sign your letter of resignation.'

Having said that, Colonel Mané took a typewritten sheet of paper from one of his pockets. Taken by surprise, the General was at a loss for words ...

'You don't know what you're doing.'

'Yes, we do, General! Léon Mignane is neither ill nor bedridden.

193

And we know what's going on behind the scenes . . . Please sign here, General.'

Colonel Mané's tone, calm and courteous, convinced the General that the course of events could not be reversed. He obeyed . . . Two Captains escorted him. Two other officers went 'to pick up the minister, Wade'. The latter confirmed that the request for assistance had been sent off to Paris. The soldiers kept him in solitary confinement. During this time, the military advisers (expatriates) were gathered together in a canteen. Colonel Mané came to tell them:

'Gentlemen, you will be our guests for a while. The higher ranking officers have seized power. We ask you to respect orders. Outside communications are not allowed. Good day.'

At about four o'clock, Commander Baïdy, Head of the Legion of Intervention, found himself alone in a cell.

Regiments stationed on the borders, and those stationed in regional capitals, received orders to close the borders, guard all large and small airfields, and confiscate or otherwise prevent the use of all amateur radio equipment.

Troops emerged from barracks with their heavy equipment: tanks, armoured cars, mobile cannons, and stationed themselves on the five main roads leading to the Plateau area. Soldiers conveyed by troop carriers took up position with their gear. Sections were stationed by French bases.

General confusion prevailed among government officials, as in embassies.

The airport was closed to traffic. Departing or transit passengers had just time enough to take off, before the landing and take-off area was obstructed by heavy lorries parked in serried ranks right on the runway.

The population was in a hurry to return home.

It was soon evening. Very soon, without twilight. The night blanketed the capital and its suburbs with a deathly stillness.

The Committee of High-ranking Officers (CHO) had sent a cable to the French, British, Soviet, American, Chinese, Belgian and German governments, as to those of all African and Arab countries, to the OAU and UN, and to all international press agencies The cable was worded as follows:

'Committee of High-ranking Officers, General Staff, Senegalese Armed Forces, have honour advise you our categorical opposition any arrival foreign troops national territory. Stop. CHO guarantees security and property foreigners resident national territory. Stop. Internal problem. Stop. Internal solution. Stop. Signed Colonel Mané on behalf CHO.'

The Committee of High-ranking Officers ordered the French Ambassador and General Bastien, Commander of the Cap-Vert base, to confine French troops to barracks. As a postscript, the CHO forbade all military and civilian flights.

General Bastien, who was expecting reinforcements from France, was disconcerted by this ultimatum. He was seething with rage. He got in touch with Jean de Savognard. 'What the hell's going on?' he demanded.

'Best do nothing, General! Respect the orders you've been given.'

'What? . . . How's that? . . . Operation . . . Ja . . . Ja . . . Damn it. (He had trouble pronouncing the word *Jaron* in Wolof). Damn . . . Operation Dolphin is under way . . . '*

'General . . .'

'Don't call me General! Just listen to me . . . Do you mean to say I'm just to sit on my arse . . . These wogs can't hold out twenty-four hours . . . Yes! Yes! . . . I know what I'm talking about . . . We're the ones who supply them with equipment and ammunitions . . . Just one day . . .'

'General, it's not a military problem; it's political . . .'

'Balls.'

'Just stay where you are! No slip-ups. Just ask the Ministry of Defence in Paris. It's political . . .' repeated Jean de Savognard before hanging up abruptly.

As soon as he had transmitted the request for application of the military assistance agreement, orders had been given to prepare the infantry companies based in Carcassonne and Castre to leave for Dakar. Eight Transalls, guided by three Bréguet-Atlantics equipped for long-distance transmission, were to convey them there.

The cable from the Committee of High-ranking Officers put an end to this plan. All Europe, Africa, Asia and the Americas were informed of the coup.

Before the plan could be carried out, the President of France, his Minister of Defence, the Under-Secretary in charge of African Affairs and their team of experts met again for the nth time. Caught between two forms of pressure, horizontal from their 'European allies', and vertical, psychological, from Africa, he decided to suspend the operation known as *Jaron*, and observe a surface neutrality.

The air fleet had left its base at six o'clock GMT, and was over the north-eastern Sahara, when it received orders to return to base, or land in a friendly African country.

That night, journalists rushed to the Quai d'Orsay, Rue Monsieur, the Elysée, in search of information. The government spokesman read them a statement:

*French military operations overseas are given code-names of tropical fish or aquatic mammals.

'We are refraining from any form of intervention. We have received the same cable as all the governments of the European Nine. We provide assistance when asked to do so. That is not now the case. However reassuring the content of this recently received message, we ask the new rulers of this country, this Senegal so dear to our French hearts! We ask them to do their utmost to protect the lives of our nationals, who went to work in their country in a spirit of self-sacrifice and humanitarian duty. As for the ex-President, Léon Mignane — that exemplary man, one of the last humanists of this century — France as a whole is ready to welcome him, and would be proud to do so. We know — through the press — that he is ill . . . Very ill. Our best doctors and hospitals are here to provide treatment for him. There is no common measure between the philosopher, the great man Léon Mignane, and the ex-Emperor Bokassa!' he said in closing, answering a journalist's question.

CHAPTER 37

Tuesday morning

'Cheikh! . . . Cheikh . . . Wake up . . . Cheikh . . .'

Djia Umrel was shaking him furiously. She rarely called him by his name; only in moments of great emotion.

'Cheikh! Wake up! The military have taken over. Cheikh, listen to the radio,' she said helplessly, sitting on the edge of the bed, both hands clasped on the old man's shoulder.

Sluggishly, with groping gestures, the man struggled to escape from drowsiness. He sat up. The skin of his face was wrinkled into folds. He moistened his lips, his coated tongue rough in his mouth, his saliva insipid. He instinctively reached for his spectacles on the bedside table.

An unfamiliar voice announced:

'Faced with a deteriorating social climate, the rule of anarchy, prevarication and corruption, the embezzlement of public funds, the systematic plundering of the national economy, the Committee of High-ranking Officers, under the direction of Colonel Mané, has been compelled to take control of the country's affairs.'

You have just heard the officer in charge of relations with the Press. This same officer stated also 'that the Committee of High-ranking Officers was prepared to return power to civilians. In the meantime, political parties are prohibited, the National Assembly dissolved, the Constitution suspended.' That, of course, was a quote.

A *xalam* solo followed.

The old man slowly and carefully got up, his limbs weak. She wanted to help him, but he pushed her arm away. Once up, he noticed that he was fully dressed. After a pause for thought, he asked: 'What happened to me?' while struggling to escape from mental confusion.

'It must have been an excess of fatigue . . . You just collapsed.'

'Maybe!' he said, moving towards the bathroom. 'What day is it?'

'Tuesday.'

'Tuesday,' he repeated, while undressing to have a hot bath . . . 'Leave the radio alone . . . I tell you, I'm starving.'

They met again at the table. Cheikh Tidiane ate with appetite. Mamadou, as delighted as a child who sees a loved one return from a long journey, waited on him with alacrity. The old woman suffered from twinges of remorse. The least gesture, the sound of an object striking another, her husband clearing his throat, attracted her gaze. She showed herself attentive to his needs, buttering his toast, touching the coffee-pot to see if the coffee were still hot. They both maintained a monastic silence.

The radio of their neighbours (Europeans) was broadcasting the same music as their own. The neighbours normally listened only to the International Network, that broadcast only in French. Today, both networks were synchronized.

Our second communiqué.

The Committee of High-ranking Officers advises all foreigners or expatriates resident in our country, whether employed in the public, parapublic or private sector, either to stay home or to go to their consular service. All schools will be closed until further notice. Public transport is forbidden throughout the national territory. All carriers, company directors, owners of businesses will be advised in due course to resume activity. This is the end of the second communiqué.

A recording of national music.

'So they've arrested Léon,' she said.

'They didn't need to arrest him to commit their misdeeds,' he said with a disillusioned air, a deep furrow between his brows. His drowsy eyes gazed at the sky. Was it the strong dose of tranquillizer? Or the sudden shock? 'I slept for a long time . . . Too long,' he kept saying obsessively.

Djia Umrel Ba lowered her eyelids. The man's suspicious gaze lingered on the woman's face. Cheikh Tidiane glimpsed guilt there. 'She drugged me,' he said to himself.

His silence widened the gulf between them. To break this denunciatory silence, that made her ill at ease, she kept asking questions about the military take-over. To be polite, Cheikh Tidiane punctuated her monologue with 'Hm! Hm! Hm!'

'Madame . . .'

'Mamadou.'

When Mamadou had that terrified, wide-eyed look, it meant he wanted to speak to her alone. Djia Umrel Ba followed him out on to the verandah. 'There's a soldier who wants to see *Joom Galle*,' he whispered to her.

'What does he want?'

'He said he wants to see *Joom Galle*.'

They went to meet him together.

'Yes, Monsieur?' she inquired. She read on the badge pinned to the intruder's pocket: 'Lieutenant Ba.' He was of the same family as herself.

'I have a letter for Mr Cheikh Tidiane Sall, from Colonel Mané.'

'The Head of the Committee of High-ranking Officers.'

'Yes, Madame.'

She held out her hand.

'I'm to give it to him in person, Madame.'

Djia Umrel looked him up and down, uneasily.

'Are you alone?'

'Yes, Madame.'

'Come with me.'

She went before him.

'*Joom Galle,* there's an officer to see you.'

He slowly looked up at the officer. The Lieutenant clicked his heels together, before handing him the letter.

Cheikh Tidiane wiped his knife and opened the letter. He read it, then looked again at the messenger.

'Shall I come with you?'

'I'm at your disposal.'

'I'll get dressed.'

He went to the bedroom.

'Won't you have some coffee, Lieutenant Ba? I too am a Ba.'

'We are related, then, Madame. I'll gladly have some coffee.'

'Mamadou, make some more coffee for the Lieutenant. Please sit down, Ba. I'll go and help *Joom Galle*.'

Mamadou muttered optimistically: 'This Ba isn't a bird of ill omen, then.'

'What does Colonel Mané want?' asked Djia Umrel when she had joined her husband.

'Please read the letter.'

She sat down on the bed, and frowned as she read the message.

CHAPTER 38

Depending on who is doing the talking, demography is a plague, a dam or a fountain of youth for African states. Economists are in favour of birth control, or family planning. For such statisticians, the growing number of children prevents the harmonious development of the country. For opposition groups, the galloping birth-rate is a good horse to ride as they denounce the ruling party for its inability to cope. Those who hold the reins of power, bewildered by the number of mouths to feed, condemned to lie, stress their efforts in building low cost housing (cages for good breeders, my aunt used to say), schools, maternity wards and workshops. Every year, they talk of readapting the plan.

Demography is the gold standard of politics.

For the young people, the result of their actions since Sunday was now evident this Tuesday. They had applauded the news of the overthrow of Léon Mignane. From dawn, like ants leaving their anthill in long processionary files, they had paraded through the streets. They encouraged the military: 'No foreign troops! No Kolwezi! No Bangui! No Chad! No N'Djaména.' The slogans burst forth in an atmosphere of youthful enthusiasm.

Two couples were walking along. The red-headed girl was pushing a pram. She had dressed hastily, without removing her curlers. Her bearded husband was carrying a two-year-old child. The other, younger couple were walking arm in arm. They were flat neighbours. They stiffened whenever they drew level with an African – civilian or military.

At the Sandaga esplanade, at the corner of President Lamine Guèye Avenue, two teenagers were taking down the sign bearing the name 'Avenue Georges Pompidou'. The (Sengalese) paratroopers standing at the centre of the intersection took no notice of them.

One of them, tall, his jeans tight over his buttocks, wearing a denim shirt, eyed the *Tubabs* insolently. He signalled to his pal, who was wearing a T-shirt with Bob Marley's likeness on it in colour. The latter was holding the street sign they had taken down.

'Going to the consulate, are you? Let us give you a hand,' the first youth offered self-confidently.

The redhead clung tightly to the pram, with a glance of alarm at her husband; he tightened his hold on the child, who began to whimper, and broke out in a cold sweat. The younger couple clasped each other more closely.

In a moment of inspiration, the lanky youth in faded jeans, with his sarcastic smile and lazy stroll, pulled out a soiled and greyish handkerchief, wound an end round his index finger and raised it on high as he headed the procession. He had seen that in a film. The second youth, wearing Bob Marley's likeness, joined him.

Was it an emblem of peace? Of human solidarity? Or an expression of triumphant vanity? Or mixed feelings? In spite of themselves, the four Europeans obediently followed him. They walked down the middle of the avenue, empty, devoid of traffic. From time to time their guide would turn round to survey his charges. The 'Baobab' (the BCEAO building) blocked the horizon. People looked at them, with their odd flag. They cut across the Place de l'Indépendance. After the Air Afrique office, on the pavement in front of the Ecole Mixte, other young people applauded them. The two Good Samaritans threw out their narrow chests under the wave of applause.

After the Nouvelles Editions Africaines, the street was blocked off. A French army commando stood guard over the embassy and consulate. Voices rose from behind the barriers.

The standard-bearer advanced to within ten metres of an armed paratrooper, a legionnaire. They eyed each other. His companion, hands on hips, stood at his side. At the sight of the Europeans, an officer opened a barrier to let them through. 'Bon voyage,' said the slim youth. A smile full of things unsaid cracked his smooth face. '*Boy nao nu go.*' Having said that, they turned back up the gentle slope.

CHAPTER 39

Taken to a cell, Daouda had quite simply fallen asleep, now that he was delivered from his fantasies. Neither the nauseating smells, nor the cold from the thick walls had disturbed him. He just lay down . . .

Last night, when a captain with his half-company had come to notify him of his arrest, he was with Guylène in the sitting-room. She had uttered a shrill cry ... or rather, the cry had broken from within her before she could cover her mouth with her hands to stifle it. Her expression was one of sheer despair. Daouda took her hands, and saw himself mirrored in her frightened gaze. They spoke to each other, each gazing into the other's eyes.

'Take care of yourself ... and the children.'

She nodded, unable to check the flood of tears flowing down her cheeks. She was sniffling.

'Listen to me, Guylène! You know Victorine ... my secretary ... Well, go and see her. She'll help you ... Don't say anything.'

She took hold of Daouda's shoulders and clung to him tightly. They stood like that for a moment.

'Come along now, Sir,' grunted the officer.

Daouda turned towards him, and chose not to engage in dialogue. He gently unwound Guylène's arms. He could hear his wife weeping behind him.

This morning he had been given some foul coffee. He rinsed his mouth with it, then was taken to the toilet before being led to Colonel Mané. In a corner of the office sat a soldier acting as secretary. Lieutenant-Colonel Gor Dia occupied a chair some distance away; behind him were the men in charge of communications. In the middle of the room were Léon Mignane and Soutapha. They were silent.

At the sight of the Venerable One, Daouda's stomach tightened in a cramp. Léon Mignane had aged. Without his daily massage, his skin had gone loose and flabby. The lines at the corners of his mouth emphasized the droop of his lower lip. His three-piece suit was wrinkled, and had lost its sharp creases; his lower trouser legs were crumpled.

'David-Daouda,' he called out in a cracked voice. 'David ... what's going on? I'm the Head of State, Commander-in-Chief of all the Armed Forces, Secretary-General of the party ...'

Daouda, seized by compassion, glanced towards the officers. He looked at the Venerable One again, and pity overcame his indignation against the military.

'... I'm still this country's President,' he proclaimed, beating himself on the chest.

He was standing in front of Daouda, who looked down upon him from his height. His eyes, striated with reddish fibres, were void of expression. There were coal-black rings under his eyes. His hair was discoloured at the roots, and had a rusty tinge. He stood on tiptoe in his kid shoes, that needed polishing, and continued his monologue:

'They want me to sign my resignation. Me? ... resign ... Out of the question, Colonel Mané. Who made you a Colonel? I did ... I ... Your pronunciamento won't get you anywhere. I'm not like some African heads of state. The people, prominent figures, will demonstrate on my behalf . . . I'm well known in Europe . . . Colonel Mané, your sedition will cost you dear . . . very dear. David, where is Wade?'

'He's been arrested.'

'Corréa?'

'Also.'

'As for me, I can be killed, but not dishonoured,' exclaimed the old man, unbuttoning his jacket to display his chest.

They all looked at each other incredulously.

'Your appeal to a foreign army has fallen through. Will you sign your resignation?' repeated Colonel Mané, pointing to the sheet of paper lying on the table.

'Foreign army . . . Who, me?' he asked. His eyes wandered from one person to another, and finally came to rest on Daouda.

Léon Mignane paused while taking a few steps backward.

'Who, me? . . . Call in a foreign army? I was ill . . . my doctor . . . Professor Fall can tell you so. General Ousmane Mbaye can testify to the fact as well . . . Corréa . . . Young Soutapha here too . . . No! . . . No . . . It wasn't me. David! David, what have you done? So it's you . . . You alone, with your ambition . . .'

Pointing his index finger at Daouda, he proceeded to exculpate himself. His wrinkled face became animated. He flashed a brief seductive smile, and glanced sideways at the soldiers before continuing his speech.

' . . . I understand . . . I understand now. Yes, I understand,' he repeated, his lower lip drooping towards his chin.

'But . . .'

'No "buts", David! That's all,' he snapped angrily. Like an incensed father, he scolded his ward: 'That's not what I taught you. You've no breeding. That's all.'

Léon Mignane suddenly turned to face the officers.

'Colonel Mané, now you know who is responsible. It's him . . .'

Without turning round, he indicated Daouda.

' . . . He's the guilty one. He betrayed my trust. He's the one to punish. He was never elected to represent the people.'

Daouda choked back the flood of words rising to his lips. He listened with amazement to the Venerable One's accusations. He was scandalized. His disillusionment made him want to vomit all his decades of submissiveness.

" . . . You and I will found the Fourth Republic," continued Léon Mignane, his back still turned to Daouda. "You understand, with my name, my influence in Europe, in conjunction with your firm and disciplined methods, Senegal in the year 2020 will be a glorious land. Don't let yourself be bamboozled by the communists. We must plan our future ourselves. David is responsible for all this. I know him . . . A very ambitious young man.'

'It's not true,' intervened Daouda, suppressing his nausea.

'David . . . David! That'll be all.'

'No! It's not all,' Daouda retorted vehemently. His height enabled him to loom over the Venerable One, looking him in the eye, 'It's not all. It's you alone who are responsible. You planned this devilish scenario. You disappeared on Thursday night. Where were you? Who killed your driver, old Siin?'

'Siin! Siin,' repeated Léon Mignane, as if suffering a sudden lapse of memory.

'Yes . . . Your personal driver? He was murdered, by whom? Colonel Mané, this man has deceived us all. Everything was done for the sake of his personal pride. He had it all planned, the crazy old fool. I was his Prime Minister, true. But he took all the decisions on his own. He controlled everything.'

'David . . . You're out of your mind. You were the head of government. What are you on about . . . Control yourself . . . Have some dignity! Stop talking nonsense,' demanded Léon Mignane, radiating an unconquerable energy. All trace of weariness had vanished from his face. He had recovered his former vigour, and added aggressively: 'Have some dignity, David! At least behave nobly, for once.'

The phrase pierced his heart. His eyes seemed to flash behind half-closed lids. His clay-doll face darkened with anger.

Like a boxer discovering his opponent's weakness, Léon Mignane pressed further, with more harsh remarks.

'David, don't evade responsibility. Be a *Guelewar*.'

'Sooner than a queer.'

'David, be careful what you say. Don't forget who you are . . .'

'What do you mean?' asked Daouda, his fury mounting to a peak.

'You know what I mean,' answered Léon Mignane, shrugging his shoulders contemptuously.

There's no telling what angered Daouda more, the implications of the words or the mocking tone in which they were said.

At all events, in two strides he had seized the Venerable One's lapels. Lifted in the air at the end of his long arm, Léon Mignane struggled, still talking. 'Come now! Come now, David . . . What are you doing?' Soutapha, his teeth bared, leapt towards Daouda. Daouda struck his face with his clenched fist. Soutapha raised his hands to his bloodied nose.

'David . . . Let me go! You'll pay for this. You know what you are . . .'

His fist pounded like a pestle at the face of the Venerable One, who howled: 'Don't hit me.' Like all wearers of spectacles, Léon Mignane had taken his off as soon as Daouda attacked him.

Colonel Mané and the others, stiff in their uniforms, listened coolly.

'Say what I am! Say it, you queer, you cuckold.'

His thirst for revenge unquenched, Daouda struck one side of his face, then the other, with the flat of his hand. He repeated his question. 'Say what I am, won't you? Say it . . .' The man's cheeks bore the marks of his fingers. Blood trickled from his nostrils and mouth, on to his tie, his shirt and the tiled floor. His split lip was bleeding.

Colonel Mané came over and released him from Daouda's grip.

'Captain, bring a medic.'

Daouda was breathing heavily, freed from the weight of his filial inhibitions. He had exorcised himself. He bureaucratically straightened his tie and shirt cuffs.

'Colonel! . . . It's for you.'

Mané took the receiver: 'First CP here . . . Colonel Mané. I read you, Gomis. Good . . . Very good! . . . Each of them must make a statement: bank accounts, here . . . or in Europe. Real estate as well . . . Yes. And their families too.'

The doctor arrived. He had Léon Mignane sit down, and began to clean his wounds. Soutapha assisted him.

'Monsieur Daouda . . . Will you please answer our questions?'

Daouda moved over to the table. The sergeant motioned towards the chair, and began.

'Do you have a bank account?'

'Yes. Here and abroad.'

'Write down the account numbers and addresses here.'

Daouda wrote.

'Thank you. How many houses or other buildings do you own?'

'None.'

'You don't own a house or flat in this country? What about abroad?' asked the sergeant once more, observing him.

'I bought a small house in France.'

'Cash or credit?'

'Credit.'

'With your own money?'

'The government endorsed it.'

'Please complete this point by noting the amount you owe, and how you intend to pay it . . . Write down the address of this house in France, too.'

Daouda did as he was asked.

'Thank you. Has anyone in your family received a loan from the state or a state-owned bank?'

'My wife.'

'How much?'

'About a hundred million.'

'CFA francs?'

'CFA'

'What was this sum used for?'

'To build a house.'

'Did you and your family live in that house?'

Daouda remained silent, and the sergeant looked up at him, his pen poised.

'I was housed in the Little Palace,' answered Daouda, struggling to control himself.

'With your family?'

'Yes.'

'What use was made of the house your wife had had built?'

'We rented it.'

'Who rented it from you? His name?'

'It was an embassy.'

'Write down the name . . . Thank you. How was the rent paid?'

'The embassy paid it into the bank.'

'Whose account?'

'My wife's.'

'Fine. Do you own any orchards or farms?'

'Orchards.'

'Inherited?'

'I bought them.'

'Before becoming PM?'

'During my time in office.'

'Do you have authenticated deeds to these properties?'

'Title deeds.'

'Did you while acting as head of government assist any friends, cousins, brothers, nephews etc. . . . . to obtain loans?'

'Yes.'

'Could you please list the names and addresses, and the amount involved?'

Seated at the table, his back straight, Daouda wrote down name after name without making a mistake, without any sense of betrayal. The sergeant was open-mouthed with admiration. He was fascinated by the smoothness and regularity of Daouda's writing.

'I may have forgotten a few,' said Daouda, pushing back the notebook.

Colonel Mané came up, and leaned over, both hands resting on the table-top, to look at the book.

'So all these people received largesse from the state's coffers?' he asked, his face three-quarters turned towards Daouda.

'Yes. One has to obey.'

'No matter.'

'No matter.'

'May I ask you a favour?'

'Ask away,' answered Colonel Mané, now turning fully towards him.

'I'd like to telephone my wife. She's at a friend's.'

The Colonel walked back across the room to consult some files, and asked:

'What is this friend's name?'

'Victorine.'

'Right. She was your secretary. You wife's there now. Sergeant . . . ring this number . . . Go ahead . . .'

Daouda got up. He went to take the receiver.

'Hullo! . . . Victorine . . . It's me, the PM', he said. 'Don't cry . . . What about your perfume . . . it was always first-class. Could I speak to Guylène . . . Yes! it's me. No . . . I'm fine. I'm ringing to let you know that everything's all right. I wanted to know how you are. I'll ring off for now . . . Have a good day, darling.'

Colonel Mané drew near Léon Mignane. There were cotton-wool swabs in his nostrils; his face was painted with mercurochrome, his upper lip swollen.

'What do you want? I have no house, neither here nor in France.'

'That's just what's so disgraceful. You own nothing . . . not even in your parents' country.'

The Colonel's disapproval stung the Venerable One.

'I've served my country faithfully and honestly.'

'You're the vilest creature there is. You don't deserve a dog's trust,' interrupted Daouda angrily.

'I served the state. I didn't make use of the state . . .'

'What about your property in France? You used other people's names . . .'

Colonel Mané took hold of Daouda's arm.

'Captain, take Daouda away.'

Daouda left the room, followed by the officer.

'You're going to sign your resignation,' stated Colonel Mané, seizing the Venerable One by the back of the neck. Léon Mignane twisted, leaned over, and bent his knees, grimacing. The two cotton swabs fell out.

'Gently, Colonel,' said Gor Dia, moving closer.

Léon Mignane was feeling his neck. Colonel Mané forced the pen into his grasp. Léon Mignane signed at the foot of the page where he voluntarily resigned his position as the country's President.

Lieutenant Ba burst in.

'Colonel, Doyen Cheikh Tidiane is waiting outside.'

'May I see Cheikh?' asked Léon Mignane.

The portable radio emitted a signal.

'It's for you, Colonel.'

Mané took the earphone.

'CP Number l. I read you, Commander . . . Black or white, it's all the same if they've French passports. Currency passing . . . Send them to the Coffin House. They're smugglers.'

This time, the telephone rang. 'Yes . . . This is General Staff. The French Embassy . . . For the ambassador. One moment please . . . I'll see if Colonel Mané is free.'

The receptionist held his hand over the receiver.

'Colonel . . . The French Ambassador wants to know if you can receive him.'

Mané held up two fingers.

'Hullo! Colonel Mané is busy. I'll ring you back in two hours' time. I'll make an appointment for you then . . . Yes, in two hours or so. It's . . . nine now . . . At eleven. OK. Thank you.'

Soutapha picked up the cotton swabs and replaced them in the Venerable One's nose.

The communications man switched from the airport to the Ministry of the Interior. 'CP 1 to CP 3 . . . You're going to be sent some currency smugglers . . . with the money . . . Two Senegalese and two Lebanese, with French passports. Give them a bit of a roughing-up, to get some information . . . *Caaf da Xëm*.'

'Colonel, Doyen Cheikh Tidiane is here.'

'Yes. Captain, put these two men together in a cell.'

'I . . .'

The rest of the query was stifled in his throat. His mouth twisted in a grimace of pain. Soutapha supported him . . . as they walked away.

CHAPTER 40

Attorney Ndaw came over as soon as the old woman rang up. 'A lieutenant came for him, with a letter from Colonel Mané,' explained Djia Umrel. She was worried. She had no confidence in the officer's polite tone.

'We'll find out what's going on,' said Ndaw resolutely.

Ndaw had heard about the arrests being made by the military junta among members of the ruling class. As many people thought, these were random arrests. In order to soothe her fears, he used the telephone to alert friends and elicit a wave of solidarity. He received the same answer time after time. People were lying low, hoping not to be noticed ... They were avoiding any compromising situations ... for the sake of a quiet future. 'After all, the doyen belonged to the old régime. He left the ship, like an old rat, before it sank.' Others sought to protect themselves, replying: 'I know the military. They're madmen! Not the least notion of democracy. Forward march, or else! Besides, when the doyen was enjoying the benefits of the régime, we were the illustrious unknown.'

Ndaw decided to go in search of news.

In front of the General Staff Headquarters, a crowd of people, young and old, men and women, were brandishing signs bearing messages of support. Photographers' flash bulbs popped. Journalists moved from one group to another, eyeing every car going in or out. Uncertain rumours were circulating. 'Léon Mignane is dead.' 'He's been killed by an officer.' Some were gathered round a transistor radio.

An intervention force was sent to Dakar last night. This airborne armada switched to another destination in mid-flight. It was learned this morning that paratroop contingents have arrived in the Central African Republic, Gabon and the Ivory Coast.

The French Government spokesman has neither confirmed nor denied these allegations.

He stated, however: 'We have mutual assistance agreements with certain African countries. When we're asked to act on these agreements ...'

'Come on, pay attention,' someone urged.
'Quiet,' ordered someone else.
'Brother, turn up the volume ...'
The listeners gathered round the 'talking box'.

Professor Porgurol, Léon Mignane's adviser for a decade, talks to us about the man. 'Professor, you knew Léon Mignane well.'

'Yes, that's true. I had the honour of approaching that illustrious man.'

'Professor, what sort of a man was he?'

'One can say without hesitation that Léon Mignane is a sincere friend of the West. An African sage. He is a far cry ... a very far cry ... from certain monarchs, emperors or heads of state for whom to rule merely means to become inordinately rich. A learned man, steeped in European as well as African culture, his opponents called him an honorary white ...'

'No need for opponents when a friend can say that,' someone commented.

Attorney Ndaw moved off among the crowd, searching the

barracks courtyard with his gaze . . .

The throng in front of the General Staff Headquarters dispersed. A flock of six sheep was wandering from one side of the pavement to another. From time to time a man kicked the side of a parked car; someone else knocked down a dustbin and dragged it some distance before abandoning it. One bright spark stood in front of the traffic-light and counted the seconds between each change of colour.

The remainder of the group – three girls and two boys – stood in a row, blocking the street. Their clenched fists raised as a token of allegiance, they shouted all together 'Long live General Mané.' The paratroopers on patrol waved at them.

They walked up the Boulevard de la République. Before them rose a massive white structure: the President's palace. They began to sing a current hit tune, their steps sounding in time to the rhythm. One of the girls, wearing jeans patched at the knees and a Rasta hairdo ornamented with beads, improvised a dance . . .

The area looked like a deserted city.

'You can't go in, kids,' said the para sergeant.

'Why?' asked the youth who seemed to have the most influence.

'Orders.'

'Orders!' repeated the boy, turning back towards the others. He added: 'OK, *grand* . . . OK . . .'

They stood uncertainly in front of the gate, then moved off, two by two. One of them crossed to the other side of the street, while the others moved along the red stone wall towards the Place de l'Indépendance.

A jeep passed with some soldiers in it.

'Hey, kids,' called out the youth on the other side of the street.

He motioned them over.

'Have a look . . . there.'

They clung to the iron railings surrounding the *'Maison Militaire'*. Pairs of eyes focused on the statue of Faidherbe, facing the palace.

'What's up, Diouf?' asked a girl whose plaited hair was parted down the middle. She was wearing a man's shirt that reached down to her knees.

'What? . . . Don't you see?' asked Diouf in an imperious tone of voice.

One of the youths, who had slanted eyes, slipped between Diouf and the girl. His sharp forehead fitted between two iron bars.

'We've got to pull it down,' announced Diouf, and read out: 'Faidherbe, 1818–1889.'

'Ropes,' suggested the youth wearing a Cabral-style woollen cap, his neck hung about with pendants.

'Where can we find ropes?'

A girl asked this ticklish question.

'There's a building site near here. Who's coming with me?'

'We ought to have a bit of explosive,' said the girl with the parted plaits, her face serious. An — imaginary — blast pulverized Faidherbe.

'I'll come with you,' boldly offered the youth with the pointed forehead.

'Let's split up in pairs.'

'Everyone bring back whatever he finds,' ordered Diouf, taking the high-explosives girl by the wrist.

They parted . . .

CHAPTER 41

As early as the third coup to take place in Africa, Cheikh Tidiane, in private conversation with Léon Mignane, had condemned the practice. 'No one in a position of responsibility can remain indifferent to these deliberate disruptions of the practice of democracy. We know who manipulates the putschists. Those people are acting on behalf of non-African interests. They're not in it for the money.'

'Cheikh, I'm against it too. But one mustn't intervene in the internal affairs of a sovereign state,' Léon Mignane had retorted. He rejoiced whenever a president was toppled who hadn't shared his ideas about power. Addressing his companion, he said 'Cheikh, you're not going to tell me that mercenaries have ideals . . . because I can't believe that.'

'What? . . . Don't be naïve, Léon. The current actions of mercenaries are based on a claim to cultural superiority. They're acting in the name of their civilization . . . Just reread . . . or read, the newspaper articles or interviews devoted to them. The French Press sees them as the heirs of the epic "empire builders". Longing for their past glory, these "lost soldiers" are a pale reflection of a bygone power . . . They perpetuate a dying civilization that still sees itself in a conquering role.'

'Cheikh, where do you get all that? Those men are fighting for money. They've nothing to do with Europe.'

'For whom are they fighting, then? . . . People fight for an ideal, and always will.'

Léon Mignane didn't answer and Cheikh Tidiane continued to be annoyed at every coup.

Doyen Cheikh Tidiane sat facing Colonel Mané, silent, his face drawn. His features were compressed in an old man's sternness. His gaze shifted from one soldier to another. He was afraid of the army: a massive undiscerning force, like an elephant crushing a lamb.

'We need your help,' said Colonel Mané once more, in a polite tone contrasting with his rough soldierly air. 'The whole Cabinet is in our hands. We want to solve the case of your ... friend, Léon Mignane.'

'What do you intend to do with him?'

'What do you suggest?'

The question answering his set the old man's chest heaving. His mocking laughter ill concealed his chagrin at hearing of his contemporary's arrest.

'You don't know what to do with him,' he replied bitterly.

Colonel Mané lit a cigarette, to give himself something to do. He was waiting ... for the answer. Léon Mignane's detention had roused a vehement debate within the CHO. Some wanted a quick trial, others were against it. A compromise had been adopted.

'What about keeping him in prison like his ministers, without a trial, and hoping that ill-health will eventually do away with him?'

The doyen was appalled at the Colonel's cynicism.

'... Precisely, we want to avoid all that,' concluded the officer.

'Then set him free,' said the old man slowly, without raising his voice.

'What would be the point of our coup then?'

'That's just what I'd like to know, Colonel.'

'Did you read the leaflets, doyen?'

'Yes ... Maybe not all ...'

'What about your speech on the occasion of Léon Mignane's seventieth birthday? Perhaps you'd rather not be reminded of it.'

'I stand by what I said.'

'Your speech alone would suffice to justify the present situation.'

'Officers weren't left out when property and funds were being distributed, so far as I know.'

'For many officers, that's true! Fortunately, it doesn't apply to everyone in the army. Whom did this institutionalized largesse benefit? Those high up in the social hierarchy. Our wish is to see Léon Mignane leave the country. He's your friend, you can convince him. You could have a word with the French Ambassador.'

'Why me?'

'We can compel him. Send him off by force ...'

'Any prominent figure could undertake this fatigue, as you would call it in your jargon,' argued Cheikh Tidiane, while searching for a gleam of sincerity in the Colonel's eyes.

'I don't think so ... In the army, the NCOs do kitchen fatigue, the men do the latrines [out of politeness, Mané refrained from using the more usual term, shit-house.]'

Cheikh Tidiane had been the unanimous choice of the CHO. The officers had a high opinion of the doyen. While his moderation in public kept him out of trouble, in private he would back down before no one.

'You must know, Colonel, that I've retired from politics. I no longer have any authority to act as a mediator.'

'Doyen,' interrupted the head of the CHO, feeling that the old man's reserve was wearing thin. He crushed his cigarette stub on the floor. 'Doyen ... if we keep Léon Mignane here, we'll have to bring him to trial ... and sentence him. In that case, all his collaborators would of course also be brought to trial and sentenced.'

'Colonel, you're in a poor position to pass judgement, after what has just happened.'

'Today and tomorrow ... maybe. In a few weeks or months, our rule will have been legalized by public opinion and international morality. People are shocked when an army takes control of public affairs ... But for how long? ... As for us, what do you know about us? We are conscious of our democratic role. Lieutenant, hand me the statements,' requested the Colonel, after craning his neck to look over to the right. 'Read these, please,' he ordered.

Cheikh Tidiane was absorbed by the list of names, ministers, principal private secretaries, company directors, heads of mixed-economy companies. Between reading two sheets, he glanced over at the officer. He was edified by this subtle form of collective denunciation.

'I must make a statement of what I own.'

'Of course ... But all in good time. You own only your house. Your son Diouldé, the deputy, owns three buildings which provide him with a substantial income. Badou, your younger son, is a notorious communist ... and penniless.'

'I've spent too much time in the political arena not to know that the generous ideas which sustain the early phases of rule gradually wear out, are corroded and turn to formaldehyde.'

'A well-turned sentence ... Feudalism is a burden of our country. All misappropriated or ill-gotten property will be requisitioned. Even our General Ousmane won't escape. Léon Mignane is no use to us. Best reunite him with his family ... over there.'

'Where is he?' asked Cheikh Tidiane, his reticence overcome.

'You'll be taken there,' said Colonel Mané, giving orders. Cheikh Tidiane pushed back his chair.

The outline of the arched veranda stood out against the tiled floor. Soldiers in battledress were busy in the courtyard. Rows of lorries were lined up, ready to leave. Outside, across from the barracks entrance, stood an anonymous throng.

212

'Cheikh! Cheikh!' called Léon Mignane, in a voice tinged with hope. He clung to the arm of the new arrival. 'They forced me to resign. It's an usurpation of power. It's illegal. I won't let them get away with it. You, you're in justice. You must make arrangements ... But ... you, Cheikh ...'

Léon Mignane stepped back. Behind the clear glass of his spectacles, his puffy eyelids were painfully distended as he stared suspiciously at his former Minister of Justice. His excitement yielded to a certain reserve. His mouth twisted in a grimace. Only one of his nostrils was plugged with cotton.

A pale anaemic light filtered through the airshaft.

'You're in it with them ... Admit it ... Admit it ... Like that bastard David-Daouda, who dared lift his hand against me. You've come to deliver the final blow ... Come on! Come on! What are you waiting for? I can be killed, but not dishonoured. You'll be my successor ... mount the throne ... You're in league with the barrack-room boys ... Why don't you say so?'

'No! No! Léon, I've nothing to do with what's happened.'

Cheikh Tidiane wanted to spare him. His heart was laden with bitterness; his limbs were heavy. Tears rose quite naturally to his eyes, and he realized then that he loved this man.

'You know I resigned, Léon,' he added to justify himself.

They fell silent. The sound of orders being given, and a lorry starting up, filled the cell. As his eyes grew accustomed to the poor light, the doyen discerned the silhouette of Soutapha, seated on the pallet.

'How are you, son?'

'Fine, doyen.'

'What happened?'

'It was Daouda.'

'The PM?'

'Yes.'

'What ingratitude! He's the cause of everything. I'll bring him to trial for assaulting the Head of State. That nobody I educated, raised to the top ...'

'Léon, you'd best leave for France.'

'They're afraid to bring me to trial. I know how to defend myself. I never misused state property. I frighten them ... They've detained me illegally. I'm going to appeal to the human rights people, to Amnesty International. It's a communist plot, using Senegalese tools. They've manipulated the military. Just listen to them talk French. Illiterates.'

Léon Mignane was breathlessly pacing the room.

'Léon.'

'Cheikh, stop trying to manoeuvre me. How do I know you're not in league with the soldiery?'

'No ... Léon ... How many have died in prison, or stagnated under house arrest, forgotten? Once overthrown, a head of state is no longer of interest to anyone. The only friends or allies the major powers acknowledge are those who serve their interests.'

'Cheikh, you're always attacking the West,' Léon Mignane objected angrily, advancing to the middle of the room. A sunbeam from the skylight fell on the back of his neck. 'You forget that I'm the initiator of Authenegraficanitus ... of Eurafrica ... I'm not like those you allude to. I've been honoured with all kinds of European distinctions. So you think that a handful of illiterate officers can replace me ... Dunces. You must be glad to see me here.'

'No, Léon, I'm not ... Do calm down,' suggested Cheikh Tidiane, deeply wounded. He wiped his eyes.

Léon Mignane took a side-step, with the calm indifference of stupidity. He launched into his theory on 'Africa, complement to Europe,' gesticulating. He let himself go, embellishing his speech with Latin, Germanic, English and French quotations. During pauses, he smiled and glanced from one corner of the room to another. He bowed his head deferentially, and murmured to himself: 'Thank you.'

'Cheikh, I'm not a fool like the others. Which of those imbeciles can take my place? ... You can tell them I said so.'

'If you insist, I'll tell them.'

'I do insist ...' shouted Léon Mignane. 'It's up to them to think of their future ... I have support ... Even in this country alone, prominent figures, religious leaders, and many more ...'

'Léon, remember Ahmet Ndour. He was very popular with those people. And when he was imprisoned, not one of them made a gesture of solidarity. For prominent people, influence is something to be cashed in ... Their god is money ... Remember Dag ... Mr H and Lumumba ... Fulbert Youlou ... the people in Dahomey, or Bénin as it is today ... The Togolese, Diori Hamani, Modibo Keita, Moktar Ould Daddah, Bokassa, Tolbert in Liberia? Think of yourself, of your family. Once in France, you'll be free to do as you please.'

'I think,' began Soutapha.

'Yes,' responded the Venerable One.

'Mr President, with your name, your renown, you could launch an appeal from France, just as General de Gaulle did in London in June 1940. I'm sure that the banks and aid funds will listen to you, and cut off supplies. The country's economy will be bankrupt. Then they'll have to call you back.'

'Yes! ... Yes! ... That's it, Soutapha. You're right. I can see it from here ... Yes! ... Yes! ...' Léon Mignane repeated quietly, his

214

forehead furrowed. He was gazing at an imaginary spot.

He alone could hear the drums playing a triumphal march. The praise-singers were singing his glory. The cathedral bells were chiming the country's deliverance. Léon Mignane savoured his victory to come. He alone could see the wrestlers, the young girls dressed in cloths the colour of gazelle pelts, the women glittering with gold, all come to welcome him and throng about him.

'Léon, we're old now. Soutapha is right.'

'Do you think so? Do you think so, Cheikh?'

'Yes, Léon! It's quite possible,' replied Cheikh Tidiane, very sceptical.

Léon Mignane drew near him. Like a conspirator, he kept an eye on the closed door, while whispering:

'We've no time to lose. That being so, just between the two of us: I'd agree to leave . . . even right now.'

Cheikh Tidiane knocked on the door. It was opened. He went to Colonel Mané's office.

'He's agreed. But only if Soutapha goes with him.'

'That's fine with us. The French Ambassador will see you. Lieutenant Ba will be your bodyguard. But he has no power of decision. If you want to contact me, tell him so. Good luck.'

The Lieutenant opened the rear door of the Peugeot for him. 'Why, there's Kad,' said the old man, seeing the journalist enter Colonel Mané's office. 'It's more honourable to accept something one could have refused, than to impose a negative point of view,' thought Cheikh Tidiane to console himself. He convinced himself that he hadn't yielded to the soldiers' demands. He had to save a companion.

'Ba, let's go by my house first,' he said, leaning back in his seat.

CHAPTER 42

Diouf and his companion, the girl with her hair done in two bunches of plaits, tossed the coil of wire to the ground.

'They're in their final year at the *lycée*.' That was how they introduced the three youths who had come with them to the first group, who had been to fetch some ropes.

They all greeted each other in Wolof-English pidgin: 'Eh . . . boy! Eh . . . boy!' and launched into an earnest discussion of how the job ought to be done.

Diouf and one of the new recruits pushed open the garden gate.

No guard or gardener in sight. They went in, followed by the rest of the gang.

Two well-dressed little boys, aged eleven and eight, emerged from the building in the Rue Boufflers and slowly drew near. The smaller of the two was eating a piece of bread spread with peanut butter.

'What are the big boys doing, Jo?' he asked, gazing up at Jo with eyes as white as cassava-flour.

'I don't know, Paul,' answered Jo, glancing back at the door from which they had just come.

They walked round the corner of the garden, to have a look.

'What are they saying, Jo?'

'They're talking Wolof.'

'Can't you talk Wolof?'

'Father told us not to.'

'Look, Jo, look . . . The big boy's climbing up.'

A youth had indeed climbed on to the pedestal, the one wearing a Cabral-style knitted cap. With care, he began to wind a rope round the statue.

'Hey! What are you doing?' shouted a sergeant, striding towards them.

'We're pulling it down. Your Lieutenant said we could,' the girl with the Rasta hairstyle said boldly. With one finger, she expertly flicked aside a plait that was out of place. The sun was in her eyes, and she moved aside a few steps.

'The Lieutenant?' said the sergeant warily. He looked round at the youthful faces.

'Yes, the Lieutenant! You know him . . . he agrees with us. This monument represents colonial rule.'

'Have you killed the Venerable One? He should be judged by a people's court . . .'

'A revolutionary people's court.'

'And all the deputies and Ministers too,' added another.

The sergeant felt out of his depth. They had been ordered to avoid all conflict with young people . . . and women. Three years ago he himself had been among those who demanded the removal of this relic of a shameful time in the nation's history. After finishing secondary school, with no scholarship and no prospect of help from his family, he had joined the army rather than join the police. He had wanted to be an electronics engineer.

'Do it properly, kids . . .'

'You can count on us, grand,' replied the girl who had wanted to use explosives.

They split into two teams, each holding an end of the rope wound round the statue. At Diouf's signal they leaned as far back as they could. 'Heave . . . ho! Heave . . . ho!' They pulled and pulled. 'Once

more, kids! Heave . . . ho! It's coming! It's coming! Heave . . . ho!'
The bronze figure wobbled as they pulled once more, then fell with a
thud, face-down in the grass.

Flushed and exultant with triumph, they congratulated one
another.

They kicked the inert mass. Diouf picked up its broken sword.
One of the late arrivals tried to climb on top of it. He lost his balance
and fell; his cut chin began to bleed. No one had noticed. The boy in
the black beret climbed on to the empty pedestal, and began to
mimic the gestures of a victorious fighter. They applauded.

'Diouf,' a girl called out, 'Sène is wounded.'

The boy called Sène was squatting, his shirt-tail stained with
blood. They gathered round him, losing interest in the fallen
monument.

'The soldiers must have medicine.'

'Let's go and ask them.'

They filed out.

'There's Daddy!' exclaimed the elder of the two little boys. His
eyelids fluttering nervously, he took hold of his brother's wrist.

A man dressed in a cardigan, pyjama trousers and bedroom
slippers was coming towards them, his face stern.

'Jo! I told you not to go out,' he thundered, gazing after the gang
of young people crossing the pavement towards the palace.

'Daddy, they pulled down Faidherbe.'

'Get back to the flat.'

His anthracite-black face crumpled into a frown as he caught sight
of the statue lying on the lawn.

CHAPTER 43

Attorney Ndaw returned without having succeeded. He found the
old woman in the company of her daughter-in-law Fatimata, who
had also come to find out what was going on.

'*Joom Galle* came back to fetch his decorations. He's gone to the
French Embassy. At his age, I was afraid the military might arrest
him. You must understand me, Attorney.'

'*Alhamdulillahi,*' said Ndaw, plucking at the crease of his trousers
before sitting down.

'You must be thirsty. Coffee, or orange juice?' asked Djia Umrel.

'Orange juice.'

'Mamadou! Oh, sorry, Ly!'

'Madame.'

'Squeeze two oranges for Attorney Ndaw. Fatimata, will you have something . . .'

'No, thank you, Mother. Nothing . . .'

'What will become of the country with the military in power?'

'It's the end of democracy,' Ndaw stated sententiously.

'The outcome depends on all of us,' said Fatimata, looking straight at him.

'How can you . . .'

Djia Umrel didn't finish her sentence. She sat up with a frightened look. The others turned their gaze in the same direction.

Diouldé's children were opening the gate. The 604 entered, with Eugénie driving. The boot was stuffed to overflowing with suitcases.

'I want to see *Joom Galle!*' said Eugénie upon emerging from the car. Her face was free of make-up. 'The army have arrested Diouldé, Mother.'

She was crying.

The old woman helped her towards the porch.

'I'll come back to see *Tonton,*' said Ndaw.

'But what about your orange juice?'

'I'll be back for it.'

'Thank you for coming.'

The women were left alone together.

The servants and children unloaded the luggage.

CHAPTER 44

The paratrooper on sentinel duty halted the Peugeot. A (white) officer came over to talk to Lieutenant Ba. 'We'll have to proceed on foot, doyen,' he said, opening the door for him.

The sentinel saluted on catching sight of the ranks of medals pinned to the old man's chest.

Behind coils of barbed wire, expatriates were huddled together; seated, or standing in groups. Volunteer helpers, dressed in white, flitted from one place to another. Discarded papers, cartons, plastic and glass bottles and tins littered the lawn, attracting flies. The sound of children shouting and crying rose above the stifled murmur of voices. Some people recognized the former Minister of Justice, and plagued him with questions: 'Is it true that the President's been killed? Why did the coup take place?' Cheikh Tidiane refrained from answering.

218

In the hall, a (white) policeman on duty presented him with a form to fill in. He did so, muttering: 'Damned bureaucracy.'

'Doyen Cheikh.'

He turned around: it was Professor Fall. Although the morning was hot, he was wearing a three-piece suit and his eternal tweed hat. He took the doyen by the arm, to lead him away from the Senegalese officer.

'What about your wife?'

'She's fine.'

'Isn't she coming?'

'Where?'

'France, of course!'

The tone of the statement made Cheikh realize what the doctor was doing on the premises. The successive questions were reminiscent of a medical consultation, except that the roles were reversed.

'Do you mean that . . .'

'I never renounced my nationality. We were French before we were Senegalese. You too, I hope . . . That . . . you . . . you see? Blacks are all crazy . . . Incapable of governing themselves. Are you going to see Jean de Savognard? He's only seeing *Tubabs*. He's letting me hang about here.'

He wiped his forehead. He caught the eye of a European who seemed to be spying on them. His pride as an authentic black-skinned Frenchman was being hurt. He continued in a plaintive tone of voice, after turning his back on the man who seemed to be watching them.

'You can't think what unpleasant things I've heard . . . about Africans.'

'It'll all sort itself out.'

'Do you think so? Everything's ruined. Completely ruined. Poor Léon, what a stupid way to die. I never wanted to go along with it.'

'Léon isn't dead.'

'Are you sure? . . . Since this morning, we've heard that he's been killed by the army . . .'

'No! He's just being detained by the army.'

'Doyen, we're expected,' announced Lieutenant Ba.

'Cheikh!' cried the Professor, clinging to his arm. It was as if he had knelt at his feet.

'Don't be afraid. You won't be forgotten.'

The civilian who had been hanging about them, entered the lift ahead of them. When they had reached their floor, he asked the Senegalese officer to hand over his weapon. The Lieutenant refused, with a look of disdain. Cheikh Tidiane intervened, saying: 'The Lieutenant will wait for me here. Does that reassure you?'

'Yes,' said the prowler.

'Don't worry, *Mawdo*' said Ba in Pulaar.

The doyen smiled at him. It gladdened his heart to hear his mother tongue.

The First Secretary ushered him into his office, affably. He showed him to an armchair.

'The ambassador will see you right away. Cigarette?'

'Thank, you, but I've stopped smoking.'

'I haven't the will-power. I stop for a month or two, then start again.'

'You must persevere.'

A light flashed. The First Secretary lifted the receiver: 'Yes! very good! . . . We'll be right there.' He rose, and adjusted his clothes, out of habit. Cheikh Tidiane did the same.

Swing doors covered in imitation leather opened to admit them to Jean de Savognard's huge office, where climbing plants clung round the window.

Jean de Savognard came to meet them. He was visibly delighted by this visit. It was his first contact with the new rulers.

The younger man withdrew.

'At last! . . . How do you do, doyen?'

'Senegalese-style.'

'That's appropriate enough, although I don't understand that expression. And that's not the only thing I don't understand these days,' said the diplomat in a regretful tone of voice.

They sat down across from the bay window looking out over the ocean, that lay very calm before them. Above the roofs and sparse greenery rose the President's palace, the national flag flying from its roof.

'We were all taken by surprise.'

'Unpleasantly so,' admitted Jean de Savognard. He continued sourly, in a godfatherly tone: 'Those who pulled it off must be very pleased with themselves.'

'Naturally,' said Cheikh Tidiane, without irony. He was not unaware of the diplomat's arrogant nature.

'They're behind the times . . . Far behind . . . The era of military take-overs is past. Look at what's happening in Ghana, in Nigeria. The army is returning to barracks, to let the civilians take over the reins of government. Do they think the Russians or Cubans are going to help them . . .?'

The European's tone, although light, betrayed his paternalism. Cheikh was annoyed. His task would not be an easy one . . . He wanted to respond to the challenge.

'I feel your government should have thought of that sooner. As for the army men to whom you refer, before returning to barracks, they'll have cleaned out the stables. In no so-called Francophone

220

State have the soldiers yet returned to barracks ... As for Bokassa...'

Great minds let themselves go only to deliver harsh truths.

Hurt, Jean de Savognard changed the subject.

'We don't intervene in the internal affairs of other states. Surely you know that. No, never!'

'No, never!' he defended himself. He perceived frank speech, coming from an ex-colonial subject, as a sign of hostility. He continued: 'We advise, and we intervene only when we're asked to.'

'I've not come here to defend or accuse anyone ... I've come to save Léon Mignane.'

'We don't intervene in your affairs ...'

The response had been quick, and the diplomat's face lit up; he savoured his revenge.

The doyen's smile relaxed the atmosphere.

'Where is he now?'

'He's in the hands of the army. They've agreed to send him to France. As soon as possible ... This evening, say.'

'You must be joking. The airport's closed.'

'They're the ones who suggested it.'

'What proof can you give?' asked the European warily. He had been making mistake after mistake, for days. Paris were after him all the time.

'My word! That's all I can offer.'

'You must be in it with them, if they have such confidence in you.'

'No, I'm not with them. They asked me to negotiate his departure.'

'What do they want in return?'

'Nothing. As you know, Léon has French nationality. I've seen him! He's agreed to leave. Otherwise, will you mount a vast humanitarian movement to send a Mystère jet to rescue him at night...'

'What do you make of current events?'

Cheikh Tidiane's gaze followed the flight of a vulture. As far as he was concerned, all African heads of state hold their positions for life. They rule, appoint heirs from their family or their party. The theatre of politics is played on a stage drenched in the people's blood. It's up to the star actor to play his part, under the media floodlights. After thinking this, Cheikh Tidiane eluded the question.

'I'm against all forms of usurpation.'

'Then why don't you become the leader of the opposition? You're widely known and trusted.'

'No,' said Cheikh Tidiane as if he were being flayed alive. 'I want to rescue a friend.'

'What about you?'

'Me? What?'

221

'Don't you want to go to France?'

The question wounded the old man's pride. He swallowed his anger in silence.

'I'm Senegalese,' he replied. He wasn't a skilful negotiator.

'Very well! I'll consult Paris.'

'With him will be Soutapha, Professor Fall and his family.'

Seated behind his desk, Jean de Savognard wrote, then summoned the young First Secretary: 'Send this top priority.'

'Oh, Pierre . . . Come in . . . May I introduce you to Doyen Cheikh Tidiane Sall, Minister of Justice in the former government. A friend of Léon Mignane. Pierre is responsible for evacuating our nationals, should it prove necessary. He works in the consulate.'

'Not an easy task,' said the old man, courteously ironical. He had recognized Pierre . . . who had wanted to disarm Lieutenant Ba . . . and who, downstairs, had been watching him and Professor Fall.

Hatchet-faced, with a crew cut and a lipless mouth, Pierre dressed like a department-store shopwalker. He sat down as if at home, and listened to Jean de Savognard informing him of the reason for the visit.

'That's strange! . . . Why do they want to send him to France?'

'Best ask them that,' answered Cheikh Tidiane. He had had negative feelings ever since Pierre had come into the room. He suspected him of being a SDEC agent.

'How is it that you were chosen as mediator?'

Pierre's question was accompanied by a glance towards the ambassador, then towards the visitor's shaven head and rows of medals.

'Why not me?'

'With your age and experience, you're exactly the right person,' said Pierre, who could not give up his paternalism, yet couldn't manage to treat him as an inferior.

Pierre, sent to help pave the way for Léon Mignane's successor, had landed on Friday evening. He had contacted Corréa and Diatta. Now that those two had vanished in the whirlwind of events, he no longer knew what was going on.

'Does Colonel Mané share your ideas?' he asked, trying to determine the nature of the link between this old man and the military.

'I know nothing about Colonel Mané.'

'Really?'

Cheikh Tidiane smiled with his eyes.

Pierre interpreted this as the typical smile of embarrassment common among black men, even elderly ones. Accustomed to making and unmaking heads of state, Pierre could not conceive that there might be some noble-minded men on the continent.

Intellectual racism is liberal.

'We can't find Adolphe.'

'Why not ask His Excellency,' said Cheikh Tidiane.

'That's just it, I haven't any word. Could you do us a favour?'

'How's that?'

'Ask them to free him along with Léon Mignane.'

'And don't forget Corréa,' added Pierre.

'I'll convey your request.'

'While waiting for Paris to reply, where can I contact you?'

'At my home.'

'Will Léon Mignane be there?'

'I'm not Léon Mignane's gaoler.'

Cheikh Tidiane took his leave, and found Lieutenant Ba waiting for him.

'Well?' asked Professor Fall as soon as they emerged from the lift.

'Everything will be all right.'

'Are you sure?' asked Fall, in Wolof so as not to be understood by the Europeans.

'Yes, I'm sure.'

'My family's here! Do you want to see them?'

'I'm in a bit of a hurry ... But don't worry.'

Back at General Staff Headquarters, he informed Colonel Mané of what had taken place.

'I'd like Léon's meals to come from my place.'

'Lieutenant Ba will come and fetch them. Thank you, doyen,' said Mané, a half-smile of satisfaction lighting up his face.

What was the Colonel thanking him for? Deep in thought, he returned home.

His grandchildren greeted him gaily. *'Joom Galle's* back! *Joom Galle's* back!'* taking him by the hands. He let them lead him in.

His two daughters-in-law kissed him. Eugénie's tears didn't surprise him. He had seen Diouldé's name in the sheaf of statements.

'Is it a revolution, *Joom Galle?'*

'Be quiet, Amath,' snapped Eugénie, his mother.

'It's not a revolution! It's a coup.'

'Joom Galle, you shouldn't tell children such things.'

'Why shouldn't children know the facts?'

'We'll discuss it, you and I,' Djia Umrel interposed decisively, looking him straight in the eye. 'Eugénie and her children are going to stay with us.'

'That's a good idea.'

'Do you want to be left alone?'

'Yes.'

'Come, children. We'll see to your rooms.'

They disappeared.

The rocking-chair's motion kept his thoughts alert.

Djia Umrel came back alone, with a glass of port on a tray.

Joom Galle examined the glass, then looked her full in the face with an unmistakeable expression. The old woman was pained by her husband's suspicion. She lowered her eyes to escape his accusing stare. She murmured 'No,' shaking her head, thus acknowledging that she had used sleeping-tablets to keep him at home. She regretted it now, and her head hung heavy with sorrow.

Cheikh Tidiane looked at her with magnanimity, before raising the glass to his lips. He drank two sips.

'Attorney Ndaw came by.'

'Good . . . By the way . . . Have lunch ready for Léon Mignane . . . Lieutenant Ba will come to fetch it.'

She withdrew with her usual quiet dignity.

CHAPTER 45

At noon, Lieutenant Ba came by for Léon Mignane's lunch: grilled chicken, green salad, peas, hard-boiled eggs, two portions of cheese, three bottles of mineral water, oranges, bananas, ice-cubes, white napkins and tableware.

'Perhaps we could try and send something to Diouldé,' suggested the mother.

'That's not necessary,' replied *Joom Galle*.

The children's racket prevented him from thinking. He withdrew to his bedroom. He wasn't hungry.

After lunch with the others, the old woman joined him. She sat in the chair at the foot of the bed.

'I've never much liked Léon,' she conceded, 'but I'd never have wished for him to end like this. It's best they should send him to France, rather than keep him in detention.'

'I'm just as guilty as he is. I've been working with him for decades.'

'That's not the same thing. What do you mean, anyway?'

He didn't answer.

' . . . You're not responsible for anything. Léon ruled alone . . . Besides, you resigned before the coup. We never took advantage of our position in the régime.'

She talked and talked, as if defending herself before an invisible judge; adducing detail after persuasive detail to show how modestly they lived.

'Don't bother me! Leave me alone,' he upbraided her.

The old woman's face grew rigid with disappointment; she looked like a Lobi goddess of maternity. Her eyes, with their liquid old-ivory gleam, glittered with sparks of silver. Dignity kept her eyelids raised.

Joom Galle returned the old woman's violent gaze for a moment, then looked away, towards the wall.

Like a silent shadow at twilight, Djia Umrel left the room.

The enforced wait revived his memories of his years of comradeship with Léon Mignane. They were the only survivors of the 1920s and 1930s. Superimposed flashbacks in rapid succession passed through his mind. Time had erased the details of faces, leaving blank profiles. Cheikh Tidiane sought to cast anchor in that past, to make himself at home in it once more. Names slowly surfaced in his mind. He recalled his last memory of Pascal Wellé.

Pascal Wellé, former deputy to the French National Assembly, had died in France but was to be buried in Dakar. He was a Catholic, but the head of the clergy denied him the right to Catholic burial. With all the vehemence of orthodoxy, the bishop stated that 'Pascal Wellé was an active freemason.' His intransigeance had dismayed the Christian community, as well as the colonial administration.

As for the Muslims, they would not consider yielding a single inch of their cemetery to a Catholic, no matter how famous he had been.

A delegation of Catholics and Muslims, friends of the dead man, asked Cheikh Tidiane Sall to help. At that time he was the only university graduate, known for his integrity; and he owed it to the dead man: 'Pascal Wellé was your guardian in Paris.' They had to find a solution! In three days, Cheikh convinced the Muslim religious leaders and the local administration to donate a small plot of ground outside the burial-ground proper. This *modus vivendi* suited everyone . . . That is how Pascal Wellé came to be buried where he is.

Dioulde and Eugénie's youngest child came into the room, babbling. He was just one year old. He began tugging at the bed-spread with his little hands.

His grandfather was looking at him. His memories faded . . . except one: emerging from other statements by Pascal Wellé, the words: 'I am a black Catholic, I married a white woman, my children are half-castes. I'm the best choice you can make.' Pascal Wellé said that in 1914. Why had he remembered it today?

The murmurs of the child trying to climb on to the bed, distracted him from his thoughts. He marvelled at the tiny boy's efforts, his grimace, the small hands clenched on the bedspread. The child managed to climb up unassisted, and began to play with his watch chain . . . 'You'll be here in the year 2020,' the old man told him. The baby clambered astride him, bouncing up and down like a rider. Both laughed.

Minutes passed.

The child relieved itself on him. He put him down on the carpet, and called: 'Umrel! Umrel!'

The baby, upset, began to cry.

'You'll have to change, won't you,' said the old woman, picking up the child and cuddling him: 'How could you do wee-wee on *Joom Galle!*' The child smiled.

Tuesday, 5.00 p.m.

'It's me! Yes, the doyen. Aha! You'll accept delivery of the parcel,' he repeated with pleasure. 'I'll contact the sender,' he said, adopting the terms used by Jean de Savognard, an inveterate thriller-reader. 'I'll contact you again in an hour, or less.'

Overjoyed, he went into his study and dialled the number of General Staff. After a minute's wait, he reached Colonel Mané: 'The parcel's been accepted,' he announced without preliminaries, parodying the ambassador. The officer replied with a 'Right' as abrupt as a hatchet-blow. 'Be at the military airport at nine o'clock for a final checkout.'

'There are some smaller parcels as well.'

'Nine o'clock, doyen,' repeated the Colonel, and hung up.

He was shocked by this brutal manner. 'Soldiers don't go in for sentiment,' he said to himself, in consolation. He informed Jean de Savognard: 'Nine o'clock, at the military airport.'

As punctual as a lawyer's clerk, Lieutenant Ba appeared.

The shadowy shapes of lorries, swallowed up by the dark, appeared in the barracks courtyard. Cigarette ends glowed. Car headlamps swept past the gateway.

'Good evening, doyen,' Colonel Mané greeted him. 'May I introduce the Committee of High-ranking Officers.'

They were all standing. As a sign of respect for him, or just a courtesy? He shook each of them by the hand. There were about ten men. He recognized most of them. The sight of these men, on whose behalf he was acting, made him feel gloomy and remote. He loathed their martial attire. He himself was a civilian through and through, even in his way of thinking. All uniformity, all levelling seemed to him a threat to freedom of thought.

'Sit down, doyen,' the Colonel invited him, and signalled to the others to do the same.

The old man controlled his anger, to avoid a pointless outburst. He thought: 'The new Political Bureau.'

'Doyen, we must ask you not to talk to journalists.'

'Conditions, already,' he muttered to himself, glancing at Colonel Mané.

'Over the telephone, you mentioned some smaller parcels.'

'Yes. There's Professor Fall, Dean of the Faculty of Medicine, Léon Mignane's personal physician, and his family. There's Adolphe too, Léon Mignane's personal adviser, whom you've detained, and Corréa . . . I myself would like some news of my son Dioulé.'

The officers looked at each other. Colonel Mané gestured with his chin towards Colonel Gomis, seated at the end of the table. In front of him were stacks of files. Gomis pushed a yellow file over towards the doyen. He adjusted his spectacles, opened it, and recognized Dioulé's writing.

'All right,' he said when he had finished reading, overcoming his own embarrassment.

'We can't make any exceptions. When we've finished the inventory of their property, they'll be released,' Colonel Mané told him.

'I understand,' he said, out of integrity. He was suffering; but out of pride, he didn't want to owe them anything. 'Professor Fall?'

With a surgeon's dexterity, Colonel Gomis shuffled through the files and read out:

'Lamine Fall, Professor of Medicine, and his family, live in a staff villa. He owns two houses which he rents to the state. He received loans from the Development Bank, without security, in order to build these houses. He has retained French nationality. Every year he renews his registration, and his family's, at the consulate.'

Gomis looked the doyen straight in the eye.

'Why are you letting him go? He's a professional man,' said Cheikh Tidiane.

'We didn't make the decision. Holding dual nationality is dishonest. We need professional men . . . but not double-dealers. The choice was his. We won't force anyone to stay . . . even in prison.'

'What about Adolphe?'

'We don't need him, nor Corréa . . .'

'That's all settled then, doyen.'

Escorted by another officer, Cheikh Tidiane went to join Léon Mignane. The room was dimly lit through the skylight.

'Léon.'

'Cheikh,' exclaimed Léon Mignane. He looked exhausted.

'Yes, Léon . . .'

The ex-President gave off a smell of old flesh left too long unaired.

'We're leaving.'

'Have the people demonstrated . . .'

'I think so, yes.'

'Did you hear that, Soutapha?'

'Yes, Mr President.'

'Soutapha, you're coming with us.'

Saying this, Cheikh Tidiane took his friend by the arm and moved towards the door.

The two septuagenarians got into the Peugeot. Lieutenant Ba sat next to the driver. There were jeeps ahead of them in the convoy . . . and lorries behind them.

Cheikh Tidiane repressed the stream of questions running through his mind: 'Where was Léon when he was arrested? How did the army get hold of him? Had he acted alone? . . . Perhaps he'd been drugged? . . . Léon Mignane remained silent. Cheikh Tidiane looked out the window.

They were going towards the Western Corniche. Silhouettes of paratroopers blended with the shadows of bushes. The reflection of street-lamps glittered on the wet tarred surface. The cloud of dust that had been hovering over Cap-Vert for the past few days, had begun to settle. A five-nights' moon, encircled by three ochre rings, reflected its orb in a dormant sea.

The convoy turned off at the first intersection in the township of Ouakam, towards the military airport. The area was all in darkness. The rotating beam of the lighthouse swept over hangar roofs, hilltops and baobab trees.

'Do you remember, Cheikh? . . . It was you who wrote to me then . . . asking me to come back here.'

'Yes, Léon! That was when we still had dreams,' replied Cheikh, as the car came to a standstill. He thought: 'Now I'm sending you off. Fate has its ironies.'

'True,' agreed Léon Mignane distinctly, without moving.

Insects were hovering round a beam of light.

'Doyen, could you come over here a moment,' asked Lieutenant Ba.

'I'll be right back, Léon.'

When he got out of the car, he felt the humidity. He shivered, and hunched his shoulders. As he followed the Lieutenant, he breathed in the iodine scent of the sea.

'Is he here?' asked Jean de Savognard, once they had exchanged the usual courtesies.

'Yes. I was with him just now. What about Professor Fall?'

'He's here too, with all his family. Adolphe and Corréa?'

'In another car.'

'Doyen, what will the country's future be now?'

The diplomat wanted to make contact with the CHO, to know what their intentions were; in other words to find out the political leanings of the new leaders.

Cheikh Tidiane refrained from answering. He didn't know what Colonel Mané intended. They heard a muffled noise, and moving circles of light appeared, aimed towards the ground.

Pierre's alert professional gaze was exploring their surroundings. The way the airport had been closed down, the psychological action of sending cables to all European and African governments as well as press agencies, couldn't have been devised by these people on their own. He prided himself on 'knowing Africans'. He moved away, to draw near a canvas-covered van.

Suddenly, a glaring light focused on him. Pierre started, his hand shielding his face. 'I say! I say! . . .' he protested.

'Get back to your place. And don't move any more. Get it?' he was told in a harsh tone.

Pierre grumbled to himself. He wasn't the one making decisions. Joining the others, he turned to see if he were being followed. He was annoyed at having failed to find anything out.

The ground-lights were switched on, lighting up the runway. The lorries started up and moved off. A line of armed guards took their place.

'Doyen, would you and these gentlemen please come with me,' a soldier came to say.

They moved towards an oblong of light.

At the top of the movable stairway, Colonel Gomis awaited them. He ushered them into the cabin. The officer halted in front of each of the departing passengers, as if at an inspection parade.

Adolphe raised his head to look at the ambassador. His prominent cheekbones stretched his roughened skin. For at least two days, he had neither shaved nor bathed. Corréa's beard covered the lower half of his face, and black circles hollowed out his eye-sockets; Professor Fall, devoid of his usual hat, revealed a completely bald scalp. A plump, exhausted little woman was huddled next to him. Their five children and their luggage took up two rows of seats. Soutapha was crying, covering his face with his hand.

'They're all here,' confirmed the Colonel, his face stiff.

Doyen Cheikh Tidiane turned towards the ambassador, who consulted Pierre, standing behind him.

'Léon Mignane is coming,' added the Colonel, moving towards the rear of the plane.

Professor Fall took advantage of the moment to whisper:

229

'Cheikh! Cheikh! I've made out a power of attorney for you. I want you to sell off my two houses.'

Cheikh Tidiane could scarcely credit Fall's mindlessness. He felt like shouting insults at him.

'I can't.'

'Cheikh! Cheikh! We're both Africans,' implored the Professor, trying to force the paper into his grasp.

'Fall, ask someone else. I . . .'

Léon Mignane's entrance put an end to the discussion. Cheikh Tidiane went to meet him, and settled him in his seat, a row in front of Soutapha.

'This gentleman is accompanying the President,' Jean de Savognard announced to Gomis.

'Lieutenant!'

'Colonel!'

'Have you searched this man's suitcase?'

'No, Colonel.'

'Please do so.'

'He's a member of the consulate,' argued the ambassador.

After the search, the Lieutenant showed the Colonel a Smith and Wesson.

'Search him too,' ordered the Colonel.

Pierre, struck dumb with astonishment, gazed inquiringly at the ambassador, while the soldier's hands passed down his sides. He pulled a 357 Magnum from its case. Pierre felt his throat tighten. He clenched his jaws. In another time and place, he would have flattened the nigger.

'Your Excellency, this Mr Pierre arrived on Friday, with confederates. He made a false statement to the police,' said Gomis, eyeing Pierre over his interlocutor's shoulder.

'My papers are in order,' said Pierre.

'That'll be enough from you,' said Gomis. 'You'll leave with the others. Your colleagues will leave tomorrow evening. As for your weapons, tomorrow we'll give your ambassador a receipt. Right? . . . Doyen . . . It's time.'

Colonel Gomis ushered out the ambassador and Cheikh Tidiane, then left the plane himself.

The doors were closed.

The plane bumped along the runway. As it moved off into the distance, its lights dwindled.

'That's that. Thank you, doyen.'

Cheikh Tidiane found himself in the Peugeot, alone with his tears.

CHAPTER 46

Wednesday morning

Cheikh Tidiane had risen wearily that morning. He was in a bad mood. He had cut himself off from the other people in the house. Eugénie and her children had come to say good morning, as if to a patriarch.

Last night, on returning from the airport, he had found only Djia Umrel, reading by lamp-light. As he sat down, he had said: 'Everything ends in memories.' The old woman understood that he had just seen off Léon Mignane.

'Kad and his woman came. I put off the dinner till tomorrow evening. Kad understood . . .'

Cheikh Tidiane passed Tuesday night with an aching heart.

This Wednesday, he felt worn out . . . Very old. He sat brooding over his sorrow. At about nine, Attorney Ndaw came by to see him. 'The old woman told me you came by yesterday. It's . . . nice of you.' After a few preliminary remarks, Cheikh Tidiane told him how he had spent the day yesterday: his meeting with the CHO, his role in bringing about Léon's departure.

'Colonel Mané isn't stupid. The way he's taken over power makes legality irrelevant,' said Ndaw cheerfully. He had just come from two hours of tennis.

'You and I believe in individual freedom. For us, that individualized freedom takes precedence over the freedom of the collectivity. Until yesterday, my notions of freedom and justice were much the same as yours . . .'

'I know that Attorney Ndaw is a great coffee drinker,' said Djia Umrel, followed by Ly bearing a tray.

'That's true . . . And your coffee is always better, Madame.'

'An old woman's secret,' she said filling their cups.

The aroma of hot coffee filled the room.

'I'll leave you men together,' she said, leaving.

After she had left, Cheikh Tidiane continued:

'The military intend to justify their action through social and collective justice. The population will see them as defenders of justice. Power gained by coercion — taking the word in its etymological sense — will thus become legal.'

'So, *Tonton,* the CHO is going to set up a socialist state?'

'Up to yesterday, the former government claimed to be socialist, while promoting embezzlement,' Cheikh Tidiane replied irritably.

'It's easy to set yourself up as arbiter when you're armed. Any officer can put two soldiers here, four over there, and overthrow a government.'

Cheikh Tidiane drank his coffee, pausing to think before stating in professorial tone:

'I can understand why you condemn their action. But shouldn't one consider what provoked them to it? A collectivity delegates a group of people to protect its interests; and those representatives misappropriate its property for their own use.'

'But *Tonton*, the army has no authorized role to play in civilian life,' protested Ndaw, his chin tightened back against his neck. 'The army doesn't take part in elections, even if they are a masquerade. Besides, the army is well provided for.'

'A mistake! That was a mistake.'

Cheikh Tidiane fell silent. He watched his grandson trotting towards them, hands outstretched. He gave him his own hands, and took him on his knee.

'. . . As I was saying, it was a mistake to try and keep soldiers out of public life, as if they and their families didn't share life's daily problems. At the same time, we wanted them to protect our institutions. An aberration . . . Either the Armed Forces are made up of mercenaries who obey whoever pays them . . . or they are the Armed Forces of the nation, and can object to a régime based on plunder.'

The toddler stood on the old man's thighs, and stuffed his fingers in his mouth. 'You're tiresome, you are,' he told him, removing the fingers.

'. . . Why do the people applaud Léon's fall from power . . . now? He was their idol . . . years ago. Now, the masses see Léon's departure as a check to fraud and the degradation of their lives. The elimination of a government they loathed makes them hope that their way of life will take a turn for the better. I wonder about what the military have done . . . Could it be that a well-organized force such as the army offers new perspectives to explore . . . ?'

'Ah! No, *Tonton* . . . a country or a state's greatness can't be measured in terms of ant-like discipline.'

'In what terms, then?'

'In terms of competence, of the citizens' high sense of their civic duty.'

'I'll grant you that, as an ultimate goal . . . Democracy can't be achieved through speeches, just as development is no longer a matter for small craftsmen. Nowadays, development is based on technical mastery. Without human capital, we won't be able to emerge from poverty. Our present states are just inflated clans. What's a country of five million people? A mere city in China, the USSR, Japan, the United States, India and Europe, being built under our very eyes.

Our subservience, even in the field of ideas, is weakening us, stifling us, stunting us.'

'That's serious! What you're saying is very serious,' objected Ndaw. He couldn't make out his mentor's motives. 'You seem to support the putsch,' he said finally.

'No! ... No ...' parried the old man. 'I was thinking about the future ... How to make use of this cataclysm.'

'All right! ... But we can't achieve anything with the army.'

'With whom, then?'

'The people, *Tonton.*'

Cheikh Tidiane gave a sugar lump to the child, who put it straight in his mouth.

'The people,' said Cheikh Tidiane, watching the child suck at his tongue. 'Unemployment, hunger, a growing population, a lack of trained personnel, compel us to make a choice. Democracy, as it's been fed to us, is nothing but a modernized, more adaptable form of feudal power. And feudalism rejects any change or renewal of traditional structures. We're told to be ourselves. That is to say, what we were a hundred years ago, during the colonial conquest. Rubbish! The African countries quickest to free themselves from dependence on others will be those where people have been half-military, half-civilian, and have fought for their freedom. Democracy comes from the base, not from the top of the pyramid.'

Attorney Ndaw was sceptical. He was beginning to lose faith in the doyen. He suspected him of being in league with the military. 'Why didn't they detain him like the others? Why is he speaking in favour of the army's actions?' He said aloud:

'*Tonton,* no military régime on the continent has proved satisfactory.'

'Except for Bokassa and Idi Amin, the others are still in power. We're more indulgent towards civilian rule. That's because we're afraid of discipline. But that's the price we'll have to pay to develop our country.'

Ndaw shifted his leg. He refrained from stating his opinions. He felt certain that his *Tonton* had gone over to the officers, and the idea left an aftertaste of rusty iron. He left, disappointed.

The old man accompanied him to the door, holding his grandson in his arms. Cheikh Tidiane was embarrassed by his nephew's conservatism.

Contrary to all likelihood, Attorney Ndaw's sudden departure didn't affect Cheikh Tidiane. He even laughed at his young friend's state of mind. As time wore on, he began to think about his autobiography, and withdrew to his study.

EPILOGUE

Wednesday evening

After a dinner party to make up for the previous night's, Diouldé's children went to their rooms. The adults were left among themselves. The upheavals in the country during the past twenty-four hours had not disrupted the house's calm and pleasant atmosphere. The servants moved quietly about their tasks. Bottles of after-dinner drinks, an ice-bucket and small glasses wers set out on the table.

Kad was conversing with Cheikh Tidiane and Djia Umrel. The old man's biography was the main topic, constantly referred to. At the other end of the table, Madjiguène was trying to comfort Eugénie, telling her: 'Diouldé will be released in a few days. Kad has told me ... You know he never says such things lightly.' Thus encouraged to hope, Eugénie revived.

Conversation became general, and reverted to local current events.

'I don't think I was the only one taken by surprise by the army's sudden appearance on the political scene. I was paying more attention to the squabbles between the two factions: Daouda against Mam Lat. When I witnessed the army's arrest of Mam Lat Soukabé and his staff, I thought they were acting on behalf of the PM, to enforce respect for the constitution.'

'Was Diouldé with Mam Lat Soukabé?'

Djia Umrel's question caught Kad's ear. He had deliberately refrained from mentioning Diouldé, so as not to pain Eugénie. He responded with a nod.

'They'll all be released,' said Cheikh Tidiane.

Ever since Léon Mignane's departure, he no longer doubted Colonel Mané's word.

'They arrested Nafissatou as well, the Minister for Women's Affairs,' added Madjiguène.

This purely feminist remark passed unnoticed. Unless no one was particularly concerned about Nafissatou and her position.

'And then?' inquired Cheikh Tidiane.

'Mam Lat was preparing his supporters for a mass demonstration. Many people were involved, from Elimane Baba Gaye, leader of the right-wing intellectuals, to the traditional chiefs, and including embittered elements, turncoats from all the political parties of the local Left, not to mention the economic operators, deputies, ministers, trade-union leaders etc. Mam Lat was planning to bring the city to a

234

standstill, and block the working of the administration. As Minister of Finance, he would delay paying the salaries of public service employees. His only purpose was to topple Daouda. But he pretended otherwise to his partners, claiming that all that was needed was to modify the clause that made the Prime Minister the heir to the presidency. When it became known that Léon Mignane had disappeared, everyone saw himself as playing a new part ... In the turmoil of subsequent events, Mam Lat's plans were never carried out ...'

'It takes courage to claim your rights when faced with an army,' mocked Cheikh Tidiane.

'As for Daouda, he planned to use Mam Lat's unsound financial management as a pretext to bring him to court. By denouncing the Minister of Finance, he was certain to discredit him. Corréa had shown him Mam Lat's secret file. It must be said to the PM's credit that he believed in abiding by the rules of democracy. Why should he yield his place to another, who hadn't been elected to it either? Inexperienced, anxious to keep his word, he hung on, not realizing that he was being manipulated ...'

'How's that?'

'*Joom Galle,*' asked Kad, 'you didn't tell me on Saturday, did you that Léon Mignane was nowhere to be found?'

Two furtive rays of light pierced the polished surface of one of his spectacles' lenses. Cheikh Tidiane shifted in his chair, to find a more comfortable position. Not finding one, he delayed his reply, then said:

'Reason of state.'

'Just so,' Kad said. 'I lacked two elements in order to discover the key to the mystery before H-hour. First, the murder of the driver Siin; secondly, Léon Mignane's disappearance ... The ministers were all used as puppets ... Even you, *Joom Galle.*'

Offended, his face grave, Cheikh Tidiane gazed levelly at Kad. The latter took a sip of whisky, disregarding the momentary annoyance of the master of the house. He continued:

'How could a President of Léon Mignane's standing, a valued asset, a stable political figure, with all that he represented for the West on the African chess-board, get away with such a childish escapade, in a country like ours, full of *barbouzes,* of all kinds of secret agents? Not to mention the advisers ensconced on every floor. So, how does one go about explaining Léon's disappearance? ...'

This series of questions troubled Cheikh Tidiane. He regretted not having questioned Léon when they were together in the car. Léon had imposed on him his own silence.

Madjiguène handed Eugénie her packet of cigarettes. She lit one and crossed her legs, tugging down her skirt out of modesty.

' ... To see things more clearly, we have to return to Daouda. Alone, without popular support, Daouda, was surrounded by Corréa, Adolphe and Soutapha ... Haïdara and Mapathé were just sidekicks. They weren't in the know ... One other person knew: Brigadier-General Ousmane Mbaye.'

'The General? Poor man, he's so good-natured,' said Djia Umrel, resting one hand on her thigh.

'Who knows, Mother! Perhaps the General was waiting for the right time to slip between the two opponents. He would then be taken for a peacemaker; there would be a coup like the one in the Congo on the *Trois Glorieuses*, or in Upper-Volta. The people would ask the army to take over. It had all been planned. The operation was named: *Caaf Xëmnë*. The General was a landowner, sour fruit and all, and an aristocrat deriving a sizeable income from his property in the city. Many of the younger high-ranking officers didn't like him ... It would have been a sort of blank shot of a coup: overthrowing Léon Mignane in order to save his face. A man like Léon could not leave the scene without applause and weeping. He needed a Shakespearian exit.'

Kad took a deep breath. He glanced at Madjiguène.

'And then?'

'Then, *Joom Galle,* the carefully planned operation stalled, then failed completely. The triumvirate – Colonel Mané, Gomis and Gor Dia – transformed the farce into a real coup. After having neutralized the General and his friends, they picked up Adolphe and Corréa ... and seized hold of Léon Mignane in his hiding-place. In order not to arouse suspicion, they kept the code-name: *Caaf Xëmnë*. After arresting the European advisers, they formed the Committee of High-ranking Officers, under the direction of Colonel Mané. The CHO immediately ordered French troops not to leave their base. They alerted the whole world. Paris, who had already sent an expeditionary force to intervene in response to a request by Senegal, was compelled to have them land elsewhere.'

Cheikh Tidiane, daunted by the journalist's revelations, gazed for a long time at his wife and daughter-in-law ...

'What about Léon?'

'Léon ... He wanted to be a prophet. Failing to leave his mark on the present, he prophesied economic independence for the year 2020. The present was giving way under his feet. Aware of the failure of his liberal policies, all that was left him were his soothing speeches throughout the world, and his unseasonable statements of opinion, running counter to the tide of African history. His European protectors could no longer moderate his greed for honorary titles. His Authenegraficanitus ideology no longer appealed to the new generation ruling other states. As for the people, politics and cullture

236

are a matter of full or empty bellies. The Léon of the 1980s was no longer the same man as the Léon of the 1940s and 1950s – or 1960s. His lustre had faded. All that was left was for him to exit in style.'

'How?'

'*Joom Galle*, on Saturday you let slip the remark: "Why was he so stubborn?" . . . Do you remember?'

Djia Umrel examined her husband. She remembered *Joom Galle's* phrase.

'. . . Why did Léon want to make Daouda his successor? He knew that Daouda wouldn't make the grade, that he was inhibited by his caste problem. Léon did it on purpose, in order to enhance his own personal renown. Daouda or General Ousmane Mbaye were six of one and half a dozen of the other. Léon Mignane would remain honorary President . . . Mam Lat hadn't a chance. He was dragging too many tin cans behind him. He might harm the Francophone alliance. In league with Muslim religious leaders of various sects, under their influence he might proclaim an Islamic Republic. And Senegal must remain in the bosom of the West. Even you, *Joom Galle*, were on the list of possible Presidents . . .'

'Who, me?'

'Yes . . . A substitute President . . . But your speech on Léon Mignane's seventieth birthday gave you the wrong image.'

Cheikh Tidiane was seething with concealed rage. Kad's assertions had convinced him. He remembered Jean de Savognard's words: 'Why don't you become leader of the opposition?' He was furious. Léon Mignane had played a double game.

'That's Machiavellian! Why do other people meddle in our problems?' he said; words failed him.

'Nothing's over and done with yet, *Joom Galle;* France has overcome her Algerian complex . . . She'll intervene again in Africa. And America's got over the Vietnamese syndrome . . . Europe? . . . The same countries that divided up Africa among themselves in Berlin in 1885, will continue penetration and pacification under other guises. Africa will be at stake for the remainder of this century, and for the first third of the next . . . The present struggle transcends our local problems.'

Kad stopped talking. The silence deepened.

'One epoch ends, another begins,' said Madjiguène, turning towards Eugénie.

'Will the times to come be easier for women?' asked Djia Umrel, to conceal her own disappointment.

237

She cast sidelong glances at her husband. The bitter lines at the corner of the old man's mouth were more pronounced. Pained to learn what had really happened, Cheikh Tidiane had withdrawn into himself. He had been used, once more. He had thought he was saving a friend ... He'd been a mere pawn. His eyebrows raised, he looked at the old woman. She smiled at him ... A constrained smile, a smile of support.

Madjiguène was saying:

'If money remains the only moral currency for men and women, nothing will have changed.'

'What if the CHO too were out to deceive the people,' asked Cheikh Tidiane abruptly.

'If you look at what's happening right now, I think you can say that's not the case. Since yesterday the CHO has been meeting with leaders of opposition parties, a few officials belonging to the old régime, Catholic and Muslim religious leaders, trade-unionists, women, pupils, students, in order to outline a general approach. They intend to publish a White Paper on the coup, a programme for economic recovery and the list of all requisitioned property. What's certain is that the interregnum will be hard. Very hard.'

'I see!' said Cheikh Tidiane, smiling faintly. He had foreseen events. 'Perspectives to explore,' he had said to Attorney Ndaw this morning. He said out loud: 'I can still be of some use to the CHO.'

'At your age!'

Djia Umrel had spoken in a sharp, authoritarian tone, making her disapproval plain. She sensed that they were all looking at her. She scarcely bowed her head, and continued: 'You'd do better to think of your book. A compendium of relevant ideas. It's time for all of us to discover or rediscover our own centres, our cultural sources. Why should we have to go to Paris, Moscow, Berlin, London, Rome, Bonne, Washington, Peking, Cairo to enhance what we already know, or gather up crumbs of knowledge derived from other people's experience? Allah isn't in Mecca, nor Jesus in Rome! Your book must anchor us in African earth.'

'Why, *Debbo*?' asked her husband.

'Your book will be useful to many people,' she replied, and fell silent.

She would tell him her thoughts and comments in bed.

After a pause, Doyen Cheikh Tidiane remarked:

'I've thought of a title for my memoirs ...'

They looked at him expectantly.

'The Last of the Empire.'

Old Djia Umrel unhesitatingly said:

'Yes.'

Other titles by Sembene Ousmane published by Heinemann

God's Bits of Wood (AWS 63)
Translated by Francis Price
This classic novel tells of the struggles of strikers on the Dakar–Niger railway line in 1948.

The Money Order with **White Genesis** (AWS 92)
Translated by Clive Wake
It might appear to be easy to change a money order. However, this man finds that the bureaucratic system erects a hurdle of literacy and numeracy at each stage. Made into a memorable film by the author.

Xala (AWS 175)
Translated by Clive Wake
The well-off businessman El Hadji Abdou Kader marries his third wife. But on the wedding night he finds he has *xala*. Not only his manhood but his business is at stake. A novel of great distinction about how the new African middle class have taken over from the colonialists as the exploiters of the people.
Illustrated with film stills.